The industrial politics of devolution

Manchester University Press

The industrial politics of devolution

Scotland in the 1960s and 1970s

Jim Phillips

Manchester University Press

Manchester and New York

distributed exclusively in the USA by Palgrave

Published by Manchester University Press
Oxford Road, Manchester M13 9NR, UK
and Room 400, 175 Fifth Avenue, New York, NY 10010, USA
www.manchesteruniversitypress.co.uk

Distributed exclusively in the USA by
Palgrave, 175 Fifth Avenue, New York,
NY 10010, USA

Distributed exclusively in Canada by
UBC Press, University of British Columbia, 2029 West Mall,
Vancouver, BC, Canada V6T 1Z2

British Library Cataloguing-in-Publication Data
A catalogue record for this book is available from the British Library

Library of Congress Cataloging-in-Publication Data applied for

ISBN   978 0 7190 7533 9   *hardback*

17 16 15 14 13 12 11 10 09 08   10 9 8 7 6 5 4 3 2 1

Typeset
by Helen Skelton, Brighton, UK
Printed in Great Britain
by The Cromwell Press Ltd, Trowbridge

Contents

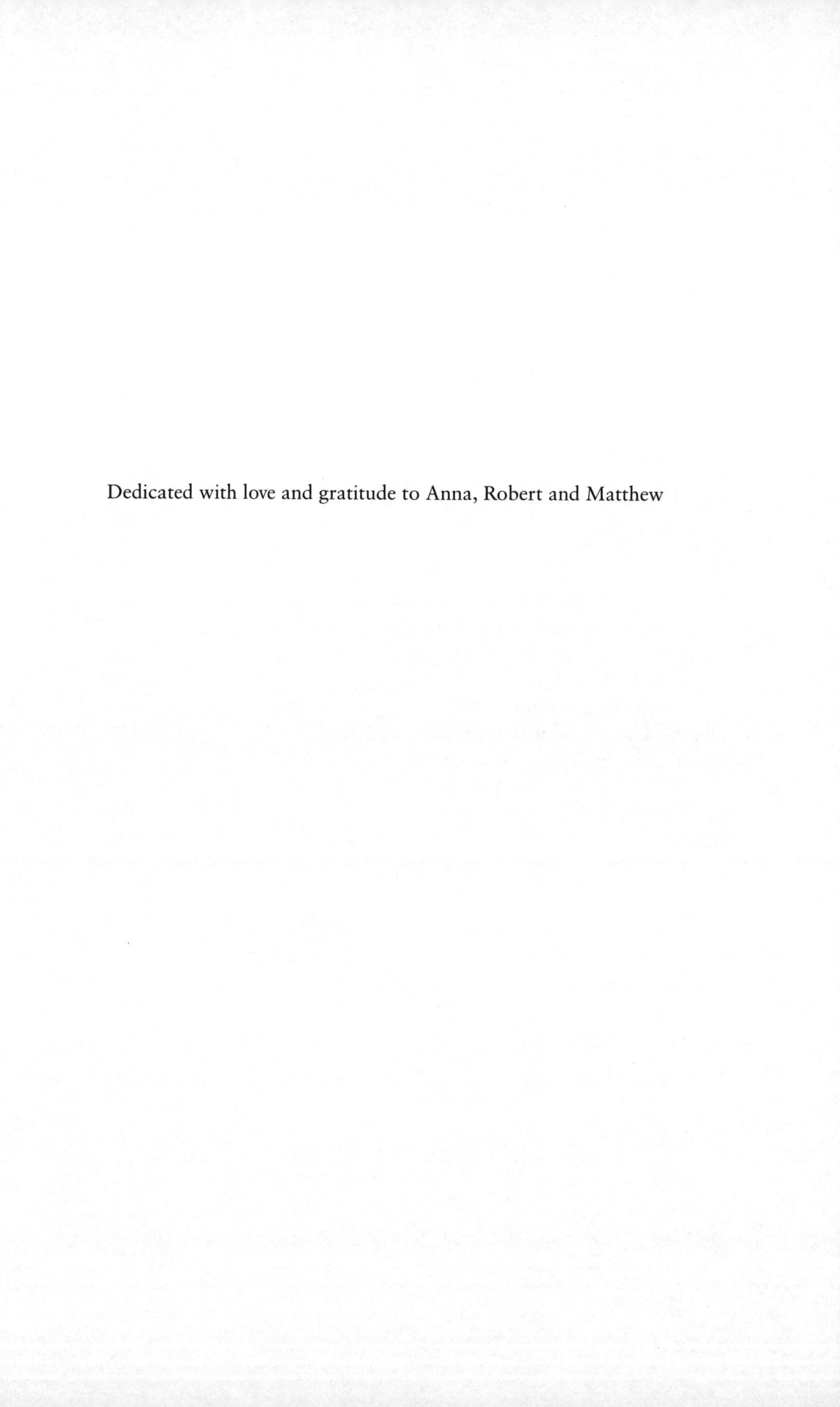

Dedicated with love and gratitude to Anna, Robert and Matthew

List of tables

Abbreviations

AEU	Amalgamated Engineering Union
BNOC	British National Oil Corporation
BP	British Petroleum
BSC	British Steel Corporation
CBI	Confederation of British Industry
CPA	Clyde Ports Authority
CPGB	Communist Party of Great Britain
DTI	Department of Trade and Industry
EEC	European Economic Community
FPA	Forth Ports Authority
MP	Member of Parliament
MSP	Member of the Scottish Parliament
NCB	National Coal Board
NPC	National Ports Council
NUM	National Union of Mineworkers
OPEC	Organisation of Petroleum Exporting Countries
PAC	(House of Commons) Public Accounts Committee
SCDI	Scottish Council for Development and Industry
SDA	Scottish Development Agency
SDD	Scottish Development Department
SHHD	Scottish Home and Health Department
SIB	Shipbuilding Industry Board
SNP	Scottish National Party
SSEB	South of Scotland Electricity Board
STUC	Scottish Trades Union Congress
STV	Scottish Television
TGWU	Transport and General Workers' Union
TUC	Trades Union Congress
UCS	Upper Clyde Shipbuilders

Acknowledgements

I have incurred many debts in writing this book, which originated in a conversation in October 2003 – aboard the 16.42 Glasgow to Aberdeen train – with Ewen Cameron. Ewen enthusiastically encouraged my involvement in the historiography of contemporary Scotland, and retained a close interest in this project as it developed. He read two versions of the manuscript and commented on its contents with great care, insight, knowledge and tact. I am extremely grateful for his help, which extended to arranging invitations to speak at the Scottish History Departmental Seminar at the University of Edinburgh in February 2005, and the Scottish Economic and Social History Society Conference in May 2006, also at the University of Edinburgh. I thank the participants at these events, along with those at the 2004 and 2005 conferences of the Association of Business Historians, for helping in the evolution of this book. I owe thanks to Martin Chick, Hugh Murphy and Jim Tomlinson, who read and commented on parts of the manuscript. Dave Whyte helped with customary enthusiasm, scepticism and perception.

My scholarly interest in the 1960s and 1970s began at the University of Aberdeen in 1989 where, as an undergraduate student, I took an Honours Special Subject on the Wilson Years, under the direction of Terry Brotherstone. Terry has remained a supportive presence over the years, and helped with this book by talking me through the politics of the Upper Clyde Shipbuilders episode. John Brown, my doctoral supervisor at the University of Edinburgh from 1990 to 1993, attended the Scottish History Departmental Seminar in 2005 and encouraged me to link developments in Scotland more directly with my original interests – cultivated at Aberdeen – in the UK industrial politics of the Wilson years, including the struggle over *In Place of Strife*.

The book was written partly on the basis of research conducted in 2002 and 2003 with the support of a grant awarded by the Carnegie Trust for the Universities of Scotland, and the practicalities of this research were greatly eased by the efficient assistance of staff at the University of Glasgow Library, the National Library of Scotland, the National Archives of Scotland, The National Archive in Kew, the Modern Records Centre at the University of Warwick, Dundee Central Library, and the University of St Andrews Library. I am grateful to Alan Wilson and Iain McTaggart of the Scottish Council for Development and Industry, who provided access to the organisation's archive materials and accommodation to view these materials in December 2004. I thank the *Scottish Historical Review* Trust and the editors and publishers of *Contemporary British History* for agreeing to the reproduction here in recast form of some material that appeared in articles published in these journals in 2005 and 2006.

I am very lucky in my working life, having found a happy home in the Department of Economic and Social History at the University of Glasgow. I thank all my colleagues there, past and present, for contributing to the stimulating and supportive environment that is such a strong characteristic of the department. I wish in particular to acknowledge a debt of gratitude to Mike French, who has helped me immensely – generously, and undemonstratively – since I joined the University in 1995.

Finally, the essential sustenance of my extended family – in Crail, Edinburgh, London and Darmstadt – must be recorded. My greatest debt, of course, is to my lovely family at home in Dundee. I thank Anna, Robert and Matthew for their very special involvement and support, and dedicate this book to them.

Introduction:
devolution and industrial change

On 17 February 1972 a crowd of 1,000 coal miners gathered outside Dunfermline Sheriff Court to celebrate the release on bail of thirteen pickets who had been arrested three days earlier at Longannet power station, charged with the highly serious offence of 'mobbing and rioting'. The pickets were attempting to close the power station to increase pressure on the Conservative government and speed the National Union of Mineworkers (NUM) to victory in a national – that is, UK-wide – strike that had been running for six weeks. The arrested men were initially denied bail and taken from court in handcuffs to Saughton jail in Edinburgh, prompting angry demonstrations from miners and vociferous protests from the Labour Party and the trade union movement. Amid escalating social and political tension the Lord Advocate, Norman Wylie, flew to Scotland and persuaded the legal authorities in Fife to arrange the early release of the miners, who were greeted by their cheering supporters on Dunfermline High Street and then taken to local union offices for a reunion with their families.

The Longannet episode is an important part of this book, the central theme of which is the political impact of long-running structural economic change in Scotland. The book shows that the growing demand for Scottish self-government was strongly rooted in the intersecting problems of the heavy industries of coal, shipbuilding and metals, and the difficulties encountered in establishing younger forms of manufacturing enterprise, notably car production. These problems were conjoined with the management by successive UK governments of perceived economic decline, industrial militancy and 'the Scottish question'. In April 1969 the Labour government's Employment Secretary, Barbara Castle, encountered the full force of this combined political, economic and industrial problem at the Rootes/Chrysler car plant in Linwood. At Linwood shopfloor unrest was highly pronounced, in the context of the shift in Scottish and especially Clydeside manufacturing from bespoke production and craft labour, with work group autonomy and pride, and embodied in shipbuilding, to automated and standardised assembly, with flow processes and deskilled – and arguably alienated – labour. Castle arrived at Linwood by helicopter from Rothesay, where she had attended the annual gathering of the Scottish Trades Union Congress (STUC), which she characterised as 'the toughest audience in the trade union world'.[1] There her plans for state intervention in industrial relations, set out in the White Paper, *In Place of Strife*, and designed to loosen the believed choking hold on economic growth exerted by unofficial strikes, demarcation disputes and other forms of shopfloor activity, were strongly opposed by a Congress that had also been sharply critical of her government's earlier attempt to manage non-inflationary economic growth through wage restraint, including a statutory freeze in 1966.[2] The STUC opposition to *In Place of Strife* had been shaped by its mining affiliates and a large one-day strike of Clydeside workers,[3] and Linwood workers used the opportunity of Castle's visit to restate in fairly pungent terms their distaste for the proposals, although they did so cheerfully enough. One man delighted the Employment Secretary by calling, 'Give us a kiss, Barbara', an invitation that she readily accepted.[4]

The Linwood plant was a product of UK regional policy, Rootes pushed there against its will in 1962 by Harold Macmillan's Conservative government, seeking to narrow the gap between Scottish and overall British economic growth. This book positions industrial politics, of which such regional policy, the miners' strike and Castle's industrial relations strategy were highly significant components, as central to the devolutionary shift in Scottish politics in the 1960s and 1970s. To a lesser extent the growth of support for nationalism and independence was also influenced by these industrial politics. These politics, it should be emphasised, were shaped essentially from below, by unheralded workers, employers, union and business representatives rather than simply constructed from above by more 'visible' politicians and other policy 'makers'. In this respect the book adapts Eric Hobsbawm's general proposition about the nature of nationalism, at least in its nineteenth- and twentieth-century post-Enlightenment guises, to conceptualise the character of devolution's emergence and evolution. Hobsbawm was opposed to nationalism, it should be emphasised, and this perhaps shaped his view that it was partly constructed from above, by elites, while being shaped ultimately by the 'assumptions, hopes, needs, longings and interests of ordinary people, which are not necessarily national and still less nationalistic'.[5] In this account, which sympathises with the broad democratic purposes of devolutionary governance, legislative or political devolution similarly emerges from the interplay between elite and 'ordinary' actors, parties and movements, some of which – notably business lobbyists – actively opposed political forms of devolution while favouring its administrative components.

This interplay of elite policy and popular pressure or agency is directly observable in the 1960s and 1970s, a crucial period, when Scotland's economic and political transition – from a predominantly industrial society, firmly embedded in the United Kingdom, to an increasingly service-based, post-industrial society, with a renegotiated position in the Union – began to accelerate. Popular resistance to the problems of economic restructuring was, as this book indicates, largely of a social or class rather than a 'nationalist' character, but it was 'answered' from 'above' by mainstream political parties – chiefly the UK Labour and Conservative parties but also the Scottish National Party (SNP) – offering non-class 'solutions' in the shape of Home Rule or, in the Nationalists' case, Independence, that would offset the costs of economic change in some significant way, although just how was seldom ventured in convincing detail. To the Labour and Conservative parties in the UK, and significant trade union and business supporters of Home Rule within Scotland, it will be argued, devolution represented a 'low-cost' and therefore attractive 'solution' to economic decline and social problems precisely because it de-emphasised questions of class conflict and inequality. Popular pressure emerged or was articulated in a number of different ways: by workers, mainly through strikes and other forms of industrial protest; and by employers, chiefly through interest group discussions with the state. In these matters two institutions operated as a conduit and sometimes a proxy for popular opinion, articulating but to some extent also shaping it: the STUC, and the Scottish Council for Development and Industry (SCDI), a pressure group that included representatives of trade unions and local authorities but was dominated by business interests. To some extent these were, of course, 'elite' bodies, but the STUC was obliged, in the age of shopfloor industrial politics, to bend to the will of its affiliated members, and the very broad industrial, financial and commercial base of the SCDI ensured that any single strand of business could not control it.

The relationship between elite positioning and popular pressure was dynamic. Chapters 1 and 2 of this book suggest that in the 1960s industrial and political elites were looking for ways of alleviating popular concerns about slow economic activity and settled upon enhanced devolutionary mechanisms for doing so, favouring increased control from within the Scottish Office of more robust regional policy. Chapters 3, 4 and 5 indicate that in the 1970s popular agency and will gained greater direct bearing on developments, with attempts to democratise and extend the trajectory of devolution following from industrial struggles in shipbuilding and coalmining, and encouraged further by the new politics of North Sea Oil. Putting more detail on this general framework, Chapter 1 opens and closes in the Rootes plant at Linwood, from its establishment in 1963 to Castle's visit in 1969. The discussion focuses on the attempts – by the UK government, by business and the trade union movement – to broaden Scotland's industrial base before and during the 1960s, the difficulties arising from these attempts and the accompanying growth of support for devolution. There is a particular emphasis here on Scottish labour's socialist critique of Harold Wilson's Labour government and the role of the STUC in articulating support for a Scottish legislature to offset the perceived anti-Scottish bias in UK macro-economic management. This involved the type of complex blurring of class and nationalist forces that Paul Ward has written about in his recent study of twentieth-century British unionist politics, with 'horizontal class identities' overlaying 'vertical union and national identities'.[6] Such forces were also evident in discussions between Scottish business and the Conservative government elected in 1970. Edward Heath, the Prime Minister, discussed Scotland's perceived problems on two occasions early in 1972 with the SCDI. These involved Baron Clydesmuir, of the Colvilles steel dynasty, who chaired the SCDI, and Sir William Lithgow, a major figure in Clydeside shipbuilding. Clydesmuir and Lithgow were the sponsors between 1969 and 1972 of a grand design, *Oceanspan*, the subject of Chapter 2, which envisaged the renewal of the old staple industries and stimulation of younger manufacturing enterprises – mainly in the foreign-owned electronics and assembly sectors – through large-scale public investment. A huge 'ocean terminal' on the Clyde, complete with steel works, would connect the Atlantic with Continental Europe across the 'land bridge' of central Scotland. The plans were designed to take advantage of Britain's impending membership of the European Economic Community (EEC), and arrest Scotland's economic decline with new residential and employment opportunities across the central belt. These opportunities would be bolstered further, it was thought, by the benefits of North Sea Oil, and Heath was invited in 1972 by the SCDI to consider the possibility that oil revenues be used to invest in the *Oceanspan* plans. It was fitting that these plans were pushed by representatives of the old, declining industries, although they were supported too by John Toothill, Chairman of Ferranti electronics, and the eponymous author of the 1961 report – examined in Chapter 1 – that emphasised the Scottish economy's urgent need for industrial diversification, which *Oceanspan* to an extent seemed to promise.

So *Oceanspan* carried substantial business support, but the imaginative plans did not secure the vital element of Exchequer funding from the UK government. In this respect the stalled regeneration of Scottish transport infrastructure and heavy industries, and the limited stimulus to new industries, pushed forward the debates about political devolution. These were developing in earnest from the late 1960s, with a Royal Commission on the future governance of Scotland reporting in 1973, and the rise of the SNP – with the famous Hamilton and Govan by-election victories of 1967 and 1973 followed by the party's broader successes in the two general elections of 1974 – pressing the Labour and Conservative parties to adopt fairly clear commitments to Home Rule.

These electoral and political developments were very strongly rooted in the social tension arising from industrial change, chiefly evident in the two economic sectors that are examined in Chapters 3 and 4 of this book, shipbuilding and coal. 'We not only build ships on the Clyde; we also build men', said Jimmy Reid, famously, during the work-in that he helped to lead in 1971–72 in the yards of Upper Clyde Shipbuilders (UCS) in Clydebank and Govan. This crisis in the industry that had earlier brought prosperity to Scotland and shaped its culture generated enormous political and social turbulence in Scotland and the UK, and mobilised powerful nationalist as well as class arguments. It also forced – from below – a dramatic change in government policy. Heath had promised in 1970 a Conservative government that would bring an end to 'uneconomic' subsidies of 'lame duck' industries and businesses. When UCS passed into liquidation in July 1971 Reid and other stewards mustered support for a novel form of resistance: the workers occupied the yards and continued production. With the Conservative Party's confidence in Scotland crumbling in the face of rising unemployment, and Glasgow's Chief Constable advising that he would be unable to guarantee the maintenance of public order were the yards to be forcibly closed, Heath's government was forced into a U-turn, announcing major new subsidies to keep UCS in business. The miners' strike, which derived considerable energy and momentum from the UCS work-in, was equally rooted in economic insecurity, arising from the coal industry's significant post-1945 contraction, with pit closures and job losses bringing anxiety to the coalfields and then, as real wages fell, increased militancy. The Scottish miners shaped the STUC's adoption of Home Rule as a political goal, and this was certainly connected to the worries aroused by the diminution of employment in the coalfields, which accelerated under the Labour government in the 1960s.

Michael McGahey, Scottish miners' President and communist, spoke at the 1969 STUC of the labour movement's need to 'come to grips' with the 'national question' to stymie the 'demagogues' of nationalism.[7] But the Labour Party took no firm position on devolution until 1974, allowing the SNP free rein to champion independence – or 'separation', as McGahey called it – as the means of exerting control over economic and industrial policy. Particular capital was made of the discovery and development of North Sea Oil, which is the subject of Chapter 5, taking the chronology forward to 1979. 'It's Scotland's Oil', was the SNP's effective campaigning slogan for a number of years from 1973 onwards, helping to secure increased Parliamentary representation in the two general elections of 1974. These saw the return of a Labour government, initially on the basis of a minority position in the Commons and then with a precarious majority of five seats that dwindled and then disappeared thereafter. The 1974 Parliaments marked the high point in the 1970s of the top-down UK government 'response' to pressures from below in Scotland, with the prospect of a devolved legislature defeated in the doomed referendum of 1979, followed closely afterwards by the election of a Conservative administration with Margaret Thatcher as Prime Minister.

In analysing these economic and political developments – and emphasising the importance of social forces that were both class and nationalist in character – this book contributes to an expanding body of literature on Scotland and its journey to Home Rule at the end of the twentieth century. David Howell, in his extended discussion of the lives and times of James Connolly, John Maclean and John Wheatley, makes some important observations about the relationships between class and nation in Scotland, Ireland and Britain. His three biographical subjects – diverse in their backgrounds and varieties of socialism – represented in different ways the commitment of the political left to devolution or independence in the 1910s, but for four decades or so from the 1920s onwards socialist orthodoxy – in both the Labour Party and the Communist Party of Great Britain (CPGB) – revolved around the possibilities of 'capturing' an unreconstructed and centralised British state as the means of delivering benefits to the manual working class in all nations of the Union.[8] This orthodoxy was gradually unpicked, however, from the mid-1960s, with trade unions and particularly the STUC – as has already been emphasised – prominent in the redevelopment of pluralist attitudes to nation, devolution and the Union on the left, although the Labour Party itself remained divided by these questions right through the 1970s, as evidenced by the developments surrounding the Home Rule legislation and the 1979 referendum.

There was a shift after 1979. Labour arguably rediscovered the pluralism of its pre-First World War origins, adopting 'sincere' support for devolution and a renegotiated position for Scotland in the UK that was distinct from its opportunistic Home Rule response to the SNP in the 1960s and 1970s.[9] This was largely related to debates about the legitimacy of Conservative governance in Scotland, which Lindsay Paterson sees as mobilising more broad-ranging support for devolution than had been evident in the 1979 referendum, and leading to the establishment of the Scottish Parliament in 1999.[10] Of particular importance here was the adoption by Thatcher's governments of policies that contributed to extremely rapid economic restructuring. Hence political devolution came to be viewed as the means of matching economic and industrial management to Scotland's particular needs.[11] In this manner Clive Lee concludes that support for devolution in the 1980s and 1990s became a proxy for support for the type of economic and social state interventionism that had been reasonably successful and popular in Scotland after 1945, but which the Thatcher governments had jettisoned. Lee relates this process to longer historical developments, noting the legacy of the disproportionate consequences in Scotland of the recurrence across the twentieth century of 'market failure' – which state policy was designed to correct – in the provision of employment and housing.[12]

This book also explores the deeper historical roots of the linkage between industrial stagnation and policy-making institutions. These can be discerned, for instance, in the 1930s, when Scottish Office officials and ministers, including Walter Elliot, the Tory – or rather the Unionist – Secretary of State for Scotland, who were conscious of the link between Scotland's narrow economic base and its high level of structural unemployment, unsuccessfully sought support from the UK government for industrial development measures that in some ways anticipated the regional policy of the late 1950s and 1960s.[13] Developments after the Second World War assumed a slightly different character. Some readers – influenced by the anti-Conservative Home Rule agenda of the 1980s and 1990s – may be surprised to see that the arguments about the dangers of 'remote' administration from Whitehall were being articulated strongly in the 1960s in Scotland from a Tory and business perspective as well as from a socialist or trade union perspective. There were precedents here in the anti-socialist and quasi-nationalist criticisms of the 1945–51 Labour governments that were mounted by Elliot and other Unionists, who talked of the 'denationalisation' of Scottish industry that was implicit in Labour's programme of nationalisation.[14] The devolutionist politics of Lithgow and Clydesmuir's *Oceanspan*, derived from the earlier Toothill analysis, were similarly ranged against the 'socialist' policies of Wilson's Labour government. These business devolutionist voices were accompanied, perhaps paradoxically, by a Scottish labour critique of unreconstructed UK administration, articulated by the NUM in Scotland and the STUC, that dwelt on the non-socialist or even anti-socialist character of Wilson's government.

So devolution has a longer history, which this book sets out. It is also important to emphasise that the economic and industrial basis of this history has often been underplayed, with devolution more normally understood – or explained – essentially in political and cultural terms. Other studies examine the character and importance of key electoral events, such as the SNP's victories in Hamilton and Govan, which are then mapped to 'responses' by the Conservative and Labour parties, notably Heath's 1968 'Declaration of Perth', where the Tory leader seemed to offer the possibility of constitutional change under a future Conservative government, or the Labour government's establishment in 1969 of the Royal Commission on the Constitution. In these accounts economic or industrial affairs in the 1950s and 1960s are briefly referred to, sometimes as examples of Whitehall governments 'shoring up' the Union through benevolent or misguided regional policy initiatives that were designed to reduce unemployment and thereby undercut the attraction of nationalism. Most established histories then discern the real origins of the relationship between economic and political developments in the 1970s, chiefly due to the debates about the potential of North Sea Oil, combined with the sharp rise in business failure and unemployment in Scotland – as elsewhere in the industrial world – that followed the four-fold rise in the price of oil after the Israeli-Arab conflict at the end of 1973.[15]

In shifting the focus of discussion of Home Rule explicitly to the slightly longer history of the economy's influence on political development, the book utilises important earlier works. Michael Hechter's competing models of core/periphery national development will be observable at different stages of the analysis,[16] although the contestable nature of the core/periphery model will also be evident. Ward's discussion of Unionism, in this connection, emphasises the very strong extent to which 'British' identities in the twentieth century were continually remade in what might be thought of as the 'periphery' – in Scotland, Wales and Northern Ireland – before passing into the mainstream of the 'core'. This process of remaking involved significant emphasis on the possibilities of devolution within the UK.[17] Here it will be remembered that Home Rule arguments within the British labour movement were advanced by Scottish trade unionists; they were then taken up by the Labour Party's UK leadership and pressed back upon the Labour Party in Scotland, which in the first half of the 1970s strongly resisted them. In the economy, meanwhile, between 'core' and 'periphery' there was some structural convergence, as Scotland moved, *inter alia*, towards vehicle building and food and drink, although there remained substantial disparity of product within 'order groups': lower value trucks rather than cars and lower volume whisky rather than processed foods prevailed, Gavin McCrone noted, adding that the outcome was continuing relatively slow growth in Scotland. This suggested that 'internal colonialism' was evident to a certain extent, with UK macro-economic management that was geared to dampening roaring growth in England's central and southern regions choking off altogether the more modest growth in Scotland.[18] This might be understood in terms of Hechter's emphasis on the domination of the periphery by the core, although this schema does not easily accommodate the diversity of conditions and experiences across Scotland. Regional policy in the 1960s, after all, involved some redistribution of resources from prosperous to less prosperous areas. The main Scottish beneficiary here was west-central Scotland, recipient of the Ravenscraig rolling strip steel mill as well as Linwood and other capital-intensive projects, and which might be seen not as an 'internal colonialist' outpost but as the epicentre of Scotland's economy and industrial politics, and capable in theory and in deed of shifting the political priorities of the UK as a whole.

The economy also featured in an earlier account of devolution, written by Henry Drucker and Gordon Brown,[19] which this book builds on – and critiques – with the benefit of the distance of time, and a different emphasis on popular agency. The book also leans on the more recent work of Christopher Harvie and John Foster, who both place industry at the core of Scotland's political trajectory from the 1950s to the 1970s.[20] The book explores the logic and some of the inconsistencies of Foster's impressive general argument that an important transition took place in the early 1970s, with political and social leadership in Scotland passing from capital to labour. During the 1950s and 1960s, he writes, Scottish politics owed more to debates and divisions within industry. This included the emergence of a powerful strand of Scottish business opinion, primarily clustered in heavy industry, that perceived its interests to be different from foreign-owned – chiefly American – manufacturing in Scotland, mainly in electronics and light engineering, and additionally in opposition to the interests of English capital. Foster links this with the successful campaign led by Sir Hugh Fraser, owner of Glasgow's largest department store, to preserve Scottish ownership of the *Glasgow Herald*, a significant event following the export of ownership during the preceding two decades of most other major newspapers, including *The Scotsman*, acquired by the Canadian, Roy Thomson, in September 1953.[21] This book suggests that these divisions within capital can be exaggerated, with light industry, for example, extremely supportive of *Oceanspan*, which Foster sees as the creature of heavy industry alone.[22]

The book also highlights the manner in which Scottish capital's devolutionary campaigning overlapped with that of the labour movement in the early 1970s. Foster's account rather suggests that organised labour, mustering around the STUC, gathered control of the Home Rule movement in 1971–72 precisely because a vacuum in social and political authority in Scotland had been created by the demise of Scottish capital. In this book it is apparent that established industrialists like Clydesmuir and Lithgow remained a force in the early 1970s, and contested vigorously the 'Scottish' leadership being assumed by the STUC. The legitimacy of this leadership, moreover, rested on the apparently broad social foundations of the Home Rule movement that was being co-ordinated. Representatives of employers' organisations, local authorities and churches as well as trade unions attended the first Scottish Assembly on Unemployment, held in Edinburgh on 14 February 1972, on the day of the Longannet arrests.[23] The broad nature of this civic, trade union and business coalition strengthened its appeal to mainstream UK political parties, which were keen to chart a path out of the social and class conflict that Longannet arguably represented.

Foster's discussion is brief, necessarily so, as part of a chapter-length contribution on the 1914–79 period to a volume encompassing a narrative of Scotland's history from the 'Earliest Times [beginning with "Pre-history"] to the Present Day', and Harvie's treatment of the 1960s and 1970s comes in an examination of the longer period from 1914. So the broad purpose of this book is to fill a major gap in the historiography by providing a detailed analysis – the first of its kind – of the role of industrial politics in shaping Scotland's development in the 1960s and 1970s. In so doing the book utilises business and trade union records and government papers that were not used by Drucker and Brown, Foster or Harvie, and these materials, combined with this book's greater detail, allow a clearer understanding of the linkages between economic and political development to emerge.

The industrial politics of devolution in the 1960s and early 1970s were, it should be emphasised, appreciably different from those that followed in the 1980s and 1990s, with significant variances in the patterns of economic structure, labour organisation and industrial ownership. The earlier years were characterised by reasonably high levels of employment in strongly unionised sectors of the economy, particularly in older manufacturing sectors like shipbuilding and engineering, along with coalmining, rail and road transport, and in the public sector, where union membership grew steadily in the 1970s, as workers who were affected by counter-inflationary public sector wage freezes sought the protection of trade unions. Hence trade union density – the proportion of the workforce that was unionised – in Scotland grew from 40 per cent in 1970 to 48 per cent in 1981. But as the process of structural economic change accelerated, particularly after the election of Thatcher's government in 1979, which presided over the privatisation of numerous state-owned industries and services, the membership of trade unions fell with the decline of their manufacturing and public sector strongholds. By 1997 union density was down to 35 per cent,[24] and the political as well as economic strength of unions was notably diminished.

The weakening of unions was consolidated by parallel developments in the ownership and control of Scottish business. In the 1960s – despite the efforts of Sir Hugh Fraser and others – foreign ownership was incrementally on the increase, although there was still a powerful role for the indigenous 'old-fashioned tycoons', as Harvie calls them. But from the mid-1970s there was a marked acceleration in the transfer of power to distant boardrooms in 'the City of London and Los Angeles'.[25] While American firms in particular had been trenchant opponents of organised labour in the 1950s, the tightening labour market conditions of the 1960s had forced them to cede recognition of unions. By the 1980s and early 1990s, however, the position had been reversed once more, symbolised by the lengthy and immensely bitter lockout at Timex in Dundee in 1993, which preceded the company's abandonment of Scottish operations altogether in its pursuit of radically lower labour costs. In the 1960s industrial politics – even and in some cases especially in Scottish-owned firms – were also characterised by a degree of social tension and conflict. Until roughly 1972, however, when their collective nerve was shaken by the twin industrial and social crises of the climax of the UCS work-in and the national miners' strike, many Scottish business leaders interpreted this tension and conflict as reinforcing the desirability of greater administrative and policy-making autonomy for Scotland. Strikes and other forms of indus-trial protest appeared – like unemployment or poor housing – as symptoms of the wider problem of slow economic growth that arose from Scotland's narrow industrial base.

Many of the workers who lost their jobs at Timex in 1993 were women. This was consistent with the broad gender profile of the workforce in electronics and other branches of younger assembly production in Scotland, and a powerful contrast with the position in ships, metals and coal, which where almost exclusively the preserve of men.[26] Devolution, as it appears in the pages of this book, was perceived by many of its advocates as the means of defending an industrial structure and a social system that included much that was meritorious: manufacturing enterprise, high levels of employment, the generation of indigenous wealth that could be (even if it was not always) re-invested in Scotland, and a prominent political role for labour representation. But the gender relations that this structure and system encompassed were not attractive. The dramatic events at Longannet in 1972 were reported in the pages of the *Scottish Miner*, a monthly paper published by the NUM in Scotland, which for its strike edition temporarily suspended the normal practice of carrying exploitative pictorial representations of women. The May 1971 edition, for example, featured a square photograph, five inches by five in scale, of a young woman in a low-cut two-piece bathing suit. She was kneeling, leaning forward towards the camera, and cupping her hands to sieve sand through her fingers. The picture was captioned: 'It's not just flying that appeals to air stewardesses but those rewarding stopovers at flight's end. Take lovely blonde JUDY PRESCOTT (22), for instance (and who wouldn't want to?). She is enjoying a relaxing day on the sands in sunny Miami, Florida. Judy has been dubbed "Highjackers' Delight"'.[27]

It may be dangerous to infer too much about industrial politics from this kind of exploitative treatment of women, which was in any case dropped from *Scottish Miner* by about 1975. But it would be entirely reasonable to argue, from a feminist perspective, that this treatment was consistent with the masculine-dominated agenda pursued by the NUM and many other trade unions in Scotland at this time.[28] Women were constructed along with the men and the ships on the Clyde: there were fetters on the lives of these women that were the condition of gender as well as class. The gradual disintegration of traditional industrial structures – accelerated in the 1980s – cut away at the strength and confidence of organised labour, yet contributed in some ways to the loosening of the constraints of gender. This benefit, at least, can be taken from the process of economic change in Scotland that in other ways – chiefly in destabilising the experience of working life – was unattractive.

Notes

1 Barbara Castle, *The Castle Diaries, 1964–76* (London, 1990), p. 322.
2 Scottish Trades Union Congress (STUC), *70th Annual Report, 1967*, pp. 416–30; and *72nd Annual Report, 1969*, pp. 412–30, 438–45.

3 Angela Tuckett, *The Scottish Trades Union Congress: The First Eighty Years, 1897–1977* (Edinburgh, 1986), pp. 381–7.

4 Castle, *Diaries*, pp. 322–3.

5 Eric Hobsbawm, *Nations and Nationalism* (London, 1992), pp. 9–10.

6 Paul Ward, *Unionism in the United Kingdom, 1918–1974* (Basingstoke, 2005), p. 9.

7 STUC, *72nd Annual Report*, p. 234.

8 David Howell, *A Lost Left: Three Studies in Socialism and Nationalism* (Chicago and Manchester, 1986), pp. 7–13.

9 Ward, *Unionism*, pp. 70–1.

10 Lindsay Paterson, *A Diverse Assembly: The Debate on a Scottish Parliament* (Edinburgh, 1998), p. 143.

11 See Robin Cook's comments in Paterson, *Diverse Assembly*, pp. 147–8.

12 C. H. Lee, 'Economic Progress: Wealth and Poverty', in T. M. Devine, C. H. Lee and G. C. Peden (eds), *The Transformation of Scotland: The Economy since 1700* (Edinburgh, 2005), pp. 154–5, and C. H. Lee, 'Unbalanced Growth: Prosperity and Deprivation', in Devine, Lee and Peden, *Transformation*, pp. 224–31.

13 R. H. Campbell, 'The Scottish Office and the Special Areas in the 1930s', *Historical Journal*, 22 (1979), 167-83.

14 Ward, *Unionism*, pp. 31-3.

15 James Kellas, *The Scottish Political System* (Cambridge, 1989); Andrew Marr, *The Battle for Scotland* (Harmondsworth, 1992), pp. 113–15, 129–30, 136–7; Lindsay Paterson, *The Autonomy of Scotland* (Edinburgh, 1994); James Mitchell, 'Scotland in the Union, 1945–95: The Changing Nature of the Union State', in T. M. Devine and R. J. Finlay, *Scotland in the Twentieth Century* (Edinburgh, 1996), pp. 85–101; R. J. Finlay, *Modern Scotland* (London, 2004), *passim* but especially pp. 257–350; Heath's speech is in Paterson, *Diverse Assembly*, pp. 26–30.

16 Michael Hechter, *Internal Colonialism: The Celtic Fringe in British National Development, 1536–1966* (London, 1975), pp. 127–61.

17 Ward, *Unionism*, p. 186.

18 Gavin McCrone, *Scotland's Economic Progress, 1951–1960* (London, 1964), pp. 121–30.

19 Henry Drucker and Gordon Brown, *The Politics of Nationalism and Devolution* (London, 1980).

20 Christopher Harvie, *No Gods and Precious Few Heroes* (Edinburgh, 1993), pp. 142–73; John Foster, 'The Twentieth Century, 1914–1979', in R. A. Houston and W. W. J. Knox (eds), *The New Penguin History of Scotland* (London, 2001), pp. 417–93.

21 *The Times*, 3 September and 28 October 1953.

22 Foster, 'Twentieth Century', pp. 467–76.

23 *The Times*, 15 February 1972.

24 Foster, 'Twentieth Century', p. 484; Christopher Harvie, 'Scotland after 1978: from Referendum to Millennium', in Houston and Knox, *History of Scotland*, p. 500.

25 Harvie, *No Gods*, p. 151.

26 W. Knox, 'Class, Work and Trade Unionism in Scotland', in A. Dickson and J. H. Treble (eds), *People and Society in Scotland: Volume III, 1914–1990* (Edinburgh, 1994), pp. 108-37.

27 *Scottish Miner*, May 1971.

28 Arthur McIvor, 'Women and Work in Twentieth Century Scotland', in Dickson and Treble, *People and Society: Vol. III*, pp. 165–8.

1 Rootes: the 1960s and the longer road to devolution

On Thursday 2 May 1963 the Duke of Edinburgh opened the Rootes car factory at Linwood, completed in just less than two years at a cost of £23.25 million. The ceremony was attended by various dignitaries, including Michael Noble, Secretary of State for Scotland, Frederick Erroll, President of the Board of Trade, William Deedes, Minister without Portfolio, and Jo Grimond, leader of the Liberal Party.[1] The Duke had spent the previous night in Glenalmond at the Scottish country home of Lord Rootes, the motor group's chairman, before driving one of the factory's new products, a Hillman Imp, to Scone airfield, attaining 70 mph on the back roads. From Scone the Duke's entourage were flown to Renfrew airport and conveyed to Linwood for a celebratory lunch. The Duke's speech congratulated the 'Clan MacRootes' for its efforts in establishing the plant:

> At this stage all the setbacks are forgotten and for one brief, glorious moment everyone can give themselves up to the feeling of splendid satisfaction that comes with achievement. It is rather like that feeling when you have had a bit of a party the night before, and you wake up and for one brief moment you believe that you haven't actually got a hangover. That moment is necessarily brief.

The Duke observed that the motor industry had 'put down Rootes in Scotland', with the Imp as the new tree's first fruit, and toured the factory after lunch before driving another Imp back to the airport. The first official sale was made to Lord Polwarth, chairman of the SCDI, who drove the car home to Edinburgh after receiving its keys from Lord Rootes.

The Imp and the Linwood plant occupy a special place in the narrative of economic and industrial change in twentieth century Scotland. The car, with its rear engine and aluminium body, assembled from parts that were mainly manufactured in and transported expensively from the midlands, has been characterised as hopelessly uneconomic and inefficient. 'Grasping for a title' for his polemical dissection of the history of Scotland's sclerotic transport system, Christopher Harvie found that 'an image of indigestible failure hove into view: the country's ghastly diet, coupled with its last attempt at the motor age: the deep-fried Hillman Imp'.[2] Stephen Young and Neil Hood, writing when the plant was still in operation, showed that in 1972 – nine years after opening – some three-quarters of parts for Linwood were sourced more than 250 miles away, and more than 60 per cent of domestic sales were at similar distance.[3] Hence Clive Lee presents the factory as a cautionary tale that encapsulates the hazards of state intervention: established at Linwood under regional development policy geared to the alleviation of unemployment, it was too remote from markets and materials to produce cars efficiently.[4] The problem of location was aggravated to a limited extent also by various labour difficulties and low productivity that were related to the problematic conjunction of a new workforce, new shop stewards, new middle management, a new car and a new factory,[5] combined with the modest scale of Rootes as a company, which inhibited its investment capacity. Peter Payne duly casts Linwood in characteristically concise terms: 'It was a disaster.'[6]

So as an economic unit the Linwood car factory was not a success, although the extent of its 'failure' has perhaps been exaggerated. More than 440,000 of the lamented Imps were produced in the plant between 1963 and 1976,[7] and, applying broader social rather than narrow economic criteria, it might be observed that for roughly two decades it provided several thousand workers with relatively well paid employment and in part off-set some of the difficulties – chiefly unemployment and low incomes – that were arising from the weakening of older industrial employment sectors. Its detailed history is certainly important, and has perhaps been obscured or distorted by the dominant narrative of its 'failure'. This chapter takes a closer look, depicting Linwood's establishment and operation as illuminating a central feature of economic, social and political life in Scotland in the second half of the twentieth century, namely the attempt to widen the country's industrial base beyond the narrow nineteenth-century-established fronts of coal, metals, ships and textiles, and the extent to which this encouraged devolutionary forms of governance.

The industrial restructuring evident at Linwood was shaped by 'regional policy', shorthand for various state incentives and implements for directing younger forms of industry to areas that had been reliant on shrinking heavy industry and which were consequently characterised by sluggish economic activity and above-average unemployment. This chapter shows that industrial restructuring and regional policy were accompanied by rising demand – from Scottish Office bureaucrats and business and labour representatives – for greater administrative autonomy for Scotland within the United Kingdom. This stemmed from the concern that the existing form of governance was not fit for the purpose of alleviating industrial decline in Scotland. This chapter emphasises that regional policy was the consequence of tension and pressure from within Scotland. Where this regional policy appeared to be inadequate, Scottish industrial politics contributed in a significant way to the growth of devolutionist pressure. The central position of social tension in policy-making is evidenced by developments at Linwood, where the frequency of shopfloor protest highlighted the immense difficulties that were associated with industrial restructuring. The Rootes plant arguably embodied dehumanised and deskilled processes of industrial assembly: much of the labour unrest was arguably related to the difficulty of accommodating car assembly within the working culture of west-central Scotland, where craft labour was embedded as the dominant element. The cultural gulf between automated assembly and bespoke production was strikingly evident in the contrast between two documentary films that are examined here and in Chapter 3, *Young In Heart* (1963) and *Seawards the Great Ships* (1960). Both were made on behalf of the Films of Scotland Committee, and in partnership with industrial employers, but they depict entirely different characteristics of industrial production.[8]

The move from bespoke to standardised production, and from skilled labour to process assembly, indirectly contributed to an important trend in the Scottish labour movement's politics towards militancy and devolution. This was more directly shaped by working-class disappointment – expressed through the STUC – with the economic management of Wilson's Labour government from 1964 to 1970. Hopes for economic expansion foundered amid a series of financial crises, culminating in devaluation of sterling in 1967, which the government attempted to resolve by counter-inflationary measures that retarded growth in Scotland, and involved a statutory freeze on wage increases. Scottish labour representatives especially resented this, and were further antagonised by subsequent government proposals for state intervention in industrial relations in 1969. These related economic and industrial pressures would shape the context of the devolutionary debates of the 1970s.

Economic and political developments from the 1930s to the 1950s

Ideas about devolution as a means of improving Scotland's economic health had been ventilated before the 1960s, gaining particular impetus during the depression of the 1930s, and then re-emerging, in different form, during the post-1945 recovery. In each of these periods Scottish Unionists – the distinct identity of Conservatives in Scotland until 1965 – were prominent. Before the Second World War they sought to soften the social antagonisms arising from large-scale unemployment and offset socialist arguments that Conservative politicians were indifferent to the difficulties of the unemployed in Scotland; after the war they attempted to undermine support for the Labour government by arguing that its economic and social policies were stripping Scotland of its distinctive identity.

In the inter-war years the historical reliance on what Ross McKibbin has called the 'fatal nexus' of coal, ships, metals and heavy engineering had exposed Scotland to substantial economic and social dislocation.[9] Large-scale and long-term unemployment resulted from falling or disrupted international demand for the products of heavy Scottish industry. The greatest trouble spots were those most reliant on the contracting branches of industry: Lanarkshire (coal, iron and steel), Glasgow (coal, ships), West Fife (coal) and Dundee (ships and jute, with 50 per cent unemployment in 1932).[10] Yet Scotland was overall more reliant on the depressed industries than England, where business and domestic demand in the densely populated midlands and south supported new industries, notably telephones and other business machinery, consumer durable goods, household furniture, and commercial and private motor vehicles. These goods contributed to the strong sense – famously recorded in J. B. Priestley's travelogue – that southern England was changing rapidly, assuming a 'modernised' appearance with wide boulevards, suburban housing, and glass-fronted and electrically lit factories.[11] These changes were slower and less pronounced in Scotland, where the narrower economic and industrial base constrained general social development.[12]

Scotland's smaller size hampered new industrial growth but contributed, perhaps, to a greater understanding of the problems of the unemployed, who were more visible and less isolated than in England. George Orwell, visiting Lancashire and Yorkshire early in 1936, noted how physical distance contributed to ignorance in the south about the scale, character and consequences of unemployment.[13] In Scotland the unemployed were not hidden in the same way. The shorter distances especially from the coalfields to the main urban centres of Glasgow and Edinburgh made it easier, for instance, for unemployed miners to stage regular demonstrations that publicised their condition, although there were longer marches also from Glasgow to Edinburgh in 1933 and Aberdeen to Glasgow in 1935.[14]

This close physical proximity between industrial 'black spots' and middle-class residential areas may explain the greater priority apparently given by Conservative – or Unionist – politicians and industrialists in Scotland than England to unemployment and other social problems before the Second World War.[15] Walter Elliot is a good example here. Unionist MP for Lanark from 1918 to 1923, and then for Glasgow Kelvingrove from 1924 to 1945, and a Cabinet Minister for much of the 1930s, Elliot was a stronger advocate of state intervention in economic and social affairs than most of his English ministerial colleagues.[16] Elliot was associated with the nutritional scientist John Boyd Orr, director of the Rowett Research Institute in Aberdeen, and the author of *Food, Health and Income*, published in 1936, which emphasised that health inequalities arose from income-related inequalities in diet and nutrition.[17] This contradicted the predominant view at the time that poor nutritional health arose from the ignorance of low-income food consumers.

Such received wisdom hampered Elliot's efforts in the 1930s, as Minister of Agriculture, Secretary of State for Scotland and then Minister of Health, to secure more progressive food and nutritional policies that would narrow inequalities in diet and health arising from class and income differentials.[18]

Elliot encouraged state activism on broader economic and industrial fronts too. As Under Secretary of State for Scotland he was instrumental in the 1920s in shifting the majority of Scottish civil servants from London to Edinburgh. This was part of a longer Unionist tradition of securing incremental extensions of administrative devolution, with enhanced Scottish Office resources and responsibilities.[19] Roy Campbell's reading of Scottish Office papers from the 1930s demonstrates Elliot's subsequent commitment, as Secretary of State for Scotland, to government support for industrial development, with an emphasis on investment in capital equipment in private sector manufacturing. This set Elliot and the Scottish Office at odds with the Treasury and other Whitehall departments, where management of the 'Special Areas' policy from 1934 onwards meant no more than basic public works in essentially non-commercial activities. In Scotland this resulted, for example, in a concentration on the development of sewerage facilities. Elliot noted – in December 1937 – that this narrow approach indicated an absence of understanding in Whitehall about the particular characteristics of Scotland's economic and industrial problems, and he forecast, with some prescience, that this would contribute to a growth of Scottish nationalist sentiment.[20]

Elliot had some limited success, at least, in establishing in 1936 the Scottish Economic Committee, devoted to industrial planning with the purpose of 'examining the possibilities of improving conditions in Scotland'. The Committee emphasised the importance of building up light industries that would be less dependent on international demand, which was cyclical and unpredictable.[21] Business interests were paramount here: the Committee was chaired by Sir James Lithgow, the Port Glasgow shipbuilder, who alleged that high labour costs – imposed by obstructive unions – was the main explanation for poor industrial performance in the 1920s and early 1930s.[22] Hence there was some disquiet in the labour movement when the STUC joined the Committee,[23] which supplemented the work of the Scottish Development Council, formed in 1931, chiefly by business representatives, to attract new industries to Scotland and offset the prolonged decline of established sectors. These important developments marked the emergence of a thick strand of business opinion in Scotland in favour of the rational planning of economic development with assistance, where possible, from government,[24] although Foster resists the view that they 'led' in linear fashion to the regional economic policies of the 1950s and 1960s. There were important discontinuities, including Elliot's political eclipse, shaped by his tortuous position on Appeasement: privately opposed, he felt bound to observe the Cabinet's policy and was subsequently passed over for office by Winston Churchill, both in the Second World War and then upon the Conservative Party's return to power in 1951.[25]

Stronger roots of post-Second World War policy were arguably put down from 1941 by Winston Churchill's Secretary of State for Scotland, the Labour leader Tom Johnston, who encouraged relocation of industry to Scotland and initiated the Clyde Valley Plan of 1946, which proposed the resettlement of large portions of the Glasgow population in new industrial towns at East Kilbride, Cumbernauld, Bishopton and Houston.[26] In the same year the Scottish Development Council merged with the Scottish Council on Industry, established by Johnston in 1942 to optimise wartime production, to form the SCDI. The SCDI enjoyed some funding from local authorities and trade unions but owed its real strength to private sector industrial and commercial sponsorship,[27] and its relations with Scottish labour were consequently not entirely harmonious. Alex Kitson, a powerful presence in the STUC by the 1960s, disliked the SCDI's politics – 'they supported the Tories up tae the hilt', he said – which tended to be veiled by its relatively low public profile.[28] Nevertheless, after the Second World War the SCDI cultivated a solid working partnership with the UK Labour government, elected in July 1945, which was seeking to draw new industrial development away from southern and central England. The Board of Trade's regional policy enabled the SCDI to foster significant inward investment. Indeed Peter Payne relates the SCDI's subsequent prominence to its 'considerable prescience' in identifying electronics as central to industrial diversification, and encouraging US electronics firms to establish plants in Scotland from 1948 onwards.[29]

The Labour government's wider economic and social programme was contested, however, in Scotland, chiefly by Unionist politicians, who objected to the nationalisation of basic industries and services, along with the expansion of state welfare provision, on the grounds that undue control over Scottish affairs was being assumed by a centralising UK government.[30] Walter Elliot spoke about the 'swamping' of Scotland's economic identity, and characterised the extension of public ownership in industry as 'not nationalisation' but the 'denationalisation' of Scottish assets.[31] This emphasis on Scottish imperatives might well, of course, have cloaked Unionism's anti-socialist prejudices, and it certainly anticipated the more trenchant anti-socialist case for devolution that would be made by Bill Lithgow in the 1960s. But it was also reasonably consistent with Elliot's pre-Second World War politics, and presumably operated as some kind of factor in Unionism's healthy electoral performance in Scotland in the 1950s. What account of Scottish twentieth-century politics is complete without the observation that only on one occasion has a political party polled more than 50 per cent of votes cast in Scotland in a UK general election, and that this was the Unionists in 1955? The Tories had regained office in the UK in 1951 (and what account of UK twentieth-century politics does not note that this was in spite of the Labour Party polling more votes?). But despite the Tories' subsequent electoral successes, in 1959 as well as 1955, the 'relaxation' of wartime and post-war controls on consumption, and the growth, apparently, of personal affluence, there gradually emerged concerns about the UK government's management of the economy.

Toothill and regional policy in the early 1960s

The Toothill Committee of Inquiry, sponsored by the SCDI, which reported in November 1961, explored the Scottish dimensions of the broader UK anxiety about economic management. Toothill established the urgent extant requirement – despite the progress in electronics and other forms of younger manufacturing enterprise – for the widening of Scotland's economic and industrial base.[32] In this respect, as George Peden observes, Toothill was retracing ground covered by the Clyde Valley Plan, which also emphasised the importance of industrial diversification, as had the report of the 1940 Royal Commission on the Distribution of the Industrial Population.[33] What marked Toothill out from these earlier investigations, perhaps, were the relatively auspicious circumstances in Scotland, by pre-1940 standards at any rate, in which the problems of unemployment, sluggish growth and narrow industrial range were highlighted.

John Toothill was managing director of Ferranti, the electronics firm that was directed by the government to Edinburgh during the Second World War, owing to a labour shortage in its native Manchester, and which became the base for the subsequent expansion of the industry in Scotland after 1945.[34] Toothill's committee included Tom Wilson, Adam Smith Professor of Political Economy at the University of Glasgow, and five businessmen: Norman Best of Ranco Ltd, J. G. S. Gammell of British Assets Trust Ltd, A. J. C. Hoskyns-Abrahall of Unilever Ltd, John Russell Lang of G. & J. Weir Ltd and W. Roxburgh of Morphy-Richards Ltd. The Committee was serviced by 'Assessors' from the Scottish Office, the Board of Trade and the Ministry of Labour.[35] Overlooking the involvement of Russell Lang – or flexibly interpreting the character of the Weir engineering group – Foster writes that Toothill excluded representatives of Scottish heavy industry. This observation develops his argument that a significant fissure had opened in Scottish economic and business life in the 1950s: 'tradition', encompassing shipbuilding and steel interests, indigenous Scottish financial groupings, including the Bank of Scotland, and the *Glasgow Herald*, was ranged against 'modernisers', composed of the SCDI and American investors and manufacturers, who enjoyed the 'open' support of the STUC and *The Scotsman*, and the 'tacit' support of John Maclay, the Secretary of State for Scotland. The two sides were in competition, chiefly for steel and skilled labour, although the extent of this competition can be overstated, and in the later 1960s – as Chapter 2 explores – the 'traditionalists' and 'modernisers' could envisage mutually beneficial development projects. Nevertheless, Foster's characterisation of Toothill's report, 'the most sophisticated presentation of the modernisers' case',[36] accurately reflects its argument that the urgent requirement of faster economic growth could only be achieved through cultivating the advance of younger forms of industrial manufacturing.

Toothill looked at employment, observing that the average rate of unemployment in Scotland between 1953 and 1959 was 3.1 per cent. In the longer history of the twentieth century this seems fairly minor, and certainly compared favourably with the inter-war years. But for Toothill the significant point was that Scottish joblessness was roughly double the UK rate of 1.6 per cent. This was linked with the continuing reliance on the older sectors – *The Times*, in commending Toothill, spoke of Scotland's industrial revolution 'hangover' – and the relatively small presence of 'the science-based' and 'consumers' durable goods' industries. This discussion of the long-running problem of unemployment was buttressed by an examination of a newer issue in debates about economic development, namely the rate of growth.[37]

Growth carries important ideological meaning, primarily in the current age because of the environmental damage of relentlessly expanding production and consumption.[38] In the 1940s, 1950s and still in the 1960s, however, the chief ideological aspect of growth was that it offered the prospect of improved living standards for all without the politically awkward redistribution of wealth. It may be significant in this context that the drive to 'measure' and promote economic growth came initially from the United Nations in the late 1940s and early 1950s, seeking development in the Third World without transferring resources from established industrial countries. In Britain the goal of growth allowed the Conservative and Labour parties to promise improved public and welfare services, and expanding living standards for all classes, without any further redistribution of wealth across income or class lines. At the same time, however, the awareness from the mid-1950s that Britain's economy was growing more slowly than other industrial economies generated an increasingly agonised discussion about relative 'decline'. Jim Tomlinson shows how the scale of this alleged decline was emphasised by the Labour opposition and numerous liberal, social democratic and leftist journalists, commentators and academics, who attributed it to the class-conscious and hidebound character of the Conservative government.[39]

The Tories' defensiveness on this question helps to explain the development of regional economic policy from the late 1950s onwards. The most notable Scottish example here was the establishment of the Colvilles steel strip mill at Ravenscraig in Motherwell in 1958, devised with the Rootes car plant in mind.[40] The idea was initially floated in May 1957 by Sir Robert Maclean, chairman of the SCDI's export committee, who rationalised the project in terms of Scotland's unemployment rate. Sir Andrew McCance, chairman of Colvilles, predicted that the project would be a 'financial disaster', but was gradually pressed to accept it by John Maclay, supported by Iain Macleod, Minister of Labour, and Sir David Eccles, President of the Board of Trade. Macleod insisted that the strip mill losses at Ravenscraig would be offset by savings on unemployment maintenance arising from direct employment at Colvilles and jobs created by the projected stimulus to light industry. McCance succumbed, fearing another party might build the strip mill and damage Colvilles by competing for supplies of coal and other materials. The Prime Minister, Harold Macmillan, duly announced the establishment of the strip mill at Ravenscraig, along with another at Newport in South Wales, in November 1958.[41] In Foster's terms this was a clear victory for the light industrial 'modernisers', who gained local access to strip metal not previously available in Scotland, and a heavy defeat for the 'traditionalists', with the directors of Colvilles rightly anticipating that the strip mill would burden the firm with massive debt and incur insurmountable losses.[42]

Toothill implicitly criticised Ravenscraig and other Tory regional policy initiatives, however, precisely because they were a response to unemployment. This, he argued, was merely the symptom of low growth; employment would be raised significantly only by altering the focus of industrial assistance, to aid younger and potentially higher-growth forms of enterprise in the first instance, chiefly in the fields of light or technologically advanced engineering. This conclusion – that growth should be the prime target of economic and industrial policy – set Toothill at slight odds from the STUC, which had a preference for extending the state direction of industry into existing 'unemployment blackspots', but *The Times* approvingly characterised it as 'an assault on traditional defensive thinking'.[43] Toothill criticised in particular the character of the 1960 Local Employment Act, which directed aid to projects in development districts that were so designated on the basis of relatively high unemployment.[44] As unemployment fell the degree of state aid was likely to fall too, thereby potentially choking off nascent expansion.[45] Toothill's recommendation, supported by the SCDI, was to widen the 'basis of eligibility' so that state assistance would not be attached so rigidly to local unemployment rates. This approach was privately endorsed by Scottish Office officials, who in January 1962 argued that in the long term this policy should be transformed from a defensive response to unemployment to an unambiguously positive drive for economic growth.[46]

The Scottish Office's enthusiasm for Toothill is worth emphasising, marking a key stage in its increasingly close relationship with the business interests represented in the SCDI. This had its antecedents in debates about unemployment policy in the 1930s, as Roy Campbell has outlined,[47] but became progressively more evident in the 1960s, when Scottish Office bureaucrats and industrialists clearly shared a common analysis of economic prospects and policy. David McCrone would possibly see this as part of the emergence of a close-knit Scottish policy-making community after 1945, which encompassed representatives of the Confederation of British Industry (CBI) in Scotland, the STUC and – from the mid-1970s – the Scottish Development Agency (SDA), as well as the Scottish Office and the SCDI. He characterises this as a 'neo-corporatist' response to heavy industrial decline, involving substantial state enterprise to mitigate unemployment and social problems. In the longer run, he adds, the formation and operation of this consensual, cross-class policy-making community contributed to Scotland's relative rejection – across the 1980s and 1990s – of Thatcherism and neo-liberalism.[48]

This argument is persuasive, yet it is worth thinking also about the extent to which this 'consensus' – in the Toothill period and beyond – was shaped to suit the interests of industrial employers rather than meet the ends of social justice. The important point here is the distinction between increasing living standards for all classes through more rapid economic growth, which was the Toothill position, and securing relatively larger improvements in living standards for manual workers through greater wealth distribution, which had been the broad position of the labour movement in the first half of the twentieth century. Of material significance here is an important strand of social scientific regulatory theory that talks of interest group 'capture' of the processes and character of public policy. The interest group – usually if not always a business group – identifies its regulatory needs and realises them through state legislation.[49] Sometimes this is the result of direct involvement with bureaucrats or legislators;[50] on other occasions the processes are subtler, revolving around the exploitation by business and particularly industrial producer interests of the privileged political status that they arguably enjoy in capitalist societies.[51] No other interest group, it has been observed, shares the ability of industrial producers to gain public and government acceptance when they claim that their interests and welfare are synonymous with those of society generally.[52] There is a fairly clear sense in the development of Scottish Office thinking that in these terms it was 'captured' by Toothill and the SCDI: there were strong and enduring personal contacts between the bureaucrats and the industrialists; the Scottish Office regional policy officials readily accepted the Toothill view that Scotland's general welfare was contingent on economic growth – as opposed to wealth redistribution – and that this required state assistance to private industrial and commercial development. But the problem for the industrialists – and this would characterise developments that are examined in Chapter 2 also – was the character of policy-making in the British state, with the Treasury and Board of Trade enjoying clear primacy over the 'territorial' Scottish Office on economic and industrial matters, and taking an interest – often a decisive and negative interest – when measures were proposed in Scotland which had implications for developments in other parts of the UK.

Such was crucially the case with the Toothill analysis, which directly related Scotland's under-development to the more pronounced economic and industrial growth of the physically congested English midlands and south. The Scottish Correspondent of *The Times* pointed to the political difficulties it raised as an 'expression' of '"economic nationalism" – the force created in the post-war years in Scotland by the active alliance of men from industry, commerce, the trade unions, politics and academic institutions, for the improvement of the Scottish economy'.[53] Toothill insisted that greater utilisation of Scotland's physical space and labour resources would benefit the UK generally, by averting the inflationary economic pressures that were partly attributable to more rapid growth in the midlands and the south. There was support in the daily press for this idea, which was described as the 'fundamental doctrine of Toothill' by J. H. McGuiness, head of the Scottish Development Department (SDD), encompassing the Scottish Office's various economic, planning and environmental responsibilities, and established in March 1962 in line with one of Toothill's recommendations.[54] McGuiness and his colleagues accepted that growth in the under-developed regions would require industrial diversification, achievable *inter alia* through regional development and improved investment, communications, transportation, housing and education.[55] Each of these triggers, particularly regional development, required changes in the character and extent of state intervention, and the Scottish Office was clearly moving strongly in the direction of ratifying Toothill's plan. Christopher Harvie observes that the Secretary of State, John Maclay, himself accepted the findings of Toothill, and it was his decision to institute the SDD.[56] But support from the UK government was not forthcoming, almost certainly because of the implications for economic and industrial development in other parts of the UK that Toothill emphasised. This became clear in the summer of 1962.

On 12 July Maclay met Toothill and Polwarth, SCDI Chairman as well as Governor of the Bank of Scotland, along with officials from various UK government departments and the Scottish Office. Polwarth indicated that the recent recession had reversed Scotland's economic development after reasonable growth from 1959 to 1961. The SCDI tabled a 'Programme for Industrial Growth', which sought convergence on unemployment between Scotland and the rest of the UK through liberalising aid to industry and so creating 120,000 new jobs in Scotland by 1970. Maclay asked the SCDI to supply detailed advice on how the terms of inducements to industry to locate in Scotland could be clarified,[57] but on the following day was sacked on Macmillan's 'night of the long knives', the reshuffling of his unpopular government that saw seven Cabinet Ministers replaced.[58] Maclay was succeeded by Michael Noble, 'inexperienced' according to Harvie, and without his predecessor's commitment to Toothill.[59] Within days Noble was struggling through a Scottish debate in the House of Commons, a 'frightening baptism of fire' according to the sympathetic *Glasgow Herald*, with the opposition 'led by the biggest gun in the Socialist armoury, Mr Hugh Gaitskell', leader of the Labour Party. The *Glasgow Herald* advised readers that the government's answer to Toothill was imminent, forecasting targets for economic growth and 'bigger carrots and sticks for industry'.[60] Instead a tentative and defensive response was published in August, *Observations by the Government on the Recommendations of the Toothill Report*, stating that the main issues of area development and uneven growth between Scotland and the congested south were so 'fundamental', involving major policy and legislative changes, that the government could not 'state [its] conclusions at this stage'. A sequence of indecisive, defensive and generalised statements followed, relating to micro-features of Toothill, such as his call for more dynamism in the government's handling of industrial relations.[61]

Polwarth, a prominent Unionist figure in Scotland, duly criticised the government's approach to Scotland at an SCDI press conference with Toothill on 22 August. Toothill said the government was ignoring the central issue, the 'promotion of Scotland's economic growth', and forecast 'a battle' with ministers over the amendment of the Local Employment Act,[62] correctly anticipating the outcome of talks that took place several days later in Glasgow between the SCDI, Michael Noble and Frederick Erroll, President of the Board of Trade. The SCDI had resolved privately to concentrate on the essence of Toothill, ignored in the government's *Observations*, that it would be in the UK national interest 'to have in Scotland and other areas with similar problems a policy of "going for growth"'. The 'clarification' requested earlier by Maclay on inducement terms was defined: loans for up to ten years, with the first three years interest free, amounting to 50 per cent of capital require-ments.[63] The talks in Glasgow were not a success, disintegrating after just two hours when it became clear that there was no prospect of agreement on the general issue of amending industrial development policy. Erroll conceded in talks with the press that the employment situation was deteriorating in Scotland, with new jobs not offsetting losses in 'contracting industries', but argued that government policy had at least prevented an even larger volume of unemployment, and rejected the notion that Scotland represented a special case.[64]

Unemployment was rising in Scotland, from 85,366 in February 1962 to 136,030 in February 1963, the highest figure since the Second World War.[65] Erroll's argument, that Scotland was not a special case, was based on the more rapid escalation of unemployment across the UK as a whole, from 453,797 to 878,363 in the same twelve months. Yet in Scotland the subsequent recovery was slower and less complete than for the UK as a whole, where by January 1964 joblessness was 2.2 per cent, close to the 2 per cent of January 1962. In

Scotland unemployment at the start of 1964 was 4.6 per cent, stubbornly ahead of the January 1962's 3.9 per cent.[66] Within this Scottish national framework of the problem there remained the long-running phenomenon of 'black spots'. In June 1963, for instance, the Scotland-wide rate of unemployment of 4.3 per cent was exceeded in Glasgow, with 5.3 per cent, in North Lanarkshire, with 7.4 per cent, and Greenock and Port Glasgow, with 8.8 per cent.[67] These phenomena – local extremities within a disproportionately high national average – seemed to contradict Erroll's assertion that Scotland was not characterised by relative disadvantage, which overlooked too the macro-economic management which shaped movements in employment and unemployment. The 'Stop-Go' policy pursued by successive Conservative Chancellors of the Exchequer was arguably geared to high growth areas and did not suit the rest of the UK. The 'Stop' phases especially – engineered by Peter Thorneycroft in 1958 and then Selwyn Lloyd in 1961 – were designed to prevent overheating in the UK aggregate economy that was primarily the result of inflationary growth in the south and midlands.[68] John Cole, labour correspondent of *The Guardian*, duly wrote early in 1962 of the perception among Scots generally – 'and not only a lunatic Nationalist fringe' – that economic policies were tailored to suit 'conditions between Brighton and Birmingham'.[69] This growing sense of remote administration in Scotland had equally been a feature of the Toothill report, which emphasised the correlation between personal communications and economic growth, including a map that detailed a very close correspondence between regions of above-average economic growth and the area within $3\frac{1}{2}$ hours of London by rail or road.[70]

Noble warned Macmillan about the political dangers to the UK government of this sense of Scotland's remote and inadequate administration from London, writing in November 1962 of the growing disquiet in Scotland, among business as well as labour representatives, about 'the "stagnant" state of our economy'. He alluded to the collapsed talks with the SCDI two months earlier, advising the Prime Minister that the government risked alienating a potentially invaluable ally, given its incorporation of 'trade union and local authority as well as employer interests'. Noble noted that despite escalating unemployment in recent months the SCDI had been both co-operative and tactful, saying and doing nothing that might 'lead to embarrassment for the Government'.[71] Polwarth had indeed persuaded his SCDI colleagues after the Glasgow talks – perhaps especially those representing trade unions – that 'a dramatic gesture at the present time was more likely to harm than to forward the Council's case' and instead secured support for a campaign of stealth, concentrating on contacts with government officials 'in the south', a recognition, perhaps, of the Scottish Office's limited purchase on UK industrial policy. In this Polwarth had been supported by another prominent Scots Unionist businessman, Lord Clydesmuir, of the Colvilles steel dynasty.[72]

Macmillan was duly persuaded by Noble to meet the SCDI early in 1963. This enabled Polwarth to tell the SCDI's AGM in December 1962 that the Prime Minister was keen to discuss Scotland's 'difficulties' openly and frankly.[73]

Macmillan was accompanied by Noble, Erroll and Reginald Maudling, the Chancellor of the Exchequer, at this meeting, on 14 February 1963, which the SCDI used to reprise the case for Toothill-inspired 'growth areas'. Macmillan made no commitments on regional policy specifics, but advised that the economy was set to enter a 'Go' phrase, observing that ministers were prepared to risk upsetting the balance of payments in order to secure expansion. Polwarth presented this news triumphantly to the SCDI, noting that pan-UK growth policy was a 'breakthrough' for Scotland. 'The door', he commented portentously, 'was now open',[74] and the Chancellor duly delivered an expansionist budget of April 1963, for which Polwarth sent hearty written thanks to the Prime Minister.[75]

Polwarth's claimed victory was ambiguous. Gavin McCrone would observe in 1964 that uneven development could only be corrected if special measures were adopted that would enable Scotland to grow *faster* than the rest of the UK and so catch up with it.[76] But at least within the Scottish Office the Toothill analysis had not been abandoned. An Official Committee on Population and Employment Policy for Creating Growth Points in Scotland had been established in August 1962. The SDD dominated this Committee, and accepted without reservation Toothill's argument that industrial policy should be shaped not by local Ministry of Labour area unemployment figures but by the needs of central Scotland as a whole, with emphasis on stimulating 'growth in those places where it is most likely to become rapidly self generating'.[77] A new inter-departmental official body had also been formed, the Scottish Development Group, which included civil servants from the various UK departments with interests in Scotland, and the efforts of these two new bureaucratic bodies were brought together in the White Paper on Central Scotland, published in November 1963 along with a similar paper on north-east England.[78] The Scottish paper proposed a programme of investment in growth-related infrastructure, especially roads, with bridges over the Forth and Tay, and housing. The suggested expenditure, an increase for two years per annum from £100 million to £140 million, was presented as providing 7 per cent of Great Britain's population with 11 per cent of total public service investment.[79] Polwarth, speaking to the press, approvingly noted that this marked a further beneficial initiative, following the expansionist budget, with the tendency in regional policy to alleviating short-term unemployment giving way to a strategy of long-term growth. James Jack, STUC general secretary was more cautious, however, likening the proposals to a fanciful promise of repayment from an extremely unreliable borrower.[80]

The STUC had been sceptical too about a related branch of Conservative 'modernisation', the major contraction of the railway network under Richard

Beeching, brought from ICI to chair the British Railways Board in 1961. The STUC had been concerned about the possible damage to industrial and social development that would follow Beeching's anticipated cuts, and reported this concern through the SCDI to the Secretary of State for Scotland in July 1962.[81] The cuts eventually announced in March 1963, although designed to secure a future for the network, were certainly received badly in Scotland. With 102 branch lines assigned for closure Scottish trade unionists denounced the plan as an 'act of sabotage'.[82] In January 1964 Macmillan's successor as Prime Minister, Alec Douglas Home, accompanied by Noble and Eric Marples, the Minister of Transport, met an SCDI delegation led by Polwarth and George Middleton of the STUC. Polwarth spoke of his anxiety that the cuts might threaten the growth strategy for central Scotland; Middleton was more direct, saying that the loss of freight services – needed to arrest 'decline' – would be sorely felt, and Beeching's 'axe was a messy instrument for achieving economic progress'. Home was unsympathetic; Noble said nothing; Marples, bizarrely, claimed that the head of the German railways was considering the adoption of a very similar programme of contraction to Beeching's.[83] The Beeching cuts duly had a major political impact, according to Christopher Harvie, costing the Tories much rural support, especially in the Highlands, and contributing to their defeat in the 1964 general election.[84]

This political context, with the deepening unpopularity of the Tories, was indeed central to the development of regional policy in the early 1960s, and an indicator that the White Paper on Central Scotland was no straightforward 'response' to Toothill. As the 1962–63 correspondence between Noble and Macmillan reveals, it was published in the context of economic slowdown and industrial stagnation that was especially damaging for the government in Scotland. This is a reminder that regional policy was not simply delivered as an act of government benevolence. Rather it was shaped by pressures from below: by the resentment of the unemployed; by the disquiet of trade unionists whose job security and wages were jeopardised by unemployment; and by the anxieties of employers, fearful about the future prospects of their businesses and the social tensions gradually being unleashed by economic stagnation and reflected in the incremental leftward shift of public and especially working-class opinion. The general election of October 1964 gave Labour a fifteen-seat majority in Scotland, its first since 1950, and enough to secure the election of a Labour government in the UK, led by Harold Wilson.

Linwood: the difficulties of industrial adjustment

The Conservative government's continuing economic and industrial problems had been evident in the opening months of operations at Linwood, where a string of industrial disputes were strongly suggestive of the difficulties of transplanting 'new' industry – with the emphasis on capital intensity and assembly production – into a region with strong craft traditions. The new plant's incorporation of advanced technology and automation was strongly emphasised in a remarkable twenty-minute documentary film, *Young In Heart*, sponsored by Rootes and produced by Glasgow Films for the Films of Scotland Committee, a state-sponsored quasi-educational agency originally established in 1936 and revived in 1954.[86] The film was part of the 'blaze of publicity' – Tom Devine's words – that capitalised on the opening ceremony attended by the Duke of Edinburgh;[87] it was written by Clifford Hanley and narrated by Bryden Murdoch, who were also involved three years earlier in the Oscar-winning *Seawards the Great Ships*, which is discussed in Chapter 3. *Young In Heart*, which was distributed and shown in theatres across the world, looked at the manufacturing process, with a lengthy sequence of images and verbal descriptions of computerised design, precision instrument cutting and shaping, and automated assembly. There was some room for skill and human agency, but this appeared chiefly in the design process, and in product checking and supervision of assembly, which itself was depicted in a distinctly disembodied manner. The overhead rail carrying parts and bodies moved slowly and quietly, with no sense of the intensity, haste, noise and friction of car plants that so strongly characterises the testimonies of those who worked in them, or the accompanying human experiences of alienation and boredom.[88]

The depiction of the processes of manufacturing in *Young In Heart* is worth consideration, for the Linwood plant was presented – by the company, by government ministers and officials, by the press covering the opening, and even by the Duke of Edinburgh – as the acme of industrial modernisation, and the template for the growth of light engineering more broadly in Scotland. There appeared to be little understanding at this stage of how far the automated processes of assembly production would cut across the particular skilled working culture of west-central Scotland,[89] or the problematic industrial relations that this would entail. Strikes and other forms of industrial protest would be a recurrent feature of the plant's history, and were sometimes presented as the chief explanation of its supposed 'failure' and ultimate closure in 1981.[90] But there are other and arguably far more persuasive ways of understanding Linwood's disappointing record of production and sales, encompassing poor product and production design, its remote position from suppliers and markets, and the weak financial position of Rootes and its successors, Chrysler and then Peugeot. These aspects of the story are told in Chapters 3 and 5. In this chapter the incidence of industrial unrest is unfolded to illustrate the extent of worker dissatisfaction stemming from the shift from skilled production to semi- and unskilled assembly.

Labour politics were briefly referred to on the opening day by the *Glasgow Herald*, the print media's chief champion of the plant. It posed the question of whether in labour relations the new plant would prove to 'be a Dagenham or a Luton?'[91] This allusion to the relatively strike-prone Ford plant and its strike-free – until 1968 – Vauxhall competitor was pursued further by the paper in a special supplement, 'Scotland's Imp', printed the following day. The upbeat conclusion here was that the 'chaos' at Dagenham would not be repeated at Linwood, chiefly – and ominously, as matters developed – because Rootes had a history of taking a firm line against the type of 'militant shop stewards' who allegedly disrupted production at Ford. At a meeting between Ministry of Labour officials and motor industry employers in December 1961, Geoffrey Rootes, chairman of the firm's Scottish enterprise from 1963, had linked strikes to 'subversive action and the increasing influence of extremists'.[92] The firm had demonstrated its willingness to confront shopfloor dissidents earlier that year, in a dispute with stewards at the British Light Steel Pressings plant at Acton, West London, when management had shut down production entirely rather than concede ground. At Ford, the *Glasgow Herald* rightly noted, shop stewards had developed their influence as a consequence of the multiplicity of unions recognised, some twenty-two in all. To cut through the complexity of dealing with each of these organisations the company had tolerated the growth of a multi-union shop stewards committee. Less accurately, perhaps, the paper also alleged that Communists controlled the Dagenham committee in order to maximise disruption. This would not be a danger at Linwood, however, as the firm had 'taken firm steps to ensure' that no Communists would be employed in the new plant.[93]

Rootes had indeed taken explicit measures to ensure that industrial relations were more 'rational' at Linwood than at Ford. The company was dealing directly with just two unions, the Amalgamated Engineering Union (AEU) and the Transport and General Workers' Union (TGWU), although a third was involved indirectly, the National Union of Vehicle Builders, which represented employees at the nearby Pressed Steel plant, where car bodies were prepared for assembly at Rootes. Rootes acquired this plant subsequently, which operated as Rootes Pressings from 1966. Industrial relations were conditioned by – and also highlighted – the central feature of British economic life that had brought Rootes to Linwood: uneven growth. In 1959 the prolonged boom in domestic consumer demand for cars – which contrasted with the erratic market of the earlier 1950s – prompted the firm to plan the establishment of a new factory, with a site ear-marked for development at Ryton in Coventry. But this was blocked by the Board of Trade, the re-elected Conservative government in 1959 keen to demonstrate the powers of its new Local Employment Act, which came into force in 1960, by directing industry to areas of high unemployment. So while Rootes went to Linwood, Ford went to Halewood on Merseyside, and the British Motor Corporation to Llanelli and Bathgate, where roughly 1,000 trucks were being produced each week by a total workforce of around 4,500 in the spring of 1963.[94] Over Linwood, Stephen Wilks has written, the Board of Trade's 'persuasion verged on pressure'.[95] Foster puts the matter more bluntly: Macmillan picked out Rootes as 'the weakest and most vulnerable of UK car producers', applied the same 'strong-arm tactics' that had been used with Colvilles, and 'persuaded' the firm to move to Linwood.[96] This was within the context of fairly broad-based Scottish political pressure in 1959, marshalled by the STUC, on the government to encourage the transplantation of car manufacturing to Scotland.[97] The *Glasgow Herald* estimated that the Linwood factory had been built with the assistance of a government loan of £10 million, at the generous rate of 5 per cent, with the firm putting £5 million of its own capital into the construction and establishment cost of £23.5 million.[98]

Despite the long lead in time at Linwood – some five years from the conception of the factory to the commencement of production – the company had not, however, reached a negotiated settlement with union representatives on all aspects of wage levels, with no joint agreement on the means of deter-mining bonus payments.[99] Instead the firm sought to impose its own bonus system on the workforce, with the resulting friction one of the chief under-lying sources of discontent in the plant. There is the sense here of Rootes executives feeling that different rules applied at Linwood, given that the firm's presence in Scotland was chiefly the result of government development policy, and despite the advance warning issued at the 1962 STUC by William Scholes, Scottish Secretary of the TGWU, that industrialists should not expect 'both cheap labour and cooperation'.[100] Towards the end of a sequence of strikes in the spring of 1964 one Rootes executive candidly told the Scottish Correspondent of *The Times* that this was the main concern of management: 'this factory was set up to give a fair amount of employment in this area – and a profit for Rootes, too, of course – and yet some workers are trying to defeat the object of it.'[101] So employees who engaged in industrial protest were duly regarded as ungrateful as well as 'irresponsible', the term used by the firm to characterise the first 'major labour difficulty' at the plant, a walkout by 350 TGWU members on 22 May 1963, just three weeks after the official opening, the men dissatisfied with the progress of a claim for additional money.[102]

The firm was understandably anxious about interruptions to production during the opening months, which were held to be crucial to the plant's future. The closing sequence of *Young In Heart* depicted three transporters leaving the factory, laden with Imps bound for distant export markets. Initial orders were promising, with 20,000 – worth £10 million – placed in just two days following the official opening of the factory. Rootes intended to produce 150,000 Imps per annum, with roughly half for export. By December 1963 the firm was more than halfway to meeting its production target, with around 1,800 cars finished per week. In January Rootes reported the establishment of dealerships in France, Belgium, Germany and Italy, with an approximate weekly export volume of 1,300. This was in line with the firm's sales target, but the expansion of production was not proceeding as intended. At this stage the shortfall was attributed to unspecified 'technical difficulties',[103] but in the spring of 1964 'labour problems' were increasingly being offered as the chief explanation for slow production growth.

These problems – manifested in a sequence of unofficial strikes from February 1964 onwards – suggested that Linwood workers had a further significant and long-running grievance, beyond the concern about bonuses, which had been evident in 1963 and continued to surface in 1964. They earned appreciably less than motor industry workers in the south and the midlands, including other Rootes employees, and this was probably the fundamental source of the Linwood troubles. This was to some extent the burden of deep historical legacy. Scotland's industrialisation in the eighteenth and nineteenth centuries had been achieved in the context of low-wage labour.[104] With a better developed labour movement in the twentieth century, which encompassed 'national' wage bargaining across the UK, this was highly problematic, with workers in Scotland resenting the survival – albeit in moderated form – of wage levels and earnings that were lower than those in England. Wage disparities across the motor industry had recurrently caused labour unrest in motor manufacturing since the mid-1950s. In parallel with the problems at Linwood were those at Ford's new plant at Halewood on Merseyside, where full production also commenced in 1963. Ford initially reached an agreement with union officials to pay hourly rates at Halewood that were one-third lower than those at the established Dagenham plant. But parity between the sites was instituted after unofficial strikes and an overtime ban at Halewood, and threatened strike action at Dagenham, where workers worried about the implications of this disparity for their job security.[105] Similar developments ensued at Linwood, where Rootes received an undertaking from the unions that there would be no attempt to claim national pay rates – that is, those pertaining in the south and the midlands – for their Scottish members. The *Glasgow Herald* correctly predicted in May 1963 that 'the militants' at Linwood, were they to emerge, would duly organise themselves around a campaign for wage parity with Rootes employees in the midlands.[106] Between opening and March 1966, when Rootes gave evidence to the Donovan Commission on industrial relations, which is discussed later in this chapter, there were forty-nine separate wage claims at Linwood that related the position to Coventry pay. During this period the differential gradually narrowed, but only marginally, so that in January 1966 the hourly rate for Rootes production workers at Coventry was still roughly one-third more than at Linwood: 14s 4d as against 9s 6d.[107]

During the 1964 unofficial strikes low wages duly served as the most commonly expressed grievance, although there were also complaints that the 'tempo' of work – driven by the speed of the track – was too high, as the firm strived to reach its weekly target of 3,000 cars.[108] In April, following an unofficial stoppage over pay rates involving 1,700 members of the 2,500-strong workforce, there were signs that management at the firm was becoming frustrated, releasing a press statement to the effect that this was the twenty-second such stoppage in just three months. An assurance was obtained from union officials that in any future disputes the workers would remain at work pending the operation of official negotiation procedures.[109]

The workers duly deployed different tactics in pursuit of their next claim for an increase several weeks later, with 270 men on the final stages of assembly slowing production to cap output at 2,100 cars per week, down from the recent weekly volume of 2,500, and well short of the firm's target. This unofficial go-slow was an echo of the attempts made by skilled workers from time to time earlier in the twentieth century to control production, particularly in engineering workshops and shipyards.[110] While union officials were persuading the men to return to normal work Rootes signalled the exhaustion of its patience by dismissing the 270 men, citing 'industrial anarchy' as jeopardising 'vital export markets'. This annoyed union officials who had in fact persuaded their members to end the go-slow, but when the sackings were announced assembly was shut down totally until a settlement was reached that relocated the dismissed men to another part of the plant. This satisfied the firm's desire to establish a new labour squad on the final stage of assembly.[111]

This suggested some recognition by the firm of the attritional nature of the work. Harvie, Lee and Knox have all related the plant's poor industrial relations to the traditional working culture of central Scotland. There are assumptions here, which may be tenuous, given the absence of definite employment histories of the workers engaged at Linwood, that the car plant recruited people who had experienced skilled, or at least varied, work in the docks, engineering and shipbuilding. Such folk – in Harvie's words – found it difficult to adjust to the 'numbing discipline of the assembly line'.[112] This view was taken by some contemporary observers, including a leader writer at *The Times*, who praised Rootes for the firm hand it showed in ending the go-slow but noted 'the basic problem' that most of the employees were new to the motor industry and 'unused to the continuous pressure of the assembly line'.[113] Union officials took a different position, remaining adamant that the real problem was the pay differential between Linwood and the midlands,[114] but on this issue management remained unsympathetic, and insisted that unions should make greater efforts to develop workforce support for the plant as it struggled to establish itself.

Before the go-slow John Boyd of AEU Scotland and I. L. R. Kealey, TGWU National Officer in Scotland, had urged the workers to ease back on their wage demands to allow Rootes to 'get on their feet'.[115] The firm expected union members to follow their officials, which was a fairly standard but arguably unrealistic expectation of internal union relations in the 1960s. The *Glasgow Herald* saw the string of disputes at Linwood as a sign that the unions were 'struggling to assert authority' over members. 'Unions are not, cannot, be run by anarchists any more than companies. They depend on an accepted and respected chain of command.'[116] Yet Linwood was clearly reflecting an emerging and fundamentally different pattern of internal union relations that was becoming evident throughout the UK in the 1960s, with union members decreasingly bound by the guidance of their officials. There was, of course, a strong tradition of workplace or work group labourism in west-central Scotland, independent of and sometimes in opposition to official trade unionism. This had been observable especially in the engineering plants of Clydeside during and immediately after the First World War. But there was a particularly 1960s feel to the disputes at Linwood. Many of the dismissed men in May 1964 were not cowed by their experience, telling the *Glasgow Herald* that 'they felt they would get other good jobs fairly easily'.[117] Even in Scotland, with the post-1963 recovery in full swing, alternative employment was available, and the sack – or threat of the sack – was not the disciplinary instrument that it had been in earlier decades (and would be again in subsequent decades) in the twentieth century.[118]

Yet the impact of high levels of employment on both industrial relations and internal union affairs was still not properly understood in 1964, and would only be partly illuminated by the 1965–68 Royal Commission on Trade Unions and Employers' Organisations, appointed by the Labour government under the chairmanship of Lord Donovan. This famously identified what one of the Commissioners, Professor Hugh Clegg of Oxford University, later described as the 'centrifugal tendencies' in British industrial relations.[119] 'Full' employment since 1945 encouraged the development of informal bargaining, between shop stewards and workplace managers, alongside formal bargaining, between union officials and employers' representatives.[120] Alan Fox and Allan Flanders, colleagues of Clegg at Oxford, spelt out the implications of these developments for the character of trade unions, challenging the conventional wisdom that these were top-down, hierarchical bureaucracies, and emphasising instead the diffused nature of authority within unions, which they saw as comprising a potential multiplicity of interests.[121] These economic and industrial processes were being bolstered by less tangible social and cultural changes in the 1960s,[122] the impact of which on industrial relations and trade unions Geoffrey Goodman briefly summarised in his assessment of the career of Frank Cousins, general secretary of the TGWU from 1955 to 1969. During these years, Goodman wrote, the grip of the 'Establishment', in all branches of economic, social and political life, including the trade unions, was weakened. Popular deference was being eroded as 'ordinary men and women' grew in confidence, and became accustomed to taking the initiative on the shop floor. This diminished the capacity of union officials to control or even to shape significantly the trajectory of industrial developments.[123]

This was evidently so at Linwood; it would be so even more emphatically in the 1971–72 work-in at Upper Clyde Shipbuilders and the 1972 miners' strike, events that form the focus of Chapters 3 and 4 of this book. The unrest at Linwood, it should be emphasised, also suggested some weaknesses in the Toothill analysis. This had conceded that the number of working days lost to strike action was proportionately higher in Scotland than the UK generally, but attributed this to structural biases in the economy. It was noted that 'certain industries' – unspecified, perhaps for reasons of tact – were 'more subject to disputes than others', and that disputes were the consequence of 'conditions in the industry' rather than a question of geography. New industries could expect much smoother relations, particularly due to the relatively slacker labour market conditions that operated in Scotland.[124] These assumptions, John Foster notes, 'turned out to be misconceived'.[125] Employers, Rootes among them, were taken aback when the workers of central Scotland exhibited an unwillingness to accept their status as a reservoir of cheap labour that could be utilised to lower production costs for manufacturers and ease inflationary pressures within the UK economy. Nor was the workforce receptive to the position implicitly adopted by Rootes managers at Linwood, that gratitude was owed to the firm which would rather have been developing its products in the midlands.

This basic unwillingness of the firm to be in Scotland at all was one of several factors that were central to the longer-term difficulties of the plant, according to Lee, along with poor industrial relations and morale, which were related – as has been noted – to the monotonous nature of assembly production and technical troubles with the line, along with the fluctuating nature of sales that were evident even in the first year, 1963–64. The market for Imps swung more markedly than the general trend in what was broadly a seasonal trade, contributing to a greater degree of short-time working and redundancies at Linwood than was the case in the midlands, where employment was markedly more stable in the 1960s than it had been in the 1950s. The 'hire and fire' approach at Linwood reinforced the tendency to industrial unrest. Stability of employment in the midlands was contingent on sustained domestic demand; Lee observes, however, that this demand was changing as well as growing, with expanding taste – along with increased means – for larger cars. This drew custom away from the small Imp.[126]

The firm's difficulties became evident in June 1964, with reports that it was to receive investment, including at Linwood, by the Chrysler Corporation, which was keen to position itself alongside Ford and General Motors as a multi-national by developing an international profile, including a presence in Europe.[127] There were some suggestions that the 270 dismissals in May had been partly designed to show Chrysler executives in Detroit that their investment would be protected by the willingness of Rootes managers to adopt a 'tougher line' in their conduct of labour relations.[128] This perhaps added to the general atmosphere of anxiety in Scotland about the proposed involvement of the US firm, which the UK government sought to soothe. Home had replaced Erroll as President of the Board of Trade with Edward Heath, who received the additional title of Secretary of State for Trade, Industry and Regional Development, and was apparently seen as understanding more clearly than his predecessor the pressing requirement for 'dynamic' economic and industrial change.[129] In this regard Heath welcomed the possibility of US investment at Linwood. Speaking in Glasgow after a tour of central Scotland, he said the Chrysler link would help to strengthen Rootes in export markets. Motor analysts in the USA as well as the UK shared the idea that the partnership between the two firms represented a 'good fit',[130] although a later Chrysler Chief Executive, Lee Iacocca, would disparage the firm's UK initiative as a distraction from the core business of 'concentrating on good cars'.[131] Meanwhile, to prevent redundancies, a four-day week was adopted at Linwood from August 1964, with the assembly lines reorganised for a new model, the Singer Chamois, Rootes observing that the Imp had not sold 'as well as hoped'.[132] Heath duly sanctioned the acquisition by Chrysler of a portion of the Rootes equity, albeit on the understanding that there would be no incursion on the UK firm's independence and no further changes to the balance of share ownership without the agreement of the UK government.[133]

The Wilson government and Scottish industrial politics

The Conservative government's position had almost been rescued by the short-term impetus provided by the expansionist budget of April 1963, the last of Macmillan's premiership. This gave rise to Maudling's famous inflationary boom, which Wilson's Labour government felt obliged to dampen with a sequence of further deflationary measures.[134] The short-term fix – often devised to 'answer' problems of overheating in the English south and midlands – would have a greater bearing on the employment position in Scotland than strategic or longer-term development plans over the next three years. This was noted by Regional Development Division officials at the Scottish Office in 1969, in a written submission to the newly established Select Committee on Scottish Affairs, which conceded that various designs for expansion in Scotland – including the Tory policy for central Scotland and Labour's more ambitious 1966 *Plan for Expansion* – had been compromised by the deflationary measures of 1965, 1966 and 1967, including those designed to protect the UK balance of payments.[135]

Labour's *Plan for Expansion* accepted that employment in Scotland's traditional sectors would continue to shrink, entailing the need for compensatory growth of 130,000 'new' jobs, spread across manufacturing (50,000), construction (20,000) and the services (60,000). These employment targets were very close to those in the SCDI's 1962 'Programme for Industrial Growth', from which the *Plan for Expansion* also borrowed by proposing that manufacturing growth be achieved through designating all of Scotland as a Development Area, allowing firms across the country to claim eligibility for a wide range of investment grants and loans.[136] This end was secured with the 1966 Industrial Development Act.[137] Taken together these measures were a large-scale if belated endorsement of Toothill's call for generous state support for the development of new industry, which some 'traditional' industrialists were starting to oppose openly in 1966 and 1967, seeking cuts to regional assistance that were seen as benefiting American firms to the disadvantage of indigenous enterprise.[138] The SCDI, continuing to champion this American investment, was bullish about the importance of regional aid, and also notably upbeat about prospects in 1966 and 1967, even although the government's response to the financial crisis of July 1966 – a massive dose of deflation – greatly reduced the possibility of the government's expansionist plans being fully realised.[139]

Wilson had worked hard to present the 1966 financial crisis as the direct consequence of a lengthy strike in pursuit of a pay claim by the National Union of Seamen from the middle of May to the end of June. There was some basis for the Prime Minister's argument. With ships tied up in port exports were delayed and short-term damage to the balance of payments resulted.[140] But he greatly antagonised trade unionists, many Labour Party members and even some of his ministers with his allegations that the seamen's strike and related unofficial stoppages by dockers were the results of a communist conspiracy. While in breach of the government's at this stage voluntary wages policy, the seamen's claim had to be seen in the context of their longer working hours and highly unusual employment environment, with discipline still shaped by the 1894 Shipping Act which imposed fines and occasionally imprisonment for disobedience.[141] The STUC supported the seamen's strike, was highly critical of Wilson's approach, and more outspoken still in its opposition to the emergency Prices and Incomes Act introduced in the summer of 1966. This placed a six-month statutory freeze on pay increases and scheduled a further six months of 'severe restraint', which was ill received by trade unionists across the UK. The restrictions seemed to fall disproportionately on weekly wage earners and especially semi- and unskilled manual labourers, and were perceived as class injustice by many on the shopfloor, with movements in profits, shares and salaries not seen as being subject to the same degree of regulation.[142] But there were particular grievances in Scotland. The 1967 STUC conference called for the repeal of the Prices and Incomes legislation, characterised by Lawrence Daly, General Secretary of the Scottish miners, as both a breach of the 'democratic right of free collective bargaining' and an instrument that consolidated the iniquitous disparity between Scottish and English wages. More galling still was the perception that wage controls on Scottish workers were designed essentially to restrain inflationary pressures that were evident only in the English south and midlands. Alex Kitson of the Scottish Commercial Motormen's Union, who outlined the 'vigorous' opposition of his members to the government freeze, supported Daly. Alluding to the power of pressure from below, Kitson added that it was the duty of 'responsible' union officials to listen and respond to workers.[143]

These two strands of the STUC critique of Wilson, that Scotland's problems were different from England's problems, and that labour leaders had to move with popular opinion, were reflected in Scottish labour's shifting approach to Home Rule. The relationship between the Scottish labour movement and Scottish 'identity' was not straightforward. Knox notes that the trend in the second half of the twentieth century in Scotland was for unions to become more British, in an institutional sense, with smaller numbers of workers organised in independent or autonomous Scottish unions. Craigen makes a similar observation, writing about the almost complete shift by the 1970s of separate Scottish into UK-wide institutions,[144] and Gregor Gall uses this trend to support his elaboration of the 'mythology' of a Scottish working class distinctive from the rest of the British working class by dint of its greater militancy. Gall's discussion is fairly plausible, although is perhaps flawed by its idiosyncratic tendency to compare quantitative trends in Scotland as a 'region' with those in 'other' regions of Britain – Yorkshire, the 'North West' and so on – rather than with those in England as a whole. This tends to obscure the comparative militancy of Clydeside, say, or West Fife, and the characterisation of Scotland as a whole but not England as a whole as a 'region' of the UK is certainly odd.[145] Nevertheless, it is true that Scottish labour institutions were losing their distinctive character in this period. Alex Kitson himself, while a prominent supporter of devolution,[146] would lead his Scottish Commercial Motormen into a merger with the UK's TGWU in 1972.[147] But identity – or national identity – was more complex, and institutional affiliations can be set against the positions adopted by union members, including and sometimes especially those who were members of British organisations. The case of the NUM in Scotland illustrates this neatly. In 1967 the Scottish miners elected as their President Michael McGahey, a Communist, who had campaigned on the basis of his opposition to the Labour government's accelerated programme of closures of pits.[148] At the 1968 STUC conference McGahey said that he would never countenance Scottish independence: he belonged to 'a national union operating in a nationalised industry which the miners would never allow to be destroyed'.[149] He followed this up in 1969 with the observation that he had 'more in common with the London dockers and the Birmingham busmen irrespective of colour or creed' than 'Alexander Home' and any other Tory Scot. Yet he was nevertheless in the vanguard of those proposing the establishment of a Scottish Parliament, which was depicted as entirely desirable from a class perspective, allowing people to take greater control over the economic, industrial and social affairs that shaped their lives.[150]

McGahey's intervention was designed to give direction to STUC policy on Home Rule, which had been fluctuating since the Second World War, and position the organised working class at the centre of the debate about the 'national question'. He argued that without a clear lead from the STUC this debate would be shaped instead by nationalist 'demagogues' who were either indifferent or hostile to working-class interests.[151] This was a response to the startling Parliamentary by-election at Hamilton of November 1967, in which Labour's safe seat was won for the SNP by Winnie Ewing. The by-election created a great stir, the SNP publicising its triumph with some panache. The victorious candidate and her family were conveyed first to Glasgow Central Station by two Linwood-manufactured Hillman Imps, courtesy of Rootes-Chrysler, and then overnight to London and thence Westminster with many of her supporters aboard a specially chartered train, the 'Tartan Express'. Ewing secured a column in the *Daily Record*, which Andrew Marr sees as contributing to her party's strong showing in local elections in May 1968, where it led the field with 34 per cent of votes cast.[152]

Labour people more broadly have concurred with McGahey's estimation of the class basis of the SNP. Gordon Brown, writing in 1980, linked the party's emergence in the 1960s to class de-alignment in electoral politics, the product in Scotland of changes in the economy and the breaking down of the skilled working class. The SNP appealed to the 'socially and politically displaced people' churned up by these economic changes.[153] McGahey's initiative, meanwhile, should also be seen in the context of Scottish labour's shifting relationship with Home Rule since the Second World War. In 1947 and 1948 the STUC pronounced support for a number of devolutionist measures, including a Scottish National Planning Commission, new Trade and Labour departments or divisions within the Scottish Office, and a 'Cabinet' of Scottish ministers.[154] These were resisted by the Labour government in the same way – although with less rhetorical disdain – that the Scottish Convention was dismissed. This Convention had grown out of the modest electoral and political gains made by the SNP during the Second World War, and encompassed a number of Scottish Assemblies between 1947 and 1949, which gathered a reasonably wide mixture of social and political support. A Covenant was prepared, recalling the independent, earnest and Presbyterian tradition of the mid-seventeenth century, with two million signatures, some of which may have been fraudulent, and presented to Parliament in Westminster, calling for Scottish Home Rule. Party political and class loyalties were not transcended by the Covenant, however, and the Labour government's rejection of Home Rule was not seriously contested in Scotland.[155]

In the Labour Party in Scotland the emergent concern about uneven economic growth in the 1950s even consolidated support for the Union, perceived as the vehicle – through the correct socialist planning from a Labour government in Whitehall – for redistributing wealth from expanding to stagnating regions.[156] This position had strong roots in the 1930s, when prolonged depression and mass unemployment encouraged the Labour Party to view centralised economic management from within the UK as the best means of directing industry and employment to Scotland. This consolidated the party's shift away from Home Rule, a process further embedded by Johnston's conduct of policy at the Scottish Office during the Second World War.[157] Within the STUC there remained some support for devolution, with Abe Moffat of the NUM and the CPGB moving a resolution in favour of a Scottish Parliament at the 1950 Congress. For Moffat this reprised his party's 'popular front' agenda of the mid-1930s, when Willie Gallacher, Communist MP for West Fife from 1935 to 1950, had campaigned with James Maxton of the Independent Labour Party and John MacCormick of the SNP – one of the leading Covenanters of the 1940s – for a Scottish Parliament that would enable Scotland to 'plan' its way out of capitalist depression.[158] But the STUC General Secretary from 1949, George Middleton, himself a former Communist – who in Stalinist mode had adopted a quick about-turn in September 1939, following the Nazi-Soviet pact, to oppose the Second World War as an 'imperialist' enterprise – swung the organisation behind Labour's centralised interpretation of the Union. He suppressed 'nationalist sentiments', according to James Craigen, an STUC officer in the 1960s and 1970s and then a Labour MP in the 1970s and 1980s, and the 'STUC had closed the door on political devolution and would concentrate on industrial development and administrative devolution'. Hence the emphasis – examined earlier in this chapter – on growth and new industries in the 1950s.[159]

James Jack, STUC General Secretary since 1963, was concerned about the political implications of McGahey's proposal at the 1968 STUC, particularly as it was faced by a potentially rival motion, from the Foundry Workers of the Amalgamated Engineers, calling for the Congress to 'repudiate' Scottish nationalism without referring to Home Rule. Jack duly secured the withdrawal of both motions,[160] but – as Campbell Christie, later General Secretary of the STUC, would write on McGahey's death – the Scottish labour movement's longer-term political goal, a devolved legislative Parliament within the UK, had now apparently been established.[161] There would be further vacillations, notably in the summer of 1970, when the STUC General Council, in evidence to the Royal Commission on the Constitution that is discussed in Chapter 2, withdrew its support for a Parliament with legislative powers, favouring instead a 'part-time' Assembly to 'exert control and give direction' to the Scottish Office.[162] But this was a temporary retreat, perhaps shaped by labour movement caution in the wake of the Conservative Party's surprise victory in the general election.[163] In the winter of 1971–72, as Chapter 3 examines, the STUC restated its commitment to a legislative Assembly within the UK, a position which it retained right through the 1970s, 1980s and 1990s.

While the Labour government was subject to increasingly sharp criticism from its traditional supporters in the STUC, the industrial leaders of the SCDI were less critical of economic developments. The SCDI's optimism in the face of deflation was partly – even perversely – based on the much greater rate of increase of unemployment that took hold in England than Scotland after 1966. In December 1967 the SCDI published a survey, *Unemployment in Scotland*, looking at the relative weights of the problem in different parts of the UK since 1952. There was 'good news' here on two fronts, allegedly. First, Scotland was now judged to be less sensitive to 'Stop-Go' than the UK as a whole. In the 1963 recession unemployment was taken as rising by 47.8 per cent in Scotland, compared with 66.8 per cent throughout the UK, although it will be remembered from earlier in this chapter that the recovery in 1964 was slightly slower and less complete in Scotland. In the 'big squeeze' from March 1966 to May 1967 unemployment in the UK had increased by 95.6 per cent but in Scotland only by 53.9 per cent. Second, and consequently, Scottish unemployment now represented a significantly smaller share of the UK-wide phenomenon: 15 per cent, compared with 18.3 per cent in 1958–59 and 17.2 per cent in 1962–63. This picture of 'improvement' was attributed to the changes in Scotland's industrial structure that had been proceeding in the 1960s. As this process of structural change was irreversible it was likely that the gap between unemployment rates in Scotland and the UK generally would continue to narrow.[164]

Yet there remained an important difference between the SCDI analysis and the position of the UK government. Toothill's observation about the complementarity of Scottish under-development and English over-development, while fully accepted at the Scottish Office, was still resisted within Whitehall. Wilson's government in 1968 established a Parliamentary Select Committee on Scottish Affairs. This was partly the government's response to the SNP victory at Hamilton the previous November, although Wilson and his Lord President and Leader of the House of Commons, Richard Crossman, had to an extent been anticipating these developments, preparing for some measures of decentralised administration in Wales and Scotland from at least May 1967.[165] In preparing a written submission to the Select Committee early in 1969 the Regional Development Division of the Scottish Office reviewed the history of development policy since the 1930s, charting the shift in thinking in the 1960s 'away from simple preoccupation with unemployment' to the encouragement of growth areas, embodied in the Toothill report, with its emphasis on the linked nature of Scottish sluggishness and English overheating described as 'accepted policy'. These references to Toothill were dropped from the published submission to the Select Committee, suggesting the existence somewhere in the bureaucracy of decisive opposition to the idea that the resolution of Scotland's difficulties required some checks on English development.[166]

So Scotland's industrial 'modernisers' were not fully in harmony with the UK government, and this was important, persuading Toothill and other light industrial leaders to offer at least conditional support for the policy initiatives of the 'traditionalists' from 1967 onwards. Steel and shipbuilding interests in Scotland had much to concern themselves with by this point, both anxious about the loss of employment in heavy industry that had accelerated, partly as a consequence of Labour's deflationary measures, since 1964. The Labour government had additionally antagonised Ronald Colville, the second Baron Clydesmuir, with the nationalisation of steel, completed in 1967.[167] The traditionalists regarded this as evidence that power was drifting away from Scotland, reinforcing extant anxieties about the growth of foreign ownership in the Scottish economy, and the attendant branch plant production syndrome.[168]

This latter anxiety was deepened with developments at Rootes in Linwood, where the problems of indifferent design and low investment had been significantly compounded by 'Stop-Go'. Labour's deflationary measures of 1966 caused particular damage for car manufacturers, with demand across the industry dropping 23 per cent on the last five months of 1966 compared with 1965. Wilks characterises the measures as having 'delivered the *coup de grâce* to Rootes'.[169] The firm's rate of losses were certainly intensified: the pre-tax loss for 1964–65 was £1.3 million; for 1965–66 it was £3 million; and for the first six months of 1966–67 alone it was £4.7 million. Tony Benn, Minister of Technology, attempted to construct a major new British manufacturer – capable of competing with US firms – by persuading the British Motor Corporation and the Leyland Motor Corporation to merge and then acquire Rootes. But this initiative was unsuccessful,[170] and so Benn reluctantly in January 1967 announced support from the UK government for a £20 million 'rescue' plan that amounted to a conditional takeover by Chrysler, which increased its share of voting equity in Rootes from 45 to 68 per cent.

Chrysler was defending its original investment, but, like other US investors in Scotland, also anticipating the access to wider markets that would follow the UK's possible future membership of the EEC. William McLean of the NUM, who in 1967 was also STUC President, said this disappointing outcome diminished the UK government's capacity to plan the Scottish economy, and offered the prospect of future profits from the plant being exported to the USA rather than reinvested in Linwood.[171] This was true, but the plant was at least saved, preserving some 7,600 jobs at Linwood, where employment would later peak at around 8,400 in the early 1970s, and by 1971, indeed, the prognosis was of stability. In his study of the economy published by Scottish Television, Thomson-owned, and so perhaps conditioned by the modernisers' optimistic agenda, George T. Murray wrote that the Chrysler investment had been beneficial, providing greater product variety at Linwood and thereby enhancing hopes for the future. In addition to Chrysler's range of medium-size cars some progress had been made in diminishing the plant's reliance on long-distance supplies of components, with rear axles and gearboxes now produced on-site at Linwood.[172]

But old practices survived these changes. There were major unofficial stoppages in March and September 1967, with production on a new Imp and the Singer Chamois suspended for several days as a consequence of disputes about pay levels and workload.[173] In 1968 there was a lengthier strike involving around 4,000 workers from 14 May to 10 June. At issue was a new wage structure and method of payment, the fixed hourly rates of 'measured day work' replacing piecework. This was designed to match pay more closely to productivity, reduce the number of 'man-hours' per car from 97 to 72, and so increase weekly production by 350. The package was designed by George Cattell, Rootes' Director of Manufacturing, who had been seconded to Linwood as Personnel Director in order to 'resolve' the firm's labour 'difficulties' there. Dave Lyddon, an authority on industrial relations in car manufacturing, notes that Rootes 'imposed' the arrangements on the workforce,[174] although there does appear to have been some consultation, with officials of the TGWU and the Vehicle Builders Union accepting the terms. The AEU, however, which represented craftsmen at the plant, did not. Barbara Castle, just in the door at the remodelled Department of Employment and Productivity, established a Court of Inquiry, where Cattell argued that the new arrangements would limit the firm's continuing losses of £4.5 million in the financial year just ended. He presented the offer as 'a sincere attempt to bring some order from a situation of chaos and, on occasion, anarchy'. The dispute was resolved without the intervention of the Court of Inquiry, which the AEU had in any case boycotted, with new proposals by the firm endorsed by union officials at talks in London and accepted by the workers in Linwood. Cattell, unable to implement his proposals without the pain of this lengthy dispute, was nevertheless appointed by Castle – with the blessing of the Trades Union Congress (TUC), the CBI and the heads of the nationalised industries – as the first Director of Manpower and Productivity at the Department of Employment.[175]

In the meantime Castle was developing her response to the Donovan Commission on Trade Unions and Employers' Organisations, which reported in June 1968. While identifying unofficial strikes as a source of significant inflationary wage drift, the Commission recommended strengthening union organisation in the workplace through a sequence of voluntary measures, consonant with established voluntarist traditions, and so narrowing the gulf between officials and members that was manifested in unofficial action.[176] This contradicted the position of employers' organisations, amplified in the business press and supported by the Conservative opposition, that agreements between employers and unions should be statutorily enforceable, effectively outlawing unofficial strikes.[177] 'What is to be done', asked John Davies, CBI Director General and Heath's future Industry Secretary, 'to these unofficial strikers who hold the country to ransom and undermine our economic life?'[178] Castle and her officials at the Department of Employment felt the pressure of this business and Tory criticism of Donovan, and were disinclined to rely on voluntary improvements alone. An unofficial stoppage late in 1968 by twenty-two machine setters at Girling Brake Works in the midlands, who refused to take orders from a foreman belonging to another union, led to the temporary redundancy of about 5,000 car assembly workers in adjacent factories, such was the integrated nature of assembly production in the industry.[179] The perceived damage to trade persuaded Castle that interventionist powers were essential, and her White Paper, *In Place of Strife*, published in January 1969, proposed fining workers engaged in unauthorised strikes, statutory ballots of members in advance of official strikes, and government-imposed resolutions of inter-union disputes such as the Girling episode.[180]

Castle recognised that these measures would be unpopular with 'her people' in the labour movement, but viewed matters from a particular socialist perspective: unofficial strikes fractured the solidarity of labour, and tended to privilege the skilled and higher paid over the unskilled and lower paid. She also emphasised – then and retrospectively – that the policy offered much of value to trade unionists, including the statutory right to union membership and state funding for union 'development', chiefly in the form of union mergers and shop steward training.[181] Even these benefits were not warmly received within the labour movement, which broadly opposed *In Place of Strife* as a major incursion on trade union prerogatives, and a breach of the 'rules' governing the relationship between the Labour Party and the unions, with a blurring of the historical boundaries between 'political' and 'industrial' matters.[182] At the STUC gathering at Rothesay in April 1969 McGahey said that granting a man the right to union membership was as presumptuous as granting him the right to breathe; he supported an emergency resolution opposing 'anti-democratic measures aimed at free trade unionism'. Kitson positioned the proposals in a continuum that incorporated the wage freeze and deflationary economic management, designed to trump the Tories and please the bankers, and the motion was carried.[183] The STUC position had been shaped by a one-day strike on Clydeside,[184] and fed into a popular UK-wide programme of resistance, which included other one-day strikes and an emergency meeting of the TUC early in June at Croydon. This proposed renewed efforts from within the labour movement – directed by the

TUC General Council – to resolve inter-union disputes and minimise unofficial disruption.[185] *In Place of Strife* was duly abandoned after discussions involving the Cabinet and the TUC General Council on 16 and 17 June, with the TUC renewing its Croydon promise to generate voluntary anti-strike measures.[186]

The first published account of this episode was called *The Battle of Downing Street*,[187] and it became customary thereafter to explain its outcome in terms of the high politics of government and the unions,[188] sometimes in relation to the perceived block-headedness of various TUC 'barons' who by taking Castle's unpalatable medicine might have avoided the brutal surgery of the Thatcher years. But events were really shaped by pressure from below, with union leaders pushed to adopt militant positions by their members who were generally disappointed with the government's economic management and particularly antagonised by the incomes policy.[189] Castle herself ought to have felt this pressure from below. On the morning of 19 April 1969 she addressed the STUC at Rothesay, where the conference president, Enoch Humphries of the Fire Brigades Union, advised her to take the message of opposition back to London.[190] She then flew on by helicopter to Linwood, where her tour of the plant was punctuated by encounters with workers who expressed their unambiguous opposition to *In Place of Strife*, including 'a young lad, jumping down from the assembly line with "Think again, Barbara" spelt out on his white jumper'.[191]

This popular resistance at Linwood to *In Place of Strife* was of a piece with the strikes of 1967 and 1968, which themselves were further reminders of the difficulties inherent in widening Scotland's economic and industrial base. Rootes was a reluctant presence at Linwood; the workers adjusted slowly, and incompletely, to the grinding monotony of assembly. The presence of US capital, initially in 1964 and then more forcefully from 1967, was an additional source of tension, and contributed to what John Foster terms the 're-emergence' of 'class politics' in the second half of the 1960s. By this he means that public debate was shaped by a polarisation along class lines, encouraged by popular anxieties about the increasing presence of multinational companies – in various branches of manufacturing – and the loss of indigenous control. A heightening of working-class consciousness had been evident in the growth of shopfloor power, at Linwood and elsewhere, with union officials – and subsequently the Labour Party also in Scotland – shifting to the left as a consequence.[192] This was reflected in the STUC debates on devolution, economic management and industrial relations. These various developments, each connected in some way to the widening of Scotland's economic base, also greatly troubled 'old-fashioned tycoons' like Clydesmuir and William Lithgow of the Clyde shipbuilding dynasty.[193] From the late 1960s to the mid-1970s Clydesmuir and Lithgow dominated the SCDI, and were concerned that efforts to build up new industries had been at excessive cost to the established industries over which they presided, and had weakened social and political stability more broadly. Their efforts to resuscitate these traditional sectors, while still nurturing the new, form the subject of the next chapter. Underlining the linkage between worries about industrial stagnation and the attraction of devolution, this involved the quest for considerably enhanced Scottish autonomy in economic and industrial policy, and an explicit attack on established economic and political links between Scotland and the rest of the UK.

Notes

1 This account of the Duke's visit to Linwood is taken from the *Glasgow Herald*, 2 and 3 May 1963, and *The Times*, 3 May 1963.
2 Christopher Harvie, *Deep Fried Hillman Imp* (Argyll, 2001), p. 14.
3 Stephen Young and Neil Hood, *Chrysler UK: A Corporation in Transition* (New York, 1977), pp. 265–7.
4 C. H. Lee, *Scotland and the United Kingdom: The Economy and the Union in the Twentieth Century* (Manchester, 1999), pp. 182–3.
5 Young and Hood, *Chrysler UK*, p. 272.
6 Peter Payne, 'New Industries', in Michael Lynch (ed.), *The Oxford Companion to Scottish History* (Oxford, 2001), p. 214.
7 Hillman Imp Exhibit Panel, Museum of Transport, Glasgow.
8 Jo Sherington, *'To Speak its Pride': The Work of the Films of Scotland Committee, 1938–1982* (Glasgow, 1996), pp. 40–3, 49; the entire output of the Films of Scotland Committee is available digitally, and can be downloaded without charge by internet users with ac.uk domains and an ATHENS identity through the Scottish Screen Archive web pages.
9 Ross McKibbin, *Classes and Cultures. England 1918–1951* (Oxford, 1998), p. 112.
10 W. W. Knox, *Industrial Nation: Scotland, 1800 to the Present* (Edinburgh, 1999), pp. 189–91.
11 J. B. Priestley, *English Journey* (Harmondsworth, 1977 reprint), pp. 9–23, 374–80.
12 Neil K. Buxton, 'Economic Growth in Scotland between the Wars: The Role of Production Structure on Rationalization', *Economic History Review*, 33 (1980), 538–55.
13 George Orwell, *The Road to Wigan Pier* (Harmondsworth, 1962 reprint), pp. 94–102.
14 Ian MacDougall, *Voices from the Hunger Marches: Volume I* (Edinburgh, 1990), pp. 111–16, 213–14; Foster, 'Twentieth Century', p. 446.
15 I. G. C. Hutchison, *Scottish Politics in the Twentieth Century* (Basingstoke, 2001), pp. 50–3.
16 Ward, *Unionism*, pp. 23–5.
17 John Boyd Orr, *Food, Health and Income: Report on a Survey of Adequacy of Diet in Relation to Income* (HMSO, 1936).
18 David F. Smith, 'The Scientific Food Committee', in David F. Smith and Jim Phillips (eds), *Food, Science, Policy and Regulation in the Twentieth Century* (London, 2000), pp. 101–2; Sir Colin Coote, 'Sir Walter Elliot', in E. T. Williams and Helen M. Palmer (eds), *Dictionary of National Biography, 1951–60* (Oxford, 1971), pp. 332–4.

19   James Mitchell, *Conservatives and the Union: A Study of Conservative Party Attitudes to the Union* (Edinburgh, 1990), pp. 17–37.

20   Campbell, 'Scottish Office in the 1930s', pp. 167–83; Elliot's prescience is noted on pp. 182–3.

21   Richard Saville, 'The Industrial Background to the Post-War Scottish Economy', in Richard Saville (ed.), *The Economic Development of Modern Scotland, 1950–1980* (Edinburgh, 1985), pp. 12–13.

22   Lewis Johnman and Hugh Murphy, *Shipbuilding in Britain since 1914: A Political Economy of Decline* (Exeter, 2002), p. 30.

23   James Craigen, 'The Scottish TUC: Scotland's Assembly of Labour', in Ian Donnachie, Christopher Harvie and Ian S. Wood (eds), *Forward! Labour Politics in Scotland, 1888–1988* (Edinburgh, 1989), pp. 141–2.

24   Iain G. C. Hutchison, 'Government', in T. M. Devine and R. J. Finlay (eds), *Scotland in the 20th Century* (Edinburgh, 1996), p. 48.

25   Foster, 'Twentieth Century', pp. 447–50; Ward, *Unionism*, pp. 29–30.

26   Lee, *Scotland*, pp. 106–7.

27   George T. Murray, *Scotland: The New Future* (Bishopbriggs, 1973), p. 28.

28   Ian MacDougall, *Voices From Work and Home* (Edinburgh, 2000), pp. 51–2.

29   Peter Payne, 'Scottish Council (Development and Industry)', in Lynch, *Oxford Companion*, pp. 574–5.

30   Mitchell, *Conservatives and the Union*, p. 27.

31   Ward, *Unionism*, pp. 31–3.

32   Committee of Inquiry appointed by the Scottish Council (Development and Industry) under the Chairmanship of J. N. Toothill, *Report on the Scottish Economy* (Edinburgh, 1961).

33   G. C. Peden, 'The Managed Economy: Scotland, 1919–2000', in Devine, Lee and Peden, *Transformation*, pp. 244–5.

34   David Newlands, 'The Regional Economies of Scotland', in Devine, Lee and Peden, *Transformation*, pp. 168–9.

35   *The Times*, 22 November 1961.

36   Foster, 'Twentieth Century', pp. 467–9.

37   Toothill, *Scottish Economy*, pp. 17, 20–23; *The Times*, 22 November 1961.

38   Larry Elliott, 'Winds of Climate Change are About to Make their Impact Felt in Many a Boardroom', *The Guardian*, 6 February 2006.

39   Jim Tomlinson, *The Politics of Decline: Understanding Post-War Britain* (Harlow, 2000), pp. 12–5, 21–5, 33–7.

40   Lee, *Scotland*, pp. 93–6.

41   Peter L. Payne, *Colvilles and the Scottish Steel Industry* (Oxford, 1979), pp. 374–83.

42   Foster, 'Twentieth Century', pp. 467–8.

43   Craigen, 'The Scottish TUC', p. 148; 'Scotland's Chance', *The Times* (editorial), 22 November 1961.

44   Peden, 'Managed Economy', p. 251.

45   Toothill, *Scottish Economy*, pp. 154–5.

46   Distribution of Industry Policy; meeting of officials in St Andrews House, 10 January 1962, chaired by J. H. McGuiness of the Scottish Development Department, SEP 10/219, National Archives of Scotland (hereafter NAS).

47   Campbell, 'Scottish Office', pp. 167–83.

48   David McCrone, 'Towards a Principled Elite: Scottish Elites in the Twentieth Century', in Dickson and Treble, *People and Society: Vol. III*, pp. 190–5.

49 George J. Stigler, 'The Theory of Economic Regulation', in George J. Stigler (ed.), *The Citizen and the State* (Chicago, 1975).

50 Donna J. Wood, 'The Strategic Use of Public Policy: Business Support for the 1906 Food and Drug Act', *Business History Review*, 59 (1985), 403-32.

51 Michael French and Jim Phillips, *Cheated Not Poisoned? Food Regulation in the United Kingdom, 1875–1938* (Manchester, 2000), pp. 6-7.

52 Ralph Miliband, *The State in Capitalist Society* (London, 1969); Charles Lindblom, *Politics and Markets: The World's Political Systems* (New York, 1977).

53 'New Government Department for Scotland Suggested', *The Times*, 22 November 1961.

54 Toothill, *Scottish Economy*, p. 191; various press clippings and note by J. H. McGuiness, in advance of a discussion between the Secretary of State and Ministers, no date but presumed January 1962, SEP 10/219, NAS.

55 Notes on Toothill by Scottish Development Department officials, January 1962, SEP 10/219, NAS; see Toothill, *Scottish Economy*, pp. 181–91 for the report's main conclusions.

56 Harvie, *No Gods*, p. 110.

57 Scottish Council for Development and Industry, 'Programme for Industrial Growth', 11 July 1962, and Minute of Meeting between the Secretary of State for Scotland and representatives of the Scottish Council, 12 July 1962, Scottish Council for Development and Industry, Campsie House, Glasgow (hereafter CH).

58 Kenneth O. Morgan, *The People's Peace: British History, 1945–1990* (Oxford, 1992), p. 224.

59 Harvie, *No Gods*, pp. 110–11.

60 'An Industrial Renaissance for Scotland?', *Glasgow Herald*, 19 July 1962, clipping in SEP 10/248, NAS.

61 *Observations by the Government on the Recommendations of the Toothill Report*, August 1962, pp. 1, 23; copy in SEP 10/248, NAS.

62 'Protest Over Toothill Reply', *The Scotsman*, 23 August 1962, clipping in SEP 10/248, NAS.

63 Scottish Council for Development and Industry, 'Notes on the Government's Observations on Toothill Report Recommendations', 29 August 1962, CH.

64 'Government Throw Out Toothill Plan', *The Scotsman*, 1 September 1962, clipping in SEP 10/248, NAS.

65 Ministry of Labour, Monthly Report on the Main Features of the Employment Position in Scotland, February 1963, SEP 10/312, NAS.

66 Ministry of Labour Notes, 'Registered Unemployment in Great Britain and Scotland', 1962–64, SEP 10/325, NAS.

67 Ministry of Labour Press Notice, 'Unemployment in Scotland', 20 June 1963, SEP 10/233, NAS.

68 John Turner, *Macmillan* (London, 1994), pp. 230–48.

69 John Cole, 'Remedies for Unemployment. 2: Scotland', *The Guardian*, January 1962, clipping in SEP 10/219, NAS; see John Cole, *As it Seemed to Me: Political Memoirs* (London, 1995), pp. 31–88, for the correspondent's general recollections of industrial politics in the 1960s.

70 Toothill, *Scottish Economy*, p. 63.

71 Michael Noble to Harold Macmillan, the Prime Minister, 30 November 1962, PREM 11/5074, The National Archives: Public Record Office, Kew (hereafter PRO).

72 SCDI, EC, 3 September 1962, CH.

73 Briefing Note for Prime Minister for Scottish Council meeting on 14 February 1963, PREM 11/5074, PRO.

74 SCDI, EC, 18 February 1963, CH.

75 Polwarth to Macmillan, 25 April 1963, PREM 11/5074, PRO.

76 McCrone, *Scotland's Economic Progress*, pp. 129–35.

77 Official Committee on Population and Employment Policy for Creating Growth Points in Scotland, Note by Scottish Development Department, 6 September 1962, SEP 10/219, NAS.

78 'White Papers Soon on North', *The Times*, 31 October 1963; Peden, 'Managed Economy', pp. 252–3.

79 *Central Scotland: Programme for Development and Growth*, Cmnd 2188 (HMSO, 1963); Memorandum by Regional Development Division of the Scottish Office, Select Committee on Scottish Affairs, *Minutes of Evidence*, 23 April– 16 July 1969 (HMSO, 1969), p. 2.

80 *The Times*, 15 November 1963.

81 Minute of Meeting between the Secretary of State for Scotland and representatives of the Scottish Council, 12 July 1962, CH.

82 Tuckett, *Scottish Trades Union Congress*, p. 366.

83 Meeting between Prime Minister and the Scottish Council, 27 January 1964, PREM 11/5074, PRO.

84 Harvie, *Deep Fried Hillman Imp*, pp. 30–4, 40–1.

85 Harvie, *No Gods*, pp. 90, 143.

86 *Young In Heart*, A Glasgow Films Production for Films of Scotland, 1963, written by Clifford Hanley and produced by David Welsh; Foster, 'Twentieth Century', p. 447.

87 T. M. Devine, *The Scottish Nation, 1700–2000* (London, 1999), p. 573.

88 Huw Beynon, *Working For Ford* (Second edition, Harmondsworth, 1984), pp. 119–31, 145–61; Beatrix Campbell, *Wigan Pier Revisited: Poverty and Politics in the Eighties* (London, 1984), pp. 117–21.

89 Knox, *Industrial Nation*, pp. 272–9.

90 Charles K. Hyde, *Riding the Roller Coaster: A History of the Chrysler Corporation* (Detroit, 2003), p. 200.

91 *Glasgow Herald*, 2 May 1963.

92 Dave Lyddon, 'The Car Industry, 1945–79: Shop Stewards and Workplace Unionism', in Chris Wrigley (ed.), *A History of British Industrial Relations, 1939–1979* (Cheltenham, 1996), p. 202.

93 'Scotland's Imp', *Glasgow Herald*, 3 May 1963; Lyddon, 'The Car Industry', pp. 193–6.

94 Ministry of Labour, Monthly Reports on the main features of the Employment Position in Scotland, February–July 1963, SEP 10/312, NAS; Chris Wrigley, 'Strikes in the Motor Car Manufacturing Industry', in Andrew Charlesworth, David Gilbert, Adrian Randall, Humphrey Southall and Chris Wrigley, *An Atlas of Industrial Protest in Britain, 1750–1990* (London, 1996), pp. 206–8.

95 Stephen Wilks, *Industrial Policy and the Motor Industry* (Manchester, 1984), p. 77.

96 Foster, 'Twentieth Century', p. 468.

97 Tuckett, *Scottish Trades Union Congress*, pp. 361–2.

98 'Scotland's Imp', *Glasgow Herald*, 3 May 1963.

99 'Scotland's Imp', *Glasgow Herald*, 3 May 1963.

100 Craigen, 'The Scottish TUC', p. 147.

101 *The Times*, 2 June 1964.

102 *The Times*, 23 May 1963.

103 Ministry of Labour, Monthly Reports on the main features of the Employment Position in Scotland, May 1963, November–December 1963, January–February 1964, SEP 10/312, NAS.

104 R. H. Campbell, *The Rise and Fall of Scottish Industry* (Edinburgh, 1980), pp. 76–100.

105 Jon Murden, 'Demands for Fair Wages and Pay Parity in the British Motor Industry in the 1960s and 1970s', *Historical Studies in Industrial Relations*, 20 (2005), 1–27, pp. 5–7.

106 'Scotland's Imp', *Glasgow Herald*, 3 May 1963.

107 Murden, 'Demands for Fair Wages', 8.

108 *The Times*, 19, 26 and 27 February 1964.

109 *The Times*, 18 and 21 April 1964.

110 Knox, 'Class, Work and Trade Unionism', pp. 116–18.

111 *The Times*, 29 May 1964; *Glasgow Herald*, 29 and 30 May 1964.

112 Harvie, *No Gods*, p. 151; Lee, *Scotland*, pp. 182–3; Knox, 'Class, Work and Trade Unionism', p. 128.

113 'Allowing Reason a Voice', *The Times*, 2 June 1964.

114 *The Times*, 2 June 1964.

115 *Glasgow Herald*, 28 May 1964.

116 *Glasgow Herald*, 30 May 1964.

117 Ibid.

118 Knox, 'Class, Work and Trade Unionism', p. 114.

119 Hugh A. Clegg, *A History of British Trade Unions Since 1889: Volume III, 1934–1951* (Oxford, 1994), p. 300.

120 *Royal Commission on Trades Unions and Employers' Associations 1965–1968*, Cmnd 3623 (HMSO, 1968), pp. 12, 261.

121 Alan Fox, *Industrial Sociology and Industrial Relations: Royal Commission on Trade Unions and Employers' Associations, Research Papers, 3* (HMSO, 1966), *passim*; Allan Flanders, 'What are Trade Unions for?', in Allan Flanders (ed.), *Management and Unions: The Theory and Reform of Industrial Relations* (London, 1970), pp. 39–45.

122 Arthur Marwick, *The Sixties* (Oxford, 1998); Mark Kurlansky, *1968: The Year that Rocked the World* (London, 2004).

123 Geoffrey Goodman, *The Awkward Warrior. Frank Cousins: His Life and Times* (London, 1979), p. 595.

124 Toothill, *Scottish Economy*, pp. 17–20, 81.

125 Foster, 'Twentieth Century', p. 470.

126 Lee, *Scotland*, pp. 182–3; Lyddon, 'The Car Industry', pp. 188–9.

127 Hyde, *Riding the Roller Coaster*, pp. 197–9.

128 Young and Hood, *Chrysler UK*, p. 273.

129 John Campbell, *Edward Heath: A Biography* (London, 1993), p. 147.

130 *The Times*, 6 June 1964; Hyde, *Riding the Roller Coaster*, p. 199.

131 Lee Iacocca, with William Novak, *Iacocca: An Autobiography* (London, 1986), pp. 162–5.

132 Ministry of Labour, Monthly Reports on the Main Features of the Employment Position in Scotland, May 1963, November–December 1963, August and October 1964, SEP 10/312, NAS.

133 Tony Benn, *Out of the Wilderness: Diaries, 1963–67* (London, 1987), p. 484.

134 Morgan, *People's Peace*, pp. 213–15, 243–6.

135 Memorandum by Regional Development Division of the Scottish Office, Select Committee on Scottish Affairs, *Minutes of Evidence*, 23 April–16 July 1969 (HMSO, 1969), p. 9.

136 *The Scottish Economy, 1965 to 1970: A Plan for Expansion* (HMSO, 1966), Cmnd 2864, pp. ix–x; see also Select Committee on Scottish Affairs, Minutes of Evidence, 23 April 1969, p. 8.

137 Craigen, 'The Scottish TUC', p. 148.

138 Foster, 'Twentieth Century', pp. 474–5.

139 Harvie, *No Gods*, p. 143.

140 Harold Wilson, *The Labour Government, 1964–1970: A Personal Record* (London, 1971), pp. 229–41.

141 Keir Thorpe, 'The "Juggernaut Method": The 1966 State of Emergency and the Wilson Government's Response to the Seamen's Strike', *Twentieth Century British History*, 12 (2001), 461–85.

142 Robert Taylor, *The Trade Union Question in British Politics* (Cambridge, 1993), pp. 138–47.

143 STUC, *70th Annual Report, 1967*, pp. 416–30.

144 Knox, 'Class, Work and Trade Unionism', p. 122; Craigen, 'The Scottish TUC', p. 154.

145 Gregor Gall, *The Political Economy of Scotland: Red Scotland? Radical Scotland?* (Cardiff, 2005), p. 14 and *passim*.

146 Drucker and Brown, *Politics of Nationalism*, p. 93.

147 MacDougall, *Voices From Work*, pp. 56–9.

148 *Scottish Miner*, January 1968.

149 Craigen, 'The Scottish TUC', p. 150.

150 STUC, *72nd Annual Report*, p. 234.

151 Ibid.

152 Marr, *Scotland*, pp. 118–19; Winnie Ewing, *Stop the World: The Autobiography of Winnie Ewing* (Edinburgh, 2004), pp. 1–15.

153 Drucker and Brown, *Politics of Nationalism*, pp. 32, 37.

154 Craigen, 'The Scottish TUC', pp. 144–5.

155 James Mitchell, *Strategies For Self Government: The Campaigns For a Scottish Parliament* (Edinburgh, 1996), pp. 85-97.

156 Drucker and Brown, *Politics of Nationalism*, pp. 24–6.

157 W. W. Knox and A. McKinlay, 'The Re-Making of Scottish Labour in the 1930s', *Twentieth Century British History*, 6 (1995), 174–93.

158 Foster, 'Twentieth Century', p. 446.

159 Craigen, 'The Scottish TUC', pp. 144–5.

160 Keith Aitken, *The Bairns O' Adam: The Story of the STUC* (Edinburgh, 1997), pp. 215–19.

161 *The Herald*, 1 February 1999.

162 *Royal Commission on the Constitution, Minutes of Evidence: IV Scotland*, 20 July 1970, pp. 111–29.

163 Aitken, *Bairns O' Adam*, p. 221.

164 SCDI, *Unemployment in Scotland* (Edinburgh, November 1967); SCDI, 'Unemployment in Scotland', Press Release, 1 December 1967; SEP 10/323, NAS.

165 Richard Crossman, *The Diaries of a Cabinet Minister: Volume Two, Lord President of the Council and Leader of the House of Commons, 1966–68* (London, 1976), pp. 344, 550.

166 Regional Development Department, 'The Machinery of Economic Planning in Scotland', draft, 19 March 1969, SEP 10/336, NAS; Select Committee on Scottish Affairs, *Minutes of Evidence*, 23 April 1969, p. 2.

167 Foster, 'Twentieth Century', p. 474.

168 Knox, 'Class, Work and Trade Unionism', p. 111.

169 Wilks, *Industrial Policy*, p. 80.

170 Benn, *Out of the Wilderness*, p. 484.

171 *Glasgow Herald*, 18 January 1967.

172 Murray, *Scotland*, pp. 78-9.

173 *Glasgow Herald*, 27 and 28 March 1967, 21–3 September 1967, 28–9 September 1967 and 3 October 1967.

174 Lyddon, 'The Car Industry', p. 199.

175 *The Times*, 9, 17, 24, 29 May 1968 and 7, 8, 11, 18 June 1968.

176 Cmnd 3623, p. 12.

177 'A Report to Forget', *The Economist*, 15 June 1968, pp. 16–17; Michael Moran, *The Politics of Industrial Relations* (London, 1977), p. 68; Alastair J. Reid, *United We Stand: A History of Britain's Trade Unions* (Harmondsworth, 2004), pp. 299–300.

178 *The Guardian*, 14 June 1968.

179 'Putting on the Brakes', *The Economist*, 7 December 1968, p. 19.

180 *In Place of Strife: A Policy for Industrial Relations*, Cmnd 3888 (HMSO, 1969), pp. 28–9.

181 Castle, *Diaries*, pp. 561, 585; Barbara Castle, *Fighting All the Way* (London, 1993), pp. 414–24.

182 Lewis Minkin, *The Contentious Alliance: Trade Unions and the Labour Party* (Edinburgh, 1992), pp. 114–16.

183 STUC, *72nd Annual Report*, pp. 412–3, 428–30.

184 Tuckett, *Scottish Trades Union Congress*, pp. 381–7.

185 *Morning Star*, 6 June 1969.

186 'In Place of Government', *The Economist*, 21 June 1969.

187 Peter Jenkins, *The Battle of Downing Street* (London, 1970).

188 Ben Pimlott, *Harold Wilson* (London, 1992), pp. 510–46.

189 Andrew Thorpe, 'The Labour Party and the Trade Unions', in John McIlroy, Nina Fishman and Alan Campbell (eds), *British Trade Unions and Industrial Politics: Volume Two, The High Tide of Trade Unionism, 1964–79* (Aldershot, 1999), pp. 138–40.

190 STUC, *72nd Annual Report*, pp. 469–79.

191 Castle, *Diaries*, p. 322.

192 Foster, 'Twentieth Century', pp. 476–7.

193 Harvie, *No Gods*, pp. 151, 164.

2   *Oceanspan*: 'Turning Scotland Sideways', 1969–72

In March 1968 *The Times* published a letter from William Lithgow, the Port Glasgow shipbuilder, outlining a critique of Harold Wilson's Labour government that was both devolutionist and anti-socialist in character. Lithgow's chief thesis was that the UK government's 'socialist' economic and social policies had 'destroyed' vital and once characteristic elements of public life in Scotland, including 'self-providence' and capital formation from low-income savers. The government's alleged assault on capitalism, defended explicitly by Lithgow as the source of the many 'disciplines which make a free society feasible', encouraged a reliance on the state that was economically and socially unhealthy, and a corresponding corrosion of 'self-respect, self-discipline and the vital spark of self-determination'.[1]

Lithgow's position, in outlining a pro-private enterprise and devolutionist critique of a Labour government, was similar to the Unionist case against nationalisation set out by Elliot in the late 1940s. It also very closely resembled the political and economic views of his father, Sir James Lithgow, chair of the inter-war Scottish Economic Committee and uncompromising critic of the labour movement.[2] Sir James would probably have endorsed the contents of his son's letter, stimulated chiefly by Labour's deflationary budget of 19 March, the first since devaluation of sterling in November 1967. The Chancellor of the Exchequer, Roy Jenkins, sought to maximise the benefits of devaluation, which was designed primarily to restore the balance of payments position, by draining domestic demand and so discouraging consumer expenditure, especially on imports. A total of £923 million was removed from the economy by an array of taxes, duties and levies.[3] Lithgow's view, that the budget was a further socialist assault on free enterprise, duly appears odd, or even perverse. After all, only modest steps were taken in the direction of greater wealth redistribution between 1964 and 1970, and the Wilson governments' recurrent doses of economic deflation were and have been interpreted – by a range of observers that encompassed Lawrence Daly, at the 1967

STUC, as well as Peter Jay, economics correspondent of *The Times* – as designed primarily to impress foreign exchange markets, ease the fears of international investors and preserve the position of the City of London.[4]

Yet Lithgow was moved by a powerful sense that Wilson's government was undermining the power and prestige of Scottish capital. He shared this analysis with other leaders of heavy industry, notably Ronald Colville, the second Baron Clydesmuir, who in 1966 became chairman of the SCDI, which Lithgow joined at the same point with a special responsibility for research.[5] While the STUC was developing a case for Home Rule from a labour or working-class perspective, Lithgow and Clydesmuir used the SCDI to press for enhanced devolutionary powers for Scotland in economic and industrial policy from a business or enterprise perspective. Historians tend to look at electoral and party politics when tracing the emergence of both nationalism and devolution in the late 1960s and early 1970s, picking out the Hamilton by-election, Heath's Declaration of Perth and Wilson's Select Committee for Scottish Affairs.[6] But the labour and business initiatives of the STUC and SCDI were arguably more important, articulating deeper concerns – based essentially on popular anxieties, expressed by trade unionists and private sector employers – about the remote nature of power and policy-making that were then reflected in electoral and party politics.

The SCDI's combination of devolutionist *and* free enterprise politics was an important feature of public debate in Scotland in the late 1960s and early 1970s that has been absent from the literature evaluating the emergence of support for Home Rule in the second half of the twentieth century. This tends to focus instead on socialist or social democratic concerns about the widening of economic and social inequality that resulted from the policies of Margaret Thatcher's Conservative governments from 1979, which enjoyed relatively modest – and from 1983 onwards markedly declining – electoral support in Scotland. Lithgow's position was roughly an inverse of the post-1979 devolu-tionary rationale, for he articulated a fairly thick strand of opinion within Scottish capital that chafed against the imposition on Scotland of 'socialist' Whitehall policies. In the previous chapter it was argued that by the early 1960s the Scottish Office had been 'captured' by business in Scotland, with civil servants adopting the Toothill position that the relative positions of Scotland on the one hand and the midlands and the south of England on the other hand were complementary and to the long-term detriment of the UK as a whole. Lithgow and Clydesmuir now mobilised the SCDI to seek to expand the administrative powers of the Scottish Office, which they saw as a supportive – or pliant – agency against the broader forces of the UK state, especially where these were being manipulated by a 'socialist' Labour govern-ment with aims and purposes that appeared to be inimical to those of indige-nous capital in Scotland. The expansion of the Scottish Office's remit would be a major stimulus to demands for a form of political devolution that would enable the electorate in Scotland to hold the administration to account more closely.[7] On this aspect of devolution, however, Scottish capital would be ambivalent, with support for a devolved Scottish Parliament tending to be stronger when Labour was in power at Westminster.

The main instrument of the SCDI campaign was *Oceanspan*, a scheme geared to promoting the long-term regeneration of central Scotland's industrial belt, and developed by Lithgow himself with assistance from Professor Ronald Nicoll of the University of Strathclyde. This was to involve substantial capital investment in cargo transport links, particularly in the Clyde and Forth ports, to facilitate the rapid west-to-east processing of raw materials from the oceanic trades, landed on the Clyde, to finished goods, manufactured in central Scotland, and exported from the Forth, mainly to continental Europe. *Oceanspan* would include the construction of a vast ore terminal and iron and steel works at Hunterston on the Ayrshire coast, which enjoyed a highly unusual combination of very deep water and an expansive area of flat land.[8] In envisaging Scotland as a 'land bridge' between the Atlantic and Europe, the SCDI pointed to a fundamental shift in the country's geographical-economic orientation. The established north-to-south axes that connected greater Glasgow and greater Edinburgh separately with England should give way to a new west-to-east axis. This involved 'Turning Scotland Sideways', as *The Economist* put it,[9] integrating the economies of western and eastern central Scotland, and positioning this Scottish economy as an offshore conduit for trade with Europe, a much larger 'home market' for Scotland than was available in the UK alone. This reconfiguration would require a much greater degree of administrative autonomy in Scotland. It would, for example, necessitate the establishment of an integrated Scottish Ports Authority, free to develop outwith the constraints of the UK Labour government's planned nationalisation of port transport, and operating under the direction of the Scottish Office rather than the Ministry of Transport.[10]

John Foster casts *Oceanspan* as a major episode in the attempt by indigenous Scottish capital, clustered around shipbuilding and steel, and with support from the Bank of Scotland, to regain economic and political influence that had been lost since the Second World War to light industry, the multinationals and more remote forms of power generally. Along with the reclamation of control of the SCDI by heavy industry, it represented 'a direct challenge to the City of London and the process of industrial centralisation'.[11] Christopher Harvie presents *Oceanspan* in similar terms, describing it as 'diametrically opposed to the Toothill orthodoxy', with Lithgow, the 'last great magnate' of indigenous heavy industry, defending free-market capitalism vigorously while other industrialists had come to terms with the Labour government and economic planning.[12] This emphasis on historical discontinuity is clearly plausible: *Oceanspan* was unmistakably designed to stimulate steel and shipbuilding. But the planned improvements to transport infrastructure, and the possibilities of the 'land bridge' between the Atlantic and Europe, were also of potential benefit to the various inward investors, light industrialists and their financial and media backers that Foster characterises as the 'modernisers'. *Oceanspan* explicitly highlighted the value of the plans to American firms in electronics and the importance of these firms to the Scottish economy was emphasised. With the goal of enhanced economic activity the plans – boosting employment – offered something too for manual workers, and so a very broad degree of support for the programme was duly mustered, and *Oceanspan* was praised in Roy Thomson's 'modernising' *The Scotsman*. The 'exciting prospect of Scotland as the industrial gateway to Europe', wrote the paper's shipping correspondent, 'is no longer just a planner's fanciful dream'.[13] Moreover, John Toothill was involved directly in negotiations with the UK government – after the 1970 election that unseated Labour in favour of a new Tory administration under Edward Heath – about ways in which the plans might be implemented. Meanwhile Douglas Young, the nationalist campaigner and writer, described the plans as 'exciting', and contrasted Lithgow's international vision, as he saw it, with the allegedly low ambition and high incompetence of the Labour Party in Scotland and Whitehall.[14]

This chapter builds on an earlier and shorter analysis of the politics of *Oceanspan*, which focused largely on its port transport dimensions,[15] by presenting it as an important episode in debates about the linkage between industrial change and the institutions of policy-making. The politics of *Oceanspan* were a qualified extension – rather than a reversal – of the Toothill-driven dynamic to greater administrative autonomy for Scotland. But there was a new element to this campaign, with the anti-socialism articulated in Lithgow's letter to *The Times* powerfully to the fore. With *Oceanspan*, the SCDI argued that Scottish economic and administrative autonomy would revive and stimulate private enterprise, diminished directly by the nationalisation of steel in 1967 and further threatened in 1969 and 1970 by the planned nationalisation of ports. The Hunterston terminal and works would re-establish a muscular and self-contained steel industry in Scotland, and ports policy would be shaped by the Scottish Office in conjunction with Scottish port authorities and port employers and users, instead of being directed from the Ministry of Transport in Whitehall. Here the SCDI drew on support from the Conservative Party in Parliament, with Tory MPs – led by Teddy Taylor – drafting amendments to the Labour government's nationalisation bill 'to seek separate and autonomous port authorities for Scotland and England'.[16]

The *Oceanspan* campaign was altered, of course, by the election of Heath's government in June 1970. The proposals were no longer presented in anti-socialist terms, but the devolutionist case remained powerful, particularly as the industrial and social tensions that were mounting, especially from 1971 onwards, were attributable to the Heath government's management of the economy. Based initially on ending subsidies to 'lame duck' enterprises and industries, and intending to promote industrial concentration and enhanced productivity prior to Britain's projected admission to the EEC,[17] this involved a considerable rise in industrial closure and unemployment in central Scotland. These developments were a disappointment to Scottish business leaders, and in the short term reinforced their attachment to *Oceanspan* as the means of ameliorating the economic and social difficulties arising from industrial change. Paradoxically, however, the very rise of industrial and social tension – evident most visibly in the 'work-in' at UCS in 1971–72 and the miners' strike in January and February 1972 – diminished the likelihood that *Oceanspan*'s grand design would be implemented. The SCDI relaxed the pressure for economic regeneration, based on greater administrative autonomy in Scotland, in order to ease the political pressure on the Heath government. This episode would reveal the complex inter-meshing of class and devolutionist or nationalist politics in Scotland in the early 1970s that would also be evident in the UCS and miners' protests that are examined in Chapters 3 and 4.

Oceanspan and the 1964–70 Labour governments

Oceanspan was based on significant dissatisfaction among Scottish business leaders with the Labour government's general economic and industrial management. This was evident in Lithgow's complaints about the 1968 budget, but also in the opposition among the 'traditionalists' to regional aid, thought to confer undue advantages to American firms.[18] In addition to these general grievances there were the two detailed problems that have already been noted as exercising Lithgow and his supporters from 1967: the nationalisation of steel and the intended nationalisation of port facilities. These are worth exploring in some detail.

Steel nationalisation had featured in the first Queen's Speech following Labour's election victory in 1964, but the narrow nature of Wilson's majority – initially five and then just three from January 1965 – precluded legislation on this matter until after the March 1966 election, which returned the government with a majority of more than a hundred.[19] Wilson duly deployed Dick Marsh as Minister of Power to see the nationalisation through, and legislation was eventually passed on 27 October 1967, at the very end of an extended Parliamentary Session that had begun in April 1966. The Iron & Steel Federation, the UK employers' organisation, had opposed nationalisation,[20] which involved establishing the British Steel Corporation (BSC), in which Scotland's interests were subsumed within a Scottish and North-Western region. This position aggrieved the industry in Scotland, which could provide a full range of steel products and saw itself as capable of standing alone, a claim recognised by the 1966 Benson Committee established by the Iron &

Steel Federation. The policy of nationalisation also stymied a major plan developed by Colvilles for a huge ore terminal at Hunterston. The politics of the situation hence represented roughly a reversal of the position in the late 1950s, when the UK government had imposed the financially disastrous but politically expedient Ravenscraig strip mill on the firm against Colvilles' will. Now the firm's positive ambition to develop a new project was being thwarted by the UK government.[21]

Clydesmuir and his associates fought back, however, apparently dominating the Scottish and North-Western division of BSC in its initial phase. At a press conference in August 1968 the division announced that it would be seeking BSC approval for a massive ore terminal and integrated steel works at Hunterston. There were echoes here of the 1929 Brassert report, with its recommendation that Scottish steel production be concentrated in a single combined import terminal and works, albeit at Erskine, on the Clyde itself.[22] The Hunterston proposal emphasised that modern bulk carriers could be accommodated in one of the deeper but relatively sheltered stretches of the Firth of Clyde; the adjacent flat land would be ideal for both the terminal and the works, which would utilise the relatively slack local labour market, and improved transport links to central Scotland would follow.[23]

Peter Payne, overlooking slightly the involvement of Tories like Clydesmuir and Lithgow, notes that the Hunterston project was quickly 'seized upon by Scottish nationalists and by leading theoretical planners to become the centrepiece of a new grand strategy for the industrial renewal of Central Scotland'.[24] The broad aims of *Oceanspan* were first publicised after a meeting of the SCDI's Executive Committee in Edinburgh in June 1969;[25] the published report followed in January 1970. This positioned Hunterston as one of the four corners of a projected central Scottish 'linear port area', the others being Greenock, also on the Clyde, and Grangemouth and Leith in the east. Greenock and Hunterston would 'pump' raw materials from the Atlantic to central belt industry, sometimes via a clearance depot at Gartsherrie in Lanarkshire; finished goods would journey back westwards for transatlantic and other oceanic destinations – in Africa, Asia and Oceania – but also eastwards through Grangemouth and Leith to the expanding continental European market. Such 'entrepot' or inter-continental endeavour had shaped Scottish trading activity during earlier periods of economic development, notably with the colonial-driven growth of the eighteenth century.[26] But the possibilities of expanding inter-European trade, enhanced by likely future UK membership of the EEC, certainly inflated the potential of these trading links, which also revolved around the envisaged closer integration of the interests of Glasgow and Edinburgh.[27] With established north-south trade links to be supplemented – and gradually supplanted – with west-east connections, *Oceanspan* was an explicit challenge to the unified British state.

The characterisation by Foster and Harvie of *Oceanspan* as reversing the

SCDI's previous emphasis on new industries, articulated chiefly in the Toothill report, has been noted.[28] The plans plainly sought to lift the fortunes of shipbuilding and steel, and so were very clearly inspired by the self-interest of Lithgow and Clydesmuir. Yet there were genuine opportunities, if admittedly less direct, for lighter industry in *Oceanspan*, which to a certain extent reprised the analysis of the early 1960s. There was not quite the same emphasis on the requirement for industrial diversification, but economic growth was still seen as the key to stimulating a variety of manufacturing activities, and this was presented as achievable through improved investment, communications, transportation, housing and education. In employment terms it was suggested that the specific proposals for the Clyde estuary – the cargo and ore terminals and steel works at Hunterston, plus a petro-chemical works and refining plant – would generate a 'peak labour force' of 10,000, stabilising at around 4,500 on completion of construction. Elsewhere the 'breeder effect' would operate, with spin-offs supporting an unspecified volume of employment across Ayrshire, up through Clydeside and across central Scotland in chemical manufacturing, power generation, steel processing, shipbuilding and repairs.[29] The importance of younger manufacturing enterprise was explicitly noted, especially in electronics, with *Oceanspan* envisaging that improved transport links and better access to Europe would encourage further growth of those industries developed by US companies since 1945. These ranged geographically from IBM in Greenock across central Scotland to NCR and Timex in Dundee.[30] Responsible for 12.3 per cent of Scottish manufacturing turnover in 1968, these companies exported 40 per cent of their output; further inward investment – and export activity – would be encouraged through *Oceanspan*.[31]

Oceanspan also offered a restatement of the Toothill-era emphasis on the physical space and potential for growth in Scotland, and the complementarity of the sluggish development in Scotland and the potential over-expansion – to the point of congestion and inflationary overheating – of central and southern England. Hunterston and Greenock were significant in this connection, removing huge transatlantic carriers from the busy traffic of the English Channel, which would be safer as well as less congested as a result.[32] *Oceanspan* suggested that hundreds of thousands of people – chiefly from Greater Glasgow – would be re-housed in new towns within the 'industrial corridor' of the 'linear port area'. In North Ayrshire employment expansion would cater for a new 'regional city' embracing Kilmarnock and Irvine, which would number 250,000 after a decade or so; in central Scotland Greater Livingston's 85,000 would increase to 185,000, and the Grangemouth to Falkirk conurbation of 120,000 would expand to 230,000 by the early 1980s. This clearly echoed Toothill's discussion of 'Overspill' and new towns, and spelt out carefully that these demographic and employment developments would arrest the concentration of people and employment in the midlands and south of England, and so ease inflationary wage pressures across the UK.[33] This would, of course, have the additional benefit of removing some of the incentive for the deflationary economic management that recurrently hindered Scotland's fragile growth.

After steel the second contested area between Scottish capital and the Labour government revealed by *Oceanspan* was port transport. There was, it should be emphasised, a longer history of business dissatisfaction in Scotland with Whitehall's conduct of ports policy. In the late 1950s and early 1960s, for example, the Ministry of Transport – in concert with the Treasury – had opposed expansion plans at Leith, which had been endorsed by the Scottish Office and were designed to secure the continued grain operations in the port of Joseph Rank Ltd.[34] The Ministry of Transport justified its opposition from 1961 largely on the grounds that a major inquiry was taking place into the operation of port transport in the UK as a whole.[35] Chaired by Lord Rochdale, the cotton industrialist, this had a bearing on future developments in Scotland, chiefly with its twin recommendations that a National Ports Authority be established to advise on investment in capital projects, and that estuarial or other regional groupings of port and harbour authorities be constructed to secure economies of scale and minimise 'wasteful' competition.[36] A National Ports Council (NPC) – rather than Authority – was duly established and the first estuarial grouping subsequently formed was the Clyde Port Authority (CPA) in 1966, a merger of four bodies, the largest being Greenock and Glasgow.[37] This was a considerable accomplishment, given the competing interests involved, especially between Greenock and Glasgow, and set in place one of *Oceanspan*'s cornerstones, the deep-water container terminal at Greenock, opened for business in June 1969 by Dick Marsh, the Minister of Transport, who had moved from the Ministry of Power in April 1968.[38]

The NPC was also involved in developing Leith, along lines envisaged in 1959, with a major lock establishing permanent, deeper water eventually completed in 1969 at a cost of £7 million. A greater Forth Ports Authority (FPA), set up shortly after the CPA, now administered the port.[39] Yet there was dissatisfaction about the scale and very slow delivery of UK government support. The Leith project, for instance, was roughly ten years in the making, from initial campaign to final completion. Scottish business discontent over ports policy was raised to a higher level, as we have already seen, by Labour's plans for nationalisation, which figured in the party's 1966 general election manifesto, and which were published in a White Paper in January 1969. Like steel nationalisation this proposed centralised management from Whitehall, with a UK-wide National Ports Authority, answering to Parliament through the Minister of Transport, to oversee subsequent investment and development.[40]

Hence the SCDI emphasised that *Oceanspan*'s grand design could not be realised within existing political and administrative arrangements. The projected 'linear port area' would only be achievable through an 'effectively autonomous Scottish Ports Authority'. This was the point at which *Oceanspan* drew upon the explicitly anti-socialist elements of Scottish devolutionary sentiment in the 1960s, with the proposed Scottish Ports Authority to operate unhindered by the Labour government's projected nationalisation of port transport under a National Ports Authority. *Oceanspan*'s Scottish Ports Authority would be accountable to the Secretary of State for Scotland rather than the Minister of Transport.[41] It is worth restating that in Parliament – until the election of Heath's government shifted the parameters of debate significantly – Conservative MPs adopted an identical position on these issues to the SCDI.[42] Lithgow discussed Labour's plans for the ports in the summer of 1969 with Sir Andrew Crichton, Chairman of the Overseas Containers Ltd shipping company, which operated routes to South America, Africa, India, the Far East and Oceania. Overseas Containers used the existing container terminal at Greenock, which the CPA was planning to supplement with a second. In the event of nationalisation this development would require the approval of the National Ports Authority, which Lithgow feared would not be forthcoming, jeopardising a major contract that the CPA was trying to agree with Overseas Containers for the utilisation of the second terminal.[43]

Alistair McCrae, CPA Chairman, conveyed these matters to Willie Ross, Labour's Secretary of State for Scotland, via J. H. McGuiness of the Scottish Office's Regional Development Department. Ross agreed to meet both McCrae and John McWilliam, Chairman of FPA, in January 1970. McCrae and McWilliam, operating closely with the SCDI's Executive Committee,[44] told Ross that nationalisation would divert investment to London and Liverpool and block Scottish developments, including the second Greenock container terminal, which would only proceed if 'London control' was diluted with enhanced Scottish Office involvement. James Mitchell has asserted that under Ross the Scottish Office in the 1960s enjoyed an unprecedented degree of 'autonomy from Westminster',[45] and McCrae and McWilliam clearly hoped that Ross would support the isolation of Scottish port transport from Whitehall's nationalisation plans. The Secretary of State certainly admitted the attraction of 'decentralisation'. But Ross has also been portrayed as a champion of non-devolved, UK-wide statism,[46] and this shaped his approach to ports policy. He observed that the Ministry of Transport was a better judge of shipping traffic than the Scottish Office and that it was 'naïve' to 'suppose' that access to the Scottish Secretary alone would secure favourable treatment for Scottish ports. He also pointed out that the Treasury would retain control over expenditure and insist that Scottish developments conform to UK national priorities. The Whitehall approach, Ross emphasised, was the 'real hope' for Scottish ports. McCrae and McWilliam accepted that the Scottish

Secretary would have some influence in the 'new machinery' but were 'apprehensive' given that 'centralisation' was the government's aim and that 'devolutionary aspects were insecurely based and still to be proved'. There was, they added, too much riding on the personal determination, temperament and inclination of the Secretary of State.[47]

Ross was expressing perhaps the dominant Scottish Labour position on *Oceanspan*. This cautious, unionist position was infused to some extent with political prejudice that was perhaps related to class sentiment. Mainstream Labour leaders could not easily accept plans that were so strongly associated with Lithgow, a stern critic of trade unions and noisy opponent of the Labour government. This was illustrated in July 1970, just after the election of Heath's government, when the state of the Scottish economy and the possibilities of *Oceanspan* were debated in the House of Lords. Labour's contribution was led by Lord Hughes, Under Secretary of State and then Minister of State at the Scottish Office under Wilson. Setting aside the STUC's criticism that Labour in office had inadequately tackled uneven development, Hughes praised his government's work between 1964 and 1970 in narrowing the income gap between Scotland and the rest of the UK, and urged the new Tory government to resist the temptations of *Oceanspan*. He talked up the costs of handling traffic in ports, asserting that the two additional handlings in Scotland of cargo bound to Europe from the Atlantic would exceed the costs of the longer, land-free shipment. Hughes conceded that there were carriers who preferred to ship across land from Greenock, sending goods southwards by British Rail's freightliner service – established by the Labour government – and hence to Europe through Harwich and Felixstowe. But Hughes was anxious that this profitable British Rail business should not be jeopardised by the rival attraction of a land bridge to the North Sea across Scotland. Other Labour figures were supportive of *Oceanspan*, however, including Lord Hoy, who as the local MP had championed the interests of Leith in the 1950s and 1960s,[48] and, in the House of Commons, George Lawson of Motherwell, who spoke about the benefits of integrating the Clyde and the Forth under a single Scottish Ports Authority. This would assist transshipment, removing the need for large vessels to make the awkward passage through the congested English Channel, and oversee improvements in road and rail links to ports, including Greenock. The package as a whole – revolving around Hunterston – would also assist the steel industry, an important issue, of course, for Lawson's Motherwell constituents.[49]

These competing views on *Oceanspan* were reflective of Scottish Labour's divisions on the broader question of how to contain the growth of nationalist sentiment in Scotland, encapsulated in the SNP's victory at Hamilton. Richard Crossman, Leader of the House of Commons, saw possibilities in extending administrative devolution, establishing the Select Committee on Scottish Affairs in 1968.[50] Much of the Select Committee's deliberations in

1968–69 were on the related questions of transport and economic development. The Ministry of Transport, presenting evidence to the Committee, defended Whitehall ports policy, noting that the NPC's first major investment scheme had been at Leith, and then reprised the position on ports outlined in Labour's Scottish *Plan for Expansion* in 1966. The *Plan* highlighted the 'natural advantages' that Scotland offered to shipping, with the narrowest distance anywhere in the UK between Atlantic and North Sea ports, but reaffirmed the benefits to Scotland of Whitehall's administration of port development, citing as evidence the NPC-approved investment schemes on the Forth and the Clyde.[51]

Crossman was trying to balance Labour's opposing impulses on devolution in Scotland, which pitted the old guard, led by Ross, against mainly younger figures, including John Mackintosh, a firm advocate of Home Rule. The Select Committee was supplemented in 1969 by the Royal Commission on the Constitution, a 'Wilsonian device', according to Andrew Marr, that allowed the Prime Minister to avoid taking sides in this internal Labour conflict. The Royal Commission, chaired by Lord Crowther and then after his death by Lord Kilbrandon, eventually reported in November 1973. Its outcome, which is further discussed in Chapter 5, was the recommendation by a majority of its members of a Scottish legislative Assembly, elected by proportional representation, and a Scottish Cabinet and Prime Minister, with a corresponding reduction in the number of MPs at Westminster and the abolition of the position of Secretary of State for Scotland.[52]

The Commission gathered written evidence late in 1969 and early in 1970, and heard oral evidence from witnesses in Scotland in May and July of 1970, before and after the general election. The business evidence, provided by the SCDI and the CBI in Scotland, was broadly in favour of further administrative devolution, but cautious about the extent to which this should be accompanied by legislative devolution.[53] This was consistent with the SCDI's general approach of seeking to strengthen the powers of the Scottish Office, which industrialists in Scotland were only too happy to work with, as Chapter 1 indicated. To these business representatives devolution of an administrative character offered the possibility of enhanced control or 'capture' of the regulatory and policy-making processes, without the inconvenience and uncertainty of public accountability or scrutiny that a legislature would provide. The CBI witnesses, giving evidence in May before the election, were quite frank on this issue. They opposed the establishment of a Scottish legislature because they felt its political complexion would be hostile to capitalism generally and the presence of international capital in Scotland in particular.[54]

The SCDI's written evidence to the Commission of November 1969 made a straightforward business case for an increase in the number of Scottish Office Ministers of State to bolster the Secretary of State and 'exert an important moderating influence' on other departments and public bodies operating in Scotland. This suggestion was duly enacted by Heath's government, which reshaped the Scottish Office in 1972. A new Scottish Economic Planning Department was established, responsible for industrial and regional policy, and buttressed by an additional Scottish Office Minister of State for North Sea Oil development,[55] Heath filling this post initially with Lord Polwarth of the SCDI and the Bank of Scotland. But the SCDI's other main proposal in 1969 was resisted, namely that the Scottish Office could be strengthened further, and devolution usefully advanced, by investing it with responsibility for a Scottish Ports Authority. This restatement of business criticism of Labour's nationalisation plans proposed that the Scottish Ports Authority be accountable to the Secretary of State in the same way as the South and North of Scotland Electricity Boards. The SCDI restated the *Oceanspan* argument that these administrative changes and transport improvements were the pre-requisite of the continuing growth of inward investment to stimulate engineering and electronics exports from the Clyde-Forth corridor.[56]

The presentation of this written evidence from the SCDI to the Commission coincided roughly with the publication of the Ports Bill that contained the nationalisation measures originally spelt out in the White Paper of January 1969. Tory opposition to this was well established. In 1966, shortly after Labour's re-election, Keith Joseph, Conservative spokesman on Transport, had complained that nationalisation would inhibit enterprise and investment in the sector. Once the Tories had been re-elected in 1970 the Minister responsible for ports, Michael Heseltine, observed that it had been 'intolerable' for Labour to announce nationalisation as an objective in 1965 and for the ports still not to have been nationalised in 1969.[57] Yet, as *The Economist* noted, the 1969 plans had scarcely raised 'a few ripples' in England, given that public authorities already owned all major ports, except Manchester. Controversy outside Westminster was also muted because the Minister of Transport, Dick Marsh, had excluded from the takeover all docks handling less than five million tons of cargo per annum, thus omitting 'vigorous enterprises' such as Felixstowe and Shoreham. This was an explicit concession to business critics of plans framed by Marsh's predecessor, Barbara Castle, meaning that nationalisation would be applied only to those ports that were stagnating or even declining.[58]

Measured against the relatively non-controversial nature of the English proposals, the opposition of the Clyde and Forth port authorities and the position adopted in Parliament by Scottish Conservative MPs were particularly significant, then, certainly when considered alongside the SCDI's argument that policy should be administered by the Scottish Office rather than the Ministry of Transport. The SCDI's Executive Council recognised, with considerable disappointment, that further lobbying would not produce any change of policy.[59] But the Ports Bill remained in the legislative queue at the House of Lords on the dissolution of Parliament in June 1970. The general election resulted in the establishment of a Conservative government under Edward Heath. Labour's position had held up reasonably well in Scotland, its share of the vote down from an all-time peak of 49.9 per cent in 1966 to 44.5 per cent, but the number of its seats cut only from forty-six to forty-four, suggesting some entrenchment of the leftward shift in public opinion that had troubled Scottish Tory businessmen across the 1960s and would continue to worry them in the 1970s. The Tories gained just one seat from Labour and three overall to take twenty-three in Scotland, but with only a marginal 0.3 per cent increase in voting share since 1966 to 38 per cent.[60] The new government very quickly announced the termination of the planned nationalisation of the ports.[61] For Lithgow and his allies this added to the pleasure of the outcome of the election, with Heath and his ministers apparently committed to quite different approaches to various strands of public policy, including industrial and ports development.

Oceanspan 2 and the Conservative government, 1970–74

John Foster writes of Scottish capital's high hopes in the summer of 1970. The Tory victory seemed to offer the prospect of governmental support for the rejuvenation of indigenous industry envisaged in *Oceanspan*. Lithgow, *Oceanspan*'s architect, enjoyed informal access to Heath as the Prime Minister's de facto 'Industrial Adviser for Scotland'.[62] Prospects for a 'new era' had further been encouraged in 1969 with the establishment of a Scottish Stock Exchange, to provide capital for 'home-based business' in Scotland. Changes at the Bank of Scotland, where ties with heavy industry remained strong, also suggested the possibility of more easily available investment capital. Clydesmuir was on the Board of the Bank, where he enjoyed a strong association with the Governor, Lord Polwarth, a close colleague also on the SCDI. Clydesmuir was also on the Board of the British Linen Bank, a subsidiary of Barclays. In 1969 – surely with Clydesmuir's guidance – the Bank of Scotland was able to increase its capital base through an alliance with the British Linen Bank.[63]

Yet the optimism of Scottish regional capital foundered in the months following the election. Heath's government encouraged multi-nationals operating in high-growth sectors, notably electronics, chemicals, pharmaceuticals, oil and car manufacturing, including the ongoing Chrysler-Rootes venture at Linwood. These were the higher growth businesses that Toothill had favoured at the beginning of the 1960s and were now seen as central to the UK's prosperity within the new context of EEC membership, which Heath secured as a core element of his programme of government.[64] The new administration was also explicit in its undertaking that there would be an end to public subsidy of the 'lame duck' enterprises and sectors that Toothill, albeit in coded terms, had been less positive about, and the economy was duly managed with a significantly higher rate of unemployment than the Labour government had tolerated. Within months this was a matter of considerable public concern in Scotland. In September 1970 a delegation from the STUC had met John Davies, recently the CBI chief, now Heath's Minister of Technology and shortly to become Secretary of State at a new Department of Trade and Industry.[65] The STUC was lobbying for policies to reverse the rising trend in Scottish unemployment, following redundancies in the west of Scotland at Singers, Burroughs, UCS and at the former British Motor Corporation truck-producing plant at Bathgate, now run by British Leyland. Clydesmuir optimistically observed that Scotland's 'share' of UK unemployment had fallen to 16 per cent at this point from 24 per cent – of a much smaller aggregate – in 1954.[66] But this was still a slight rise from the 15 per cent share – again of a smaller aggregate – which the SCDI had welcomed late in 1967,[67] and the employment position progressively deteriorated in 1971, partly because of Heath's continuing determination to loosen support for declining industry in pursuit of rapid economic restructuring.[68] This allowed UCS to enter liquidation in June 1971, with the probable disappearance of 8,000 jobs in Glasgow and Clydebank. Not only labour voices were raised in protest at this development, which extended a depressing sequence of job losses across Scotland, particularly in the west. In December 1971 Davies was advised by R. B. Anderson, chairman of the Conservative Party's Glasgow Regional Council, that this organisation had recently passed a motion calling on the government to offset the 'social consequences' of rising unemployment and the UCS crisis by establishing a deep-sea port and 'steel complex' at Hunterson.[69]

So *Oceanspan* remained an attractive proposition for Tory and business opinion in Scotland, despite the change of government. But as early as July 1970, during the Lords debate on the Scottish economy, Heath's administration signalled its likely resistance to the grand scheme, suggesting a fissure within Conservative as well as Labour ranks on the question of Scotland's economic development and its position within the UK. Speaking for the government was the new Minister of State, the newly ennobled Baroness Tweedsmuir, formerly MP for Aberdeen South. Regional Development Division officials at the Scottish Office prepared a draft speech for Tweedsmuir that emphasised the modernisation of economic policy thinking in Scotland and the UK, with development no longer seen as a 'social handout' but as the means of securing growth points and 'easing the pressures in the more congested areas'. These Toothill-inspired sentiments were set aside by Tweedsmuir, who preferred to focus more directly on the case against *Oceanspan*, which she knew would be praised by Clydesmuir and the Earl of Perth, the Tory peer who was initiating the debate.[70] Tweedsmuir's own speech drew on her experience as a Director since 1966 of Cunard, part of the

Atlantic Container Line consortium that had been utilising the new Greenock terminal. She presented this experience as unambiguous expertise, which guided her to the conclusion that the costs of trans-shipping across Scotland – even were east-west links to be improved – would decisively exceed those of shipping through the Channel or round the north of Scotland.[71]

Yet Tweedsmuir – as a Cunard Director – was hardly an objective witness. Like Clydesmuir or Lithgow her capital interests surely shaped her political judgements. Shipowners, after all, had different material interests from others – shipbuilders, for example – who were engaged in port and maritime transport. A revolution in port transport, with the shift to containerised carriage, offered more or less unalloyed commercial opportunities for shipbuilders, including Lithgow, with his Port Glasgow yards adjacent to the deep Clyde water that the SCDI was recurrently characterising as one of Scotland's major economic assets. But for shipowners the benefits of the revolution in cargo shipment were less clear-cut. Cunard owned many non-container as well as container cargo vessels: the spread of container facilities in ports was rendering the former obsolete, potentially well in advance of their scheduled dates for decommissioning. Public debates on the slow pace of modernisation of port facilities in the 1960s tended to focus on dockers' resistance to change and the mismanagement or low ambitions of port authorities.[72] But the inbuilt conservatism of shipowners, with fleets of vessels serviced economically enough by existing facilities, represented an extremely powerful impediment to innovation.[73] Tweedsmuir ignored these competing material concerns in her speech, which Clydesmuir also overlooked in his reply, accentuating instead those elements of *Oceanspan* that were either in place or 'programmed to happen', including the Greenock terminal, the improving road links across central Scotland, and the growing trade between the Forth and Continental Europe.[74] *The Scotsman* gave some prominence to Clydesmuir's contribution, but headlined its coverage 'Doubts on heavy cost of Forth-Clyde land bridge' and emphasised the consensus across the Tory and Labour front benches that Scotland and the UK could not afford to jeopardise established north-south links in pursuit of the SCDI's risky and potentially expensive alternatives.[75]

The Lords debate was thus important, drawing some sting out of the *Oceanspan* campaign, and marking a second significant defeat for the Lithgow-Clydesmuir axis since the publication of the plans at the beginning of 1970. The first had been the BSC restructuring in March 1970. Peter Payne describes this as a direct result of *Oceanspan*, the area divisions being replaced with product divisions in order to strengthen the command of the centre and preclude the recurrence of regional political lobbying. This, he concluded, marked the termination of the 'phantom' post-nationalisation presence and influence of Colvilles in the industry.[76] But Clydesmuir and the SCDI did not concede defeat, continuing to lobby for the combined terminal and works at Hunterston and the additional investment and administrative devolution of ports policy that were incorporated in *Oceanspan*. A new document was drawn up, *Oceanspan 2*, and published in October 1971. This was used by the SCDI to negotiate directly with Edward Heath on Scottish industrial and ports policy in the difficult winter of 1971–72, as unemployment and industrial failures accelerated.[77]

The revised plans reflect Andrew Marr's characterisation of Scottish politics in the early 1970s, which were 'nudged along', he says, by three issues: 'oil, jobs and Europe'.[78] Oil had been discovered off Scotland's east coast in 1969 and the huge fields of Forties and Brent located amid much publicity and political debate in 1971. The SCDI in *Oceanspan 2* presented these finds as a major *Scottish* windfall. Extraction would generate demand for indigenous Scottish manufacturing; revenue from sales would finance significant capital investment. *Oceanspan 2*'s amplification of the European context, meanwhile, was in tune with Heath's drive towards EEC membership, but should not be interpreted as opportunism on the part of the SCDI. The original *Oceanspan* had been sub-titled *A Maritime-Based Development Strategy for a European Scotland*, and Toothill – still a driving force on the SCDI – had been a consistent advocate of EEC membership. In January 1970, at a conference organised by the Scottish Committee of the United Europe Association, Toothill punned that 'unless we get in [to the EEC] we have had our chips'.[79]

In one further important aspect, however, *Oceanspan 2* was more clearly distinct from its predecessor, being published in the context of escalating economic difficulties and social class and industrial tensions in 1971 and 1972 which made its provisions all the more desirable from a business perspective. The growing economic and social problems in Scotland were encapsulated, arguably, in the UCS crisis. In February 1972 the government reversed its original position by deciding to provide subsidies that would keep the yards open. This was partly influenced by the perhaps mistaken view that civil disorder would arise in the event of the yards being closed. Cabinet Ministers were preoccupied at this point also with the national miners' strike. This had a powerful Scottish dimension, with the massive Longannet power station in Fife kept open only as a result of a major police operation, amid picketing that was characterised by serious civil disorder and considerable social conflict.

Both of these events, the UCS crisis and the miners' strike, examined in detail in Chapters 3 and 4, involved a significant defeat for Heath's UK government, and had a very large bearing on *Oceanspan 2* which, it must be emphasised, appeared during a substantial economic, social and political crisis. Hence, perhaps, the very broad base of business support for the plans, with *The Scotsman* – often, remember, associated with the 'modernisers' of inward investment and light industry – welcoming a 'Vision splendid' and envisaging that the scheme would be 'painlessly financed' from oil. In framing its package in the conjunction of oil revenues and EEC membership, the SCDI recommended a development fund for the expansion of roads and ports, likening the possibilities to those of the Toothill era, when popular pressures forced Macmillan, eventually, to adopt an interventionist regional policy shaped by various industrial incentives in 1963. Clydesmuir, *The Scotsman* suggested, was articulating a 'Scottish consensus', based on economic devolution but ignored by both Labour and Tory parties in London. The 'modernising' paper aimed one subtle barb at the 'traditionalist' Lithgow, suggesting that the SCDI was now restored to relevance after the alleged stagnation of the mid- to late-1960s: the period, in other words, when the 'traditionalist' shipbuilder was finding his feet as the organisation's Research Director.[80]

Oceanspan 2's oil-based development fund is worth emphasising, given the subsequent history of the North Sea's 'wasted windfall'. Christopher Harvie, among others, has dwelt on the missed opportunities of the 1970s and 1980s, with successive Labour and Conservative governments dissipating oil revenues on tax cuts for the fortunate and welfare support for the unfortunate.[81] But it was Heath's administration that established rapid extraction as the central priority of policy, with fundamental long-term consequences for Scotland and North Sea policy. This increased the government's reliance on the major oil producers and narrowed the possibilities of regenerating indigenous industry on the basis of servicing production in the North Sea with new ships, rigs, pipes, drills and other equipment. Indeed, in the long run the emphasis on maximising production probably accelerated the narrowing of Britain's industrial base. The revenues generated transformed sterling into a petro-currency, diminishing the competitive position of British manufactures in international markets.[82]

A different trajectory for oil policy – and Scotland's economic development – was at least projected, however, at a ministerial lunch hosted by the Prime Minister on 12 January 1972, in advance of talks with the SCDI about *Oceanspan 2*. Heath's lunch guests were John Davies, Gordon Campbell, the Secretary of State for Scotland, and Sir William McEwen Younger, the industrial brewer who was associated with the *Oceanspan* plans through his membership of the Executive Committee of the SCDI. Younger, like Clydesmuir, was also on the Board of the British Linen Bank, and as Scottish Conservative Chairman had devised the party's response to the devolution debate and the advance of the SNP by drafting limited Home Rule proposals. These were quietly shelved following the 1970 general election, principally because the Nationalists' forward march appeared to have halted. The SNP won about 11 per cent of the vote, but Winnie Ewing lost Hamilton to Labour and its sole success, taking the Western Isles from Labour, has been ascribed to 'local rather than national factors'.[83] The Tory plans were also downgraded, however, in the light of the clear distaste for devolution among Conservative Party activists, who in large number had been angered as well as surprised by Heath's initial Declaration of Perth.[84] Drawing on his SCDI membership and activities Younger was, nevertheless, enthusiastic about *Oceanspan 2*, writing a paper in December 1971, 'Regional Policy: Scotland', read by Heath, Davies and Campbell before the January lunch. The paper absorbed the unease of Tory activists in western Scotland, revealed in the approach from the party's Glasgow Regional Council to Davies at the beginning of December 1971. Younger expounded the political disadvantages to the Conservative Party of rising unemployment and falling business confidence in western Scotland, and the need for dramatic public investment to engineer rapid industrial restructuring. He was especially anxious about the 'disastrous' political consequences for the Tories in Scotland if North Sea Oil was viewed as 'a purely extractive industry' and recommended an oil-based fund for economic development in Scotland. So *Oceanspan 2* was presented as a political necessity, a mechanism for bolstering the Tories' position in west Scotland. It would also transform regional policy, going beyond the 'modest' achievement of inward investment in electronics and subsidising 'non-viable' undertakings or the unsustainably imbalanced industrial structure.[85]

There was broad support for *Oceanspan 2* from within the Scottish Office, consistent with its established links with the SCDI. This worried officials at the Department of Trade and Industry (DTI), who warned Davies that Campbell would support Younger's paper and the SCDI in the meetings ahead. The DTI opposed the plans as not costed fully, covering industrial plants, installations for oil, petrochemicals, steel and aluminia works, but containing no estimates for port and other transport developments or the acquisition of land, construction of housing and other linked aspects on the Forth. These would be significant and ultimately the government's responsibility, so no 'firm commitment' could be given to the SCDI.[86] The Prime Minister shared this view, explaining to his colleagues that the 'bold step' favoured by Younger and the SCDI – and Lithgow, unable to secure much of a return, it would seem, on his position as Heath's Industrial Adviser – could not be taken. Heath was determined to take a different path on Scottish economic development from Macmillan in the late 1950s and early 1960s, whose various 'dramatic' industrial initiatives – including the Ravenscraig steel mill – he ruminated upon. Thinking perhaps also of the Rootes car plant at Linwood, Heath described these earlier subsidised developments as gravely mistaken, and 'unrewarding from every point of view. It was important to work with the grain and not against it'. In this connection he and Younger disagreed over the broad political and economic condition of Scotland. Unusually frank notes of this exchange were made by one of Heath's officials:

> The Prime Minister expressed general pessimism about the political and economic good sense of the Scots. Sir William said that he should not be misled by the neurotic state of a few businessmen in the West of Scotland. It was true that there was a dearth of enterprising business talent in Scotland, but he was not too gloomy about the chance of the political holding operation which as Chairman of the Party in Scotland he was now conducting.[87]

Heath at least assuaged Younger by holding out the possibility at this stage of assisting the Tories' 'holding operation' by considering an oil development fund for Scotland, separate from regular Exchequer revenue and expenditure. Labelling the revenues 'as Scottish, and used for Scottish development, instead of English money', would work to the 'advantage' of both Scotland and the Conservative Party.[88]

The meeting with the SCDI took place on the following day, 13 January 1972, the fifth day, incidentally, of the national miners' strike. The *Glasgow Herald*, in a clear exhibition of what Douglas Young characterised as its 'highly Tory' politics,[89] praised the restraint, moderation and good sense of these Scottish business leaders. 'Unlike some visitors to Whitehall', the paper noted, in a fairly transparent criticism of labour representatives, including NUM and UCS union officials and stewards, 'the Scottish Council do not resort to demands for such meetings at every deterioration in a situation which the Government may or may not be in a position to influence'. Despite the disproportionate concentration of unemployment in Scotland, Clydesmuir and his colleagues, Toothill and Polwarth, were not going to 'moan about unemployment' but explore the possibilities of the Hunterston steel plant and a European strategy embracing petrochemicals, oil and steel.[90] A leader in *The Times*, perhaps surprisingly, was also upbeat about *Oceanspan 2* and government subsidy,[91] and the meeting was apparently conducted in a positive atmosphere. Clydesmuir summarised *Oceanspan 2*; Heath praised the SCDI's ambitions and the emphasis on the EEC context. Clydesmuir then asked that government take full 'cognisance' of *Oceanspan 2* when shaping ports policy, which should be transferred to the Scottish Office. Gordon Campbell said the Scottish Office was examining the report; Davies noted that an ore terminal at Hunterston would be established before too long, although he said nothing about its proposed scale, and added that BSC was still considering both the question and possible location of a new works.[92] At the beginning of February BSC duly agreed to open talks with the CPA about establishing a terminal at Hunterston capable of handling ships up to 250,000 tons initially, with a possible extension later to accommodate vessels of 350,000 tons. This was further encouragement for the SCDI and the Secretary of State, who – prematurely, as we will see – described the Hunterston proposal as a 'first class investment in the future of Scotland'.[93]

Heath wrote to Clydesmuir on 17 January, praising the SCDI's 'constructive and forward-looking approach' to Scottish economic problems. The

Prime Minister appreciated the European context of the discussions, stating that, 'your determination to take full advantage of our entry into the EEC gave me much encouragement'. On 21 February Clydesmuir duly spoke to the SCDI Executive in positive terms about the meeting with Heath, which seemed to promise an end to 'short-term' crises and some hope for 'long-term' difficulties.[94] The immediate industrial and social pressures were certainly eased by the government's announcement of the 'rescue' of UCS on 28 February. This coincided exactly with the resumption of work that day by the miners after their successful strike. The apparent conclusion of these crises was followed by the expansionist budget of 21 March and the Industry Bill, unveiled on 22 March, to assist industry in the longer term through general tax allowances and provisions for specific companies.[95] The SCDI approved these initiatives, particularly the Industry Bill's proposed assistance to existing firms and operations as well as new ones,[96] and a further meeting – again involving Heath, Davies and Campbell on the ministerial side – took place in Edinburgh on 12 May 1972.[97] There seemed to be little disagreement now, with the shared approach encapsulated, perhaps, by the presence at this meeting of Polwarth in his new capacity as Minister of State for Scotland, with Scottish Office responsibility for North Sea policy.[98] This was consistent with the SCDI's persistent call for enhanced administrative devolution and additional ministerial personnel at the Scottish Office, and seemed to indicate a serious government commitment to the measured development of the North Sea that the SCDI also advocated. But this hope, as Chapter 5 details, would prove to be illusory in the long term.

In the short term the SCDI also received some disappointing news, which offset the positive developments surrounding the budget and the Industry Bill. In November 1972 Heath wrote to Clydesmuir, outlining the government's final decision on the SCDI's two long-standing requests: the Scottish Office would not be given responsibility for the ports; and there would be no substantial public investment in the *Oceanspan* proposals. Heath claimed that the 'balance of advantage lies in treating ports in the United Kingdom as a whole',[99] with policy in all parts of the UK to remain the province of Department of the Environment, the Ministry of Transport's departmental successor in 1970. To answer the long-running criticism that Whitehall administration of ports policy was too remote from Scotland, the Department of the Environment established a separate branch of its Ports Directorate in St Andrew's House to work with Scottish port authorities, the Scottish Office and the NPC to 'advance' the position of Scottish ports, as Heath put it to Clydesmuir. This was at the suggestion of Scottish Office officials, who continued to insist that the future prosperity of west-central Scotland especially was contingent on significant port investment and development.[100]

This was the end of *Oceanspan*, which had been an imaginative response to deindustrialisation, but the planned regeneration of older industries and expansion of the new were constrained by Scotland's physical situation and geographical characteristics. *Oceanspan* was based on the premise that these features were in Scotland's favour. Deep water on the Clyde, combined with Scotland's position between the Atlantic Ocean and Continental Europe, would enable large, ocean-going vessels to drop goods on the Clyde for onward shipment to other points in Europe. There was strong support for this optimistic view in Scotland's daily press,[101] and inter-continental endeavour had, of course, characterised Scottish trading activity during earlier periods of economic development, notably with the colonial-driven growth of the eighteenth century.[102] In August 2004 a report commissioned by the Scottish Executive, written by Professor Alf Baird of Napier University, would reprise the case for Scotland as a trans-shipment base for inter-continental trade, with deep-water container ports proposed at Hunterston and Scapa Flow in Orkney.[103] This can be taken as a sign of the enduring allure of casting Scotland as a hive of 'entrepot' activity. Yet the English south coast was closer to large segments of both the UK and European markets, and the deep North Sea water near Rotterdam was in any case preferable to the Clyde for ocean-going vessels carrying goods to Continental destinations. The pioneer of containerised transportation, the American firm Sea Land, subsequently maintained its established practice of calling first at Rotterdam's Europort, and then trans-shipping to British and other European destinations.[104] Other big container firms followed suit, rather than vice versa, as Lithgow and his colleagues had hoped.[105] The impact of this geography on *Oceanspan*, constraining its potential, recalls the long-term structural environmental factors that Fernand Braudel wrote about in his celebrated history of the Mediterranean. The imperceptibly changing features of land, mountain, river, valley and sea, Braudel emphasised, are the decisive causal factors in shaping historical development, and Lithgow and the SCDI could not transcend these profound physical characteristics.[106]

At Hunterston there was no grand design. Plans for an ore terminal that could accommodate ships of up to 250,000 or even 350,000 tons, welcomed at the beginning of February 1972 by Gordon Campbell, who was anxious, no doubt, for a good news story in the fourth week of the miners' strike,[107] were revised downwards. The *Glasgow Herald*'s correspondent, David Murray, had forecast troubles ahead, emphasising the fundamentally conflicting interests of BSC, which was interested only in establishing a moderately sized ore terminal, and the CPA, which was seeking a much larger and multi-purpose port.[108] BSC was the more powerful of these two bodies, and in December 1972 it put an end to five years or so of speculation by announcing that an ore terminal would be constructed at Hunterston at a cost of £27 million. This followed last-minute lobbying of the Secretaries of State for Industry and Scotland by the SCDI,[109] but the terminal would accommodate vessels up to

35,000 tons only; construction began in 1973 and was finished in 1978. Although modest in scale, relative to the SCDI's original projection, this would come to assume great political as well as economic significance by facilitating coal as well as ore imports. These weakened the impact of the 1984–85 miners' strike, examined in Chapter 6, with Hunterston the scene of considerable disorder as striking miners attempted unsuccessfully to blockade the terminal.[110] Meanwhile, 'the vision of a major greenfield steelworks at Hunterston is dead', wrote George Murray, early in 1973; although proposals for the iron and steel works were in fact developed, and work even begun, these were not completed.[111]

The SCDI was now in retreat, hampered from the closing months of 1972 by a severe shortage of cash, chiefly the consequence of mergers and closures affecting its private sector subscribers.[112] The eclipse of *Oceanspan 2* seemed to mark the defeat of indigenous Scottish capital, clustered around steel and shipbuilding, and brought to an end, for the time being, a powerful business case for devolution in Scotland. The leadership of this campaign would now pass into the hands of organised labour, which shifted the focus from administrative to legislative devolution, true to the STUC's earlier support, articulated by McGahey in 1969, for democratic measures that would enable people to influence the decisions that shaped their lives.[113] The shift was symbolised by the STUC convening a Scottish Assembly in Edinburgh, at the Usher Hall, on 14 February 1972. This was attended by MPs and representatives of political parties, including William McEwen Younger, as well as members of churches, educational bodies and delegates from the SCDI and the CBI in Scotland. These business representatives remained ambivalent on the question of legislative devolution, but were pulled towards it for the time being by the STUC, which was deftly directing the momentum generated by the popular movements of the UCS work-in and the miners' strike. The Assembly's purpose was to focus attention on how economic policies could be devised to meet the particular conditions and problems that existed in Scotland. The idea of a separate Parliament was duly discussed, and a charter of proposals was drawn up which included a call for public investment in the ore terminal and works at Hunterston.[114] John Foster examines this transition in the leadership of the devolution campaign, but situates it in the months between Heath's election and the passing of UCS into bankruptcy in June 1971, which stripped the 'traditional leaders of Scottish capital' of their confidence. They were defeated, he implies, by more powerful aggregates of capital, chiefly located in the City of London and multi-national enterprises engaged in more modern manufacturing sectors. The revolt of Scottish capital, he writes, was then followed by a different revolt, by the shipyard workers of the Clyde, supported by the labour movement more broadly.[115]

On the basis of the evidence examined in this chapter it would appear, however, that the two revolts actually overlapped, and drew strength from the other in an observably dialectical manner. *Oceanspan 2* – witness Younger's paper of January 1972 on regional development – was cast as the means of mitigating the economic and industrial problems that formed the basis of working class discontent in Scotland. Yet the very mounting of these economic and industrial problems weakened the authority of Scottish industrial leaders and thereby diminished the likelihood that the type of devolutionist measures envisaged in *Oceanspan 2* would be brought forward. Clydesmuir and Polwarth instead put themselves in Heath's unreconstructed Unionist hands, trusting these might bring a restoration of the economic, industrial and social stability that was threatened by the UCS work-in and the miners' strike. So much was this the case that the SCDI's progress with *Oceanspan* was arguably stymied more by indigenous Scottish labour than multi-national capital. In this connection, however, it should be emphasised that the balance of power between labour and capital in Scotland was only slightly tipping towards the former. In the chapter that follows it will be seen that the 'victory' won by the workers over the UCS crisis was constrained, with Scottish business exerting significant leverage over the conduct and outcome of the work-in. These events would add colourful Scottish lustre to the model of social relations more broadly in post-Second World War Britain sketched out by Peregrine Worsthorne, the Tory journalist and author in 1959. Worsthorne disputed the idea that these social relations amounted to a consensus or partnership between the Labour and Conservative parties and the working and middle classes whose material interests they roughly encompassed. Instead he wrote of the existence of a grudge-ridden 'stalemate' between essentially irreconcilable social forces.[116] In Scotland, as in the UK more broadly, labour and capital clearly had the capacity to resist but not to defeat each other.

Heath's appetite for 'Scottish' ventures was certainly waning as he faced the industrial and economic consequences of this class stalemate. Just as support for political devolution was abated by the apparent containment of the SNP, at least as measured by the result of the 1970 general election, so economic or industrial measures that were designed to respond to the specific threat of Scottish nationalism, sentiments and circumstances also appeared superfluous. The early 1970s, in Scotland as elsewhere in the UK, were characterised by an upsurge in industrial unrest and, arguably, class conflict, generated in substantial measure by Heath's attempt to 'reform' industrial relations while withdrawing public subsidies for 'uneconomic' industrial enterprises. In this respect it is worth emphasising that Heath was encountering economic and industrial problems on much broader sectoral and geographical fronts. The 1971 Industrial Relations Act, overturning 'voluntarist' traditions with state regulation of trade unions to minimise the economic impact of industrial unrest, and related attempts to control pay inflation with incomes policies, met huge resistance from organised labour, starting with the miners, as we shall see in Chapter 4. But there was a powerful Scottish dimension to this economic, social and political crisis, manifested most visibly in the UCS work-in, which is taken up in the next chapter. This particular difficulty framed Heath's contacts with the SCDI in 1971–72, and was at the root of the Scottish business anxieties that Sir William McEwan Younger attributed to the 'neurotic state' of some industrialists in western Scotland.

Notes

1 William Lithgow, 'Taxes of the Rich', Letter to *The Times*, 28 March 1968.
2 Anthony Slaven, 'Sir James Lithgow', in Anthony Slaven and Sidney Checkland (eds), *Dictionary of Scottish Business Biography: Volume I, The Staple Industries* (Aberdeen, 1986), pp. 222–7.
3 *The Times*, 21 March 1968; Morgan, *People's Peace*, p. 279.
4 Paul Foot, *The Politics of Harold Wilson* (Harmondsworth, 1968), pp. 155–98; *The Times*, 21 March 1968; Ralph Miliband, *Parliamentary Socialism. A Study in the Politics of Labour* (Second edition, London, 1972), pp. 350–77; David Howell, 'Wilson and History. "1966 And All That"', *Twentieth Century British History*, 4 (1993), 174–87; STUC, *70th Annual Report*, p. 416.
5 Foster, 'Twentieth Century', p. 474.
6 Finlay, *Modern Scotland*, pp. 320–2.
7 Drucker and Brown, *Politics of Nationalism*, p. 23.
8 Murray, *Scotland*, p. 67.
9 'Turning Scotland Sideways', *The Economist*, 21 June 1969, p. 60.
10 Scottish Council for Development and Industry, *Oceanspan: A Maritime-Based Development Strategy for a European Scotland, 1970–2000* (Edinburgh, 1970), pp. 1, 8–9, 24–6.
11 Foster, 'Twentieth Century', p. 474.
12 Christopher Harvie, *Scotland & Nationalism: Scottish Society and Politics, 1707–1994* (Second edition, London, 1994), pp. 135–6.
13 *The Scotsman*, 27 January 1970.
14 Douglas Young, *Scotland* (London, 1971), pp. 155–9, 163–4.
15 Jim Phillips, 'Oceanspan: Deindustrialisation and Devolution in Scotland, c. 1960–1974', *The Scottish Historical Review*, 84 (2005), 63–84.
16 *Glasgow Herald*, 23 January 1970.
17 Robert Taylor, 'The Heath Government and Industrial Relations: Myth and Reality', in Stuart Ball and Anthony Seldon (eds), *The Heath Government, 1970–1974: A Reappraisal* (London, 1996), pp. 161–4.
18 Foster, 'Twentieth Century', p. 475.
19 Pimlott, *Harold Wilson*, pp. 355–9, 400.
20 Wilson, *Labour Government*, pp. 219, 235, 446.
21 Lee, *Scotland and the United Kingdom*, pp. 93–6; Murray, *Scotland*, p. 66.
22 Payne, *Colvilles*, pp. 170–80, 417–23.
23 Murray, *Scotland*, p. 67.
24 Payne, *Colvilles*, p. 421.
25 SCDI, EC, 16 June 1969 and 16 February 1970, CH.

26 T. M. Devine, *The Tobacco Lords: A Study of the Tobacco Merchants of Glasgow and their Activities* (Edinburgh, 1975).
27 'Turning Scotland Sideways', *The Economist*, 21 June 1969, p. 60.
28 See also Harvie, *No Gods*, pp. 62–3.
29 *Oceanspan*, pp. 30–2.
30 Alan McKinlay and Bill Knox, 'Working for the Yankee Dollar: US Inward Investment and Scottish Labour, 1945–1970', *Historical Studies in Industrial Relations*, 7 (1999), 1–26.
31 *Oceanspan*, p. 33.
32 Harvie, *Scotland & Nationalism*, pp. 135–6.
33 *Oceanspan*, pp. 40–7; Toothill, *Scottish Economy*, pp. 129–44.
34 Memo from Joseph Rank Ltd, 27 September 1960, addressed to General Manager, Leith Dock Corporation, 27 September 1960; General Manager, Leith Dock Corporation, 'Supplementary Memo', October 1960; Johnson of the Scottish Office to Pearson of the Ministry of Transport, 17 March 1960; correspondence between Dunnett and Winnifrith, 6 January and 6 February 1961; Scottish Home Department note for the Secretary of State, 16 December 1960; all in SEP 5/38, NAS.
35 Note to Scottish Secretary of State from Scottish Home Department, 16 December 1960, SEP 5/38, NAS.
36 *Report into the Major Ports of Great Britain*, Cmnd 1824 (HMSO, 1962), pp. 40–1, 53–9.
37 Murray, *Scotland*, p. 161.
38 Alistair G. McCrae (CPA chairman), 'Estuarial Grouping of Ports', paper submitted to the Scottish Office, March 1969; note for Scottish Economic Planning Council, September 1969; SEP 5/45, NAS; Wilson, *Labour Government*, p. 522.
39 National Ports Council, Port Development Series, DK 1/36, various materials, PRO.
40 Ministry of Transport, *The Reorganisation of the Ports*, Cmnd 3903 (HMSO, January 1969), pp. 5–6.
41 *Oceanspan*, pp. 1, 9, 17, 24, 26.
42 *Glasgow Herald*, 23 January 1970.
43 A. McCrae to J. H. McGuiness, 25 August 1969, SEP 5/45, NAS; *The Economist*, 14 September 1968, p. xiv.
44 SCDI, EC, 16 February 1970, CH.
45 Mitchell, 'Scotland in the Union', p. 96.
46 Harvie, *No Gods*, p. 146.
47 Note of meeting between the Secretary of State for Scotland and the Chairmen of the Forth and Clyde Port Authorities, 23 January 1970, SEP 5/45, NAS.
48 *Parliamentary Debates, Fifth Series, Lords*, 311, 750–6, 764–8, 16 July 1970.
49 *Parliamentary Debates, Fifth Series, Commons*, 803, 1410–15, 14 July 1970.
50 Crossman, *Diaries of a Cabinet Minister: Vol. Two*, pp. 736, 739, 759.
51 *Select Committee on Scottish Affairs, Session 1968–69. Minutes of Evidence, 23 April to 16 July 1969* (HMSO, 1969), pp. 301–11; Cmnd 2864, pp. xii, 73.
52 *Royal Commission on the Constitution: Volume I, Report*, Cmnd 5460 (HMSO, 1973), pp. 335–44.
53 *Royal Commission on the Constitution, Minutes of Evidence: IV, Scotland, 5 May 1970*, pp. 74–86, 89–96.
54 Ibid., p. 86.
55 Lee, *Scotland and the United Kingdom*, p. 160.

56 Submission by the SCDI to the Royal Commission on the Constitution, 'Administration and Constitutional Arrangements As They Affect Industry', November 1969, HO 221/59, PRO.

57 *Parliamentary Debates, Fifth Series, Commons*, 729, 58–68, 23 May 1966, and 803, 1423–6, 14 July 1970.

58 Castle, *Diaries, 1964–76*, p. 133; 'Docks: Rational Reorganisation', *The Economist*, 1 February 1969, p. 67.

59 SCDI, EC, 16 February 1970, CH.

60 Harvie, *No Gods*, p. 90.

61 *Parliamentary Debates, Fifth Series, Commons*, 803, 1421–6, 14 July 1970.

62 Hugh Murphy, who has interviewed Sir William, provided this insight by e-mail to the author on 8 June 2005.

63 Foster, 'Twentieth Century', pp. 474–5; for biographical information on Clydesmuir see *Who's Who in Scotland*, 1988–89 (Second edition, Ayr, 1988).

64 John Foster and Charles Woolfson, 'How Workers on the Clyde Gained the Capacity for Class Struggle: the Upper Clyde Shipbuilders' Work-In, 1971–2', in McIlroy, Fishman and Campbell, *British Trade Unions*, p. 301.

65 Campbell, *Edward Heath*, pp. 303–5.

66 'Scotland's Jobless Fears May Bring a Winter of Discontent', (by Chris Baur of *The Scotsman*), *The Times*, 22 September 1970.

67 SCDI, *Unemployment in Scotland*, SEP 10/323, NAS.

68 Lee, *Scotland and the United Kingdom*, pp. 184–5.

69 R. B. Anderson to John Davies, 6 December 1971, SEP 4/4424, NAS.

70 Draft Speech, 'Scottish Economy and Oceanspan', 7–8 July 1970; Morison (Dover House) to Miss M. J. Alexander (Regional Development Division), 9 July 1970; SEP 10/409, NAS.

71 *Parliamentary Debates, Fifth Series, Lords*, 311, 758–63, 16 July 1970.

72 For a summary of evidence submitted to various inquiries on port transport see Jim Phillips, 'Class and Industrial Relations in Britain: The 'Long' Mid-Century and the Case of Port Transport, c. 1920–1970', *Twentieth Century British History*, 16 (2005), 52–73.

73 Professor Derek Oddy of the University of Westminster articulated this perspective, speaking in his capacity as a maritime historian, at the Association of Business Historians Conference at the University of Nottingham, 24–25 June 2004.

74 *Parliamentary Debates, Fifth Series, Lords*, 311, 768-73, 16 July 1970.

75 *The Scotsman*, 17 July 1970.

76 Payne, *Colvilles*, p. 423.

77 Scottish Council for Development and Industry, *Oceanspan 2. Eurospan: A Study of Port and Industrial Development in Western Europe* (Edinburgh, 1971).

78 Marr, *Battle for Scotland*, p. 131.

79 *Glasgow Herald*, 23 January 1970.

80 *The Scotsman*, 21 December 1971; clipping in PREM 15/1190, PRO.

81 Christopher Harvie, *Fool's Gold: The Story of North Sea Oil* (Harmondsworth, 1994).

82 Foster, 'Twentieth Century', pp. 479–81.

83 Hutchison, *Scottish Politics*, p. 99.

84 Marr, *Battle for Scotland*, pp. 123–7.

85 'Regional Policy: Scotland', 8 December 1971, PREM 15/1190, PRO.

86 Notes for Secretary of State for Trade and Industry in advance of meeting with SCDI, 12 January 1972, PREM 15/1190, PRO.

87 Official Note of Lunch given by Prime Minister for Secretary of State for Trade and Industry and Secretary of State for Scotland and Sir William McEwan Younger, 12 January 1972, PREM 15/1190, PRO.

88 Ibid.

89 Young, *Scotland*, p. 140.

90 *Glasgow Herald*, 11 January 1972; clipping in PREM 15/1190, PRO.

91 'Scotland Puts Forward Her Case', *The Times*, 13 January 1972.

92 Official Minute of Meeting between the Prime Minister and representatives of the Scottish Council (Development and Industry), 13 January 1970, PREM 15/1190, PRO.

93 Chris Baur, 'BSC to start talks on £26 million ore terminal at Hunterston', *The Scotsman*, 1 February 1972.

94 SCDI, EC, 21 February 1972, CH.

95 Campbell, *Edward Heath*, pp. 443–9.

96 SCDI, EC, 24 April 1972, CH.

97 *The Times*, 12 May 1972.

98 Note in advance of meeting between the Prime Minister and the SCDI; and minute of meeting, 12 May 1972, PREM 15/1190, PRO.

99 Heath to Clydesmuir, 29 November 1972, SEP 10/115, NAS.

100 Undated DOE commentary, SEP 10/115, NAS.

101 *Glasgow Herald*, 23 August 1969; *The Scotsman*, 27 January 1970; clippings in SEP 5/45, NAS.

102 Devine, *Tobacco Lords*.

103 'Port Proposals Could Signal Economy Boost', *The Herald*, 20 August 2004.

104 Jameson W. Doig, *Empire on the Hudson. Entrepreneurial Vision and Political Power at the Port of New York Authority* (New York, 2001), pp. 375–6.

105 National Ports Council, *Transshipment in the Seventies: A Study of Container Transport, Report prepared by Arthur D. Little* (London, June 1969), pp. 5, 9–11.

106 Fernand Braudel, *The Mediterranean and the Mediterranean in the Age of Philip II* (London, 1992).

107 Chris Baur, 'BSC to Start Talks on £26 Million Ore Terminal at Hunterston', *The Scotsman*, 1 February 1972.

108 *Glasgow Herald*, 23 February 1972.

109 SCDI, EC, 18 December 1972, CH.

110 *The Times*, 9 May 1984.

111 Murray, *Scotland*, p. 67; Lee, *Scotland and the United Kingdom*, p. 89.

112 'Cash Crisis for Scottish Council: No Reserves Left', *The Times*, 10 October 1972.

113 STUC, *72nd Annual Report*, p. 234.

114 Tuckett, *The Scottish Trades Union Congress*, p. 402; 'Scots Charter on Workless Goes to Mr Heath', *The Times*, 15 February 1972.

115 Foster, 'Twentieth Century', pp. 475–6.

116 Peregrine Worsthorne, 'Class and Conflict in British Foreign Policy', *Foreign Affairs*, 37, 3 (1959), 419–31, pp. 421, 428.

3 Ships: the UCS work-in, 1971–72

> "Let them eat cake" made no bones about it.
> But we say let them eat the hope deferred
> and that will sicken them. We have preferred
> silent slipways to the riveters' wit.
> And don't deny it – that's the ugly bit.
> Ministers' tears might well have launched a herd
> of bucking tankers if they'd been transferred
> from Whitehall to the Clyde. And smiles don't fit
> either. "There'll be no bevvying" said Reid
> at the work-in. But all the dignity you muster
> can only give you back a mouth to feed
> and rent to pay if what you lose in bluster
> is no more than win patience with "I need"
> while distant blackboards use you as their duster.

This, the fifth of Edwin Morgan's ten *Glasgow Sonnets*, published in 1973,[1] illuminates the class and nationalist politics and ultimately ambivalent outcome of the 1971–72 work-in at the Clydebank and Glasgow yards of UCS, which contributed significantly to the growth of support for devolution across Scotland. The work-in, led by a body of stewards, some of whom, including Jimmy Reid, Jimmy Airlie and Sam Barr, were Communists, was the workforce's response to the liquidation of the combine in June 1971. UCS was at this point dependent on state subsidy, which Edward Heath's Conservative government – eschewing determinedly any continued support for 'lame ducks' – refused to perpetuate.

The work-in generated widespread social and political support, encompassing in Clydeside a large fraction of business opinion and the Progressive Lord Provost of Glasgow, Sir Donald Liddle, who was broadly an ally of the Conservative Party but criticised volubly the government's perceived 'abandonment' of the yards. The labour movement in Scotland and the UK, already mobilising against the government's Industrial Relations Bill, provided the UCS workers with major moral and financial support. On Wednesday 23 June 1971 40,000 people participated in a demonstration that marked the beginning of the public campaign to save the yards, marching from George Square to Glasgow Green, with an accompanying half-day regional strike in Clydeside. The work-in commenced across the threatened yards on 30 July after a House of Commons announcement by John Davies, Secretary of State for Trade and Industry, that no further support from the government would be forthcoming. A larger demonstration still, attended by 80,000, and a one-day strike, observed by 200,000 workers across Clydeside, took place on Wednesday 18 August. In the face of this concerted opposition – which incorporated those 'neurotic' Tory businessmen on Clydeside whom William McEwen Younger complained about during the *Oceanspan* discussions of January 1972, but whom Heath could not, on grounds of political expediency, ignore – the government reversed its position. Major new subsidies were announced in February 1972, which kept the yards open, although employment was reduced from around 8,500 to 6,300.

This outcome seemed to represent a victory for the workers, the Clyde and Scotland more generally. 'Protest was seen to work', writes Tom Devine, whose very brief account of this very important episode – in a very large book on Scotland from 1700 to 2000 that has been criticised for its relatively slight coverage of industrial developments – mistakenly situates the 80,000-strong demonstration in June 1972.[2] Many other assessments have been offered. Irene Maver and Christopher Harvie both record the 'pugnacious' efforts of the stewards and the workforce, but are sceptical about the nature of the workers' apparent victory. The necessary 'modernisation' and 'reorganisation' of the yards was not achieved, and so the Heath reinvestment provided short-term comfort but no lasting industrial benefit.[3] Lewis Johnman and Hugh Murphy provide a similar verdict in their analysis of twentieth-century British shipbuilding, concluding that the 1972 rescue was geared to 'the sustenance of the industry rather than its reform'.[4]

These more recent works follow a number of instant histories, published either during or shortly after the work-in, and each written from a distinctive political or ideological position. An early example of these is an arresting portrait written at the end of 1971 by Alasdair Buchan, a *Daily Record* journalist and son of Janey and Norman Buchan, central figures in the Clydeside labour movement. This sympathised with the position of the workforce and the leaders of the work-in, praised the contribution to the campaign to save the yards of Labour Party leaders, notably Harold Wilson, who provided an appreciative introduction to the book, and was highly critical of the Conservative government. Another journalist, Jack McGill, industrial correspondent of the *Scottish Daily Express*, wrote an important mainstream Tory and business interpretation, explaining the 'crisis' in terms of – in ascending order of importance – the incompetence of management, the block-headed intransigence of the workforce and the outgoing Labour government's maladministration of shipbuilding policy.[5] Before too long a proto-Thatcherite account appeared, Frank Broadway's *Upper Clyde Shipbuilders*, published by the Centre for Policy Studies with a preface by Sir Keith Joseph. This railed against the 'Luddism' of the workforce, the opportunism of the Labour Party in supporting the work-in and the further damage to Britain's allegedly poor productivity that arose from Heath's eventual 'bail-out'.[6]

A very different contemporary account was written by Willie Thompson and Finlay Hart, its Communist sympathies signalled by the inclusion of a foreword by Jimmy Reid, although it presented his famous and fundamentally Scottish paean to sobriety in the shipyards – captured in Morgan's sonnet – as, 'There will be no *drinking*'.[7] The Thompson and Hart book contained two fairly clear analytical strands. First, the work-in was central to the emergence of a peculiarly Scottish set of political formations, with the CPGB part of a broader left pan-nationalist alliance. Second, the aims and purposes of UK government policy were linked to the capitalist identities, associations and interests of the *English* Conservative practitioners of this policy. These two strands are also present in the later publications of John Foster and Charles Woolfson, which chart the relationship between the work-in and the trajectories of working-class, labourist and nationalist politics. Foster's self-authored contribution to the 2001 *Penguin History of Scotland* emphasises the strong causal connection between the decline of heavy industry and a growth of support for political devolution in Scotland, and presents the UCS episode as central to this relationship. The triumph of the UCS work-in accelerated the labour movement's forward march in Scotland, according to Foster, enhancing its leadership of the Scottish 'proletarian nation', as evidenced by the numerical growth of trade union membership and the Labour Party's 'success' in the general election of 1979 when, in the face of Thatcher's UK triumph, there was a significant swing to Labour in Scotland.[8]

Labour's electoral improvement in 1979 was, however, largely at the SNP's expense. Labour's vote was up from 36.3 to 42 per cent and number of MPs up from forty-one to forty-four; the SNP were down from about 30 per cent to 18 per cent and from eleven MPs to just two. Meanwhile the Tories – and this would not be surmised from Foster's account – made gains on 1974, and arguably capitalised even further than Labour on the SNP's collapse by increasing their share of the Scottish vote, from 24.7 to 30 per cent, and their number of MPs, from sixteen to twenty-two.[9] So there must be some resistance to the idea that 1979 was a victory for Labour in Scotland, certainly when set against the subsequent rebalancing of power in favour of employers and capital which Thatcher's government encouraged. Its policies can be presented as an assault on the organised working class, and drew on a large reservoir of business and Tory resentment that accumulated in the 1960s and 1970s. The UCS episode was central to this resentment, with Tory ministers humbled by the eventual about-turn on the Clyde. This contributed to the Heath government's larger sense of defeat, shaped also by its struggle to impose the Industrial Relations Act and the embarrassing surrenders to the NUM in 1972 and 1973–74, the first of which overlapped with the collapse of the 'lame ducks' approach on the Clyde and is examined in Chapter 4.

In this longer historical sense then, the outcome of the work-in was ambiguous. In the short term too the workers' victory was far from complete. Roughly one-quarter of the 8,500 jobs in the yard were lost and the employment of those who remained was highly insecure. The precarious balance of forces on the Clyde duly resembled Peregrine Worsthorne's model of social relations in Britain more generally after the Second World War, the 'stalemate' between capital and labour.[10] This stalemate was almost broken on a number of occasions in the early 1970s, but over the UCS, as elsewhere, it remained intact, with neither labour nor capital able to assert itself over the other. In this connection the Trotskyist Socialist Labour League and its paper, *Workers Press*, questioned the 'success' of the work-in in highly robust terms. In a further instant history of the UCS episode Stephen Johns, the *Workers Press* correspondent, criticised the 'Stalinist' CPGB and the stewards, especially Reid, who dampened the class forces apparently unleashed by the crisis by reaching a 'solution' in co-operation with business interests and the Conservative government. The rescue deals consolidated capitalist property rights – retreating from an initial demand for nationalisation – and made the position of the workers even more vulnerable.[11]

The Trotskyist critique also encompassed the stewards' presentation of the work-in as an explicitly and particularly *Scottish* phenomenon, which de-emphasised its connections with workers' struggles in other parts of the UK, or the structural features of capitalism that resulted in a global crisis of over-capacity in ships and shipbuilding. Instead the insecurity of employment on the Clyde was related by the stewards to the remote administration of power, a familiar theme in Scottish economic life since the 1930s and especially from the Toothill era onwards. For the *Workers Press* this was an undoubted expression of 'false consciousness', but the work-in nevertheless stimulated further the growth of support for Scottish devolutionary mechanisms. The loss – or potential loss – of skilled and craft-based employment in shipbuilding was seen across Scotland as politically unacceptable. So in this sense Thompson and Hart and Foster and Woolfson were not wrong: the presentation of the work-in as a *Scottish* phenomenon allowed the labour movement to take a greater lead in the campaign for enhanced Scottish administrative and political autonomy, and the social and political influence of indigenous industrial leaders, by comparison, was progressively uncertain. The *Oceanspan* episode illustrated that traditional Scottish industrialists, while determined and even imaginative, enjoyed limited political capital in Whitehall and Westminster, although the government listened to their voices on the specific question of rescuing UCS. These industrialists, it might be added, were the more willing to support UCS because of the progressively moderate position adopted on the issue by labour leaders, including the stewards.

Yet the work-in was only a Scottish affair in so much as broader questions, tensions and difficulties that were developing in a UK context were overlooked. One of the striking features of the episode is the extent to which most of its historiography – from Devine, Maver and Harvie through to Foster and Woolfson – has generally privileged its particularly Scottish features. These appear prominently in this account also, although the linkages between the Clyde and wider UK industrial and labour phenomena are emphasised too, and shaped the government's reversal over subsidies. A more critical approach is adopted here towards other aspects of the work-in, including the involvement of the CPGB, which is presented by Foster and Woolfson and Thompson and Hart largely as an unambiguously 'progressive' force. Edwin Morgan, in his poetic instant history, viewed the outcome of the work-in with caution and even pessimism, noting the tendency of even ostensibly militant working-class leaders to adopt positions that ultimately made little impact on existing configurations of economic and social authority. This was partly the purpose of the Reid reference: working-class and 'socialist' dignity, along with restraint and forbearance, were admirable enough but counted for little against the remote administration – the 'distant blackboards' – of unrestrained corporate and reactionary political power. The tendency, then, of Communists to control rather than heighten working-class militancy is duly highlighted in this account, and in this sense the *Workers Press* analysis is certainly instructive. The chapter utilises Cabinet, Scottish Office and Department of Trade and Industry papers that were not available to Foster and Woolfson and other scholars, and so pays closer attention to the position of the Conservative government and its various difficulties – and resentments accrued – in the conduct of economic policy and industrial relations. The discussion duly measures the work-in against the events outlined in Chapter 6, the deferred revenge visited on organised workers – of the Clyde, Scotland and elsewhere in the UK – by the Conservative government that took office in 1979, which ruptured Worsthorne's 'stalemate' decisively in the interests of capital but, in so doing, inadvertently helped to advance Scotland's progress to devolution.

Seawards the Great Ships: industrial insecurity and craft skill

Two structural features of shipbuilding triggered the UCS crisis: long-running but 'glacial' decline that accelerated in the 1960s; and the powerful presence of craft skill, which heightened the sense of loss when the group entered liquidation.

Shipbuilding in Scotland followed the general UK pattern of slow decline from its late Victorian and Edwardian position of global pre-eminence. The Second World War and then increased demand for merchant shipping in the late 1940s and early 1950s offered the industry an opportunity which it failed to take, according to Johnman and Murphy, who observe that shipbuilding was characterised by lower investment – as share of net output – and higher share dividends than other branches of British manufacturing.[12] Total employment in Scottish shipbuilding gradually fell. On the Clyde shipyard employment had contracted from around 50,000 after the Second World War to roughly 20,000 by 1971. But the yards that remained, clustered on the lower and upper reaches of the Clyde, retained a substantial industrial profile.[13]

This industrial significance was reflected in shipbuilding's cultural prominence, with many important artistic representations of the industry and its workforce. Stanley Spencer's phenomenal *Shipbuilding on the Clyde* series, incorporating hundreds of drawings and dozens of paintings, was completed from studies conducted in Port Glasgow during the Second World War. Spencer's major paintings in the series detail the many branches of highly developed craft skill deployed in the yards: *Caulking* (1940), *Burners* (1940), *Welders* (1941), *Riveters* (1941), *The Template* (1942), *Bending the Keel Plate* (1943), *Riggers* (1944), *Plumbers* (1944–45).[14] This theme of craft skill was evident in *Seawards the Great Ships*, which won the 1961 Oscar for Best Live Action Short.[15] Produced by Templar Film Studios for the Clyde Shipbuilders' Association and Films of Scotland Committee, this depicted shipbuilding as a great historical project, based on bespoke production and the human input of craft skill. In this it fundamentally differed from *Young In Heart*, discussed in Chapter 1, which dwelt on the computerised and mechanised technologies of car production, and unwittingly outlined the human ennui that shaped the Linwood labour unrest. In *Seawards the Great Ships* the 'men of the Clyde', 'tough in sinew, warm in spirit', were central to the skilled and precise production processes, and depicted in their hundreds and even thousands, with very little visual representation, by comparison, of the bosses who had commissioned the film.

This tribute to labour power and craft skill, produced on behalf of the employers, conveys much about shipbuilding in the early 1960s. The emphasis on craft- and labour-intensive methods and bespoke production reflected the industry's commitment to high-value passenger and cargo liners, for which demand was falling, and its reluctance to manufacture standardised tankers, increasingly in demand but not viewed by industrialists, according to Johnman and Murphy, as 'real' shipbuilding. The same industrial conservatism would be evident in the later 1960s, in the reluctance to consider new ship designs, including container vessels and roll-on/roll-off passenger and cargo ferries.[16] But the film also says much about broader industrial politics in Scotland in the 1960s. The public and formalised courtesies extended to the workers were indicative of labour's enhanced social and political power, despite fluctuating product and labour market conditions. The work-in sprang from this rise in working-class expectations and self-confidence, reflected in the stewards' emphasis on the right to work. It also indicated the extent to which male craft skill would continue to represent a central feature of working-class identity early in the 1970s.

Seawards the Great Ships arguably caught the final phase of the busy post-Second World War years, which were giving way in the 1960s to fluctuating order books and levels of employment. In April 1963 the Managing Director of John Brown's at Clydebank told Ministry of Labour officials that he could not compete with the Swedish and Japanese firms that were offering 'suicide prices'.[17] There was then an increase – roughly 35 per cent – in the volume of work 'in hand' in the industry in the year from September 1963. This owed something to government assistance, through the £30 million government Shipping Loan Fund. Late in 1964 John Brown's received a much anticipated major order, the 58,000-tons passenger liner – provisionally named *Q4* – for Cunard, which it was expected would employ a thousand additional men at Clydebank.[18] Yet even this would prove an ambiguous industrial lifeline as costs escalated, in the tradition of the damagingly expensive *Queen Mary* and *Queen Elizabeth*.[19] A loss exceeding £1 million on the *Q4* alone was duly inherited by the grouping of shipyards formed as Upper Clyde Shipbuilders in September 1967, encompassing John Brown's, Yarrow's, Fairfield's, Stephen's and Connell's. A Committee of Inquiry, established by Wilson's Labour government in 1965, and chaired by Reay Geddes of Dunlop, had recommended the grouping concept for the industry as a whole.[20] On the Clyde's lower reaches the Scott-Lithgow group was established, centred on Greenock and Port Glasgow. The government also followed the Geddes Inquiry by setting up the Shipbuilding Industry Board (SIB) in 1966 to oversee the process of estuarial grouping and disburse strategic public investment in the industry.[21]

With the terms of the UCS merger being finalised, *Q4* took to the water on 20 September 1967, defying the pessimism of Sir Basil Smallpeice, Chairman of Cunard, who had told Harold Wilson in July that falling global demand was such that many of his firm's 'famous' ships would have to be laid up and that the new ship would remain un-launched.[22] But launched it was, as *Queen Elizabeth II*, a 'good' name, according to Charles Oakley, Glasgow Chamber of Commerce President, but described as an 'insult' to Scotland by Gordon Wilson of the SNP, reviving the 1952–53 controversy surrounding the coronation of the first Scottish Elizabeth. Hugh Wyper of Glasgow District Trades Council – echoing the politics of *Seaward the Great Ships* – argued that the ship ought to have been named for the men, the skills, the river and the industry that had produced it, suggesting in these terms *The Endeavour*.[23] More serious trouble followed the launch, with a public dispute early in 1969 between Cunard and UCS over the vessel's turbines, resolved only after Tony Benn, Minister of Technology, appointed the mediating services of the Institute of Mechanical Engineers. But Cunard remained unhappy about the late delivery of the vessel, with speculation continuing over several years about a possible claim for damages against UCS.[24]

The turbines dispute compounded the difficulties facing UCS in 1969. In August its accounts showed total losses of £8.39 million, including £3.55 million in inherited losses – one-third arising from the *QE II* – and roughly £5 million in losses on post-merger contracts.[25] UCS had been hampered by the industry's structural weaknesses, evident across the UK and not just on the Clyde. The consequence of low capital investment and the embedded reliance on labour intensive production methods was a highly problematic and confrontational pattern of industrial relations, noted and lamented by a variety of observers, including Reay Geddes in 1965–66.[26] With good historical reason workers were highly suspicious of managerial incursions on their craft privileges. Jack McGill of the *Scottish Daily Express* wrote of the tendency of shipyard workers to 'screw' their bosses but related this to management's short-term and adversarial employment practices.[27] There has, of course, been a lengthy discussion in economics, historical and management literature on the linkage between industrial relations and industrial performance. Those adhering to the 'decline' thesis – that there was a substantial but avoidable decline in British manufacturing enterprise after the Second World War – sometimes relate this to multi-plant unionism and multi-unionism within plants, and what is seen as the consequently high incidence of strikes and 'restrictive practices'. Derek Aldcroft and Michael Oliver, for instance, directly link collective bargaining and industrial unrest with 'sub-optimal economic performance', seeing shipbuilding, car production, coal, steel, port transport and printing as sectors where strikes were especially 'endemic', resulting in 'more than a marginal influence in terms of lost production and progress'.[28]

Yet this terrain is highly ideological. To some scholars 'decline' itself is exaggerated. Alan Booth has indicated that manufacturing industry actually performed reasonably well in the post-1945 period, and sees criticism of unions and workers as particularly overblown, outlining the limited impact of strikes – especially in the allegedly 'crisis' years of the early 1970s – and the low union 'mark up' in wages, which in any event continued to rise even in the declining years of organised labour in the 1980s.[29] Jim Tomlinson, in similar vein, has presented 'decline' as political construct rather than economic or industrial fact, grounded to a large extent in the contested terrain of electoral politics in the 1950s and 1960s, and picked up – for different reasons, of course – by both Labour and Conservative parties.[30] Reviewing the economic and business history literature, meanwhile, David Edgerton has noted the inclination of scholars to accept the 'decline of declinism'.[31] It would seem plausible, on this basis, to extend Tomlinson's model of decline as a constructed process to encompass the ideological 'scapegoating' of labour: anti-labour forces mustered 'declinist' arguments, rooted in criticisms of organised workers, as strategic elements in the conduct of industrial politics. This is strongly suggested, for instance, in Tim Claydon's analysis of press coverage of disputes in car manufacturing, with much editorial coverage of their alleged impact on production and sales and little on their underlying industrial and social causes.[32] It is more substantially demonstrated in Theo Nichols's significant critique of the anti-worker declinist model, which was published in 1986, when Thatcherite-fuelled ideas about decline and poor worker performance were at their zenith.

Nichols examined the particular question of productivity, and argued that economists who sought to demonstrate the culpability of workers in this area were guided by a narrow managerial agenda, focusing on the outcome of the labour process but ignoring its contents. These encompassed three powerful general contingencies: the long history of the social organisation of production in Britain, including the legacy of 'atomised' industrial structure, which reduced economies of scale and undermined investment; the relative degree of democracy in Britain over time, which reduced the availability of 'vulnerable' and highly exploitable labour; and the tendency in macro-economic management over several generations to privilege the interests of the financial sector over the productive sector. There were, moreover, many important micro-contingencies that shaped economic performance. Within industry there were significant structural weaknesses, notably plant size, design and age, and there were also various management deficiencies, including the modest educational qualifications and technical expertise of managers, and the indifferent or poor design of the organisation of produc-tion. Collectively these macro- and micro-contingencies offered a very wide and deep history of industrial under-performance that indicated very strongly the limitations of worker performance as an explanation for Britain's relative shortfall in productivity.[33]

Nichols's analysis might be linked to the history of the Rootes-Chrysler plant, examined in Chapter 1, where disappointing output was commonly attributed to intermittent or sometimes even 'constant' labour 'difficulties' or 'unrest', which 'cut production and reduced efficiency'.[34] But this emphasis on labour can be read as a means of deflecting attention from other explanations of poor performance: poor industrial relations at Linwood were arguably the symptom rather than the source of the plant's difficulties, which arose from limited investment and probable deficiencies in design and marketing. These managerial questions were probably the key in most industrial sectors, including shipbuilding, where of additional structural significance was the fact that the upper Clyde was tortuously winding and narrow, like the upper reaches of other British estuaries, and ill-designed for bulk carriers.

These various difficulties in shipbuilding – including managerial attitudes and class prejudices – received full expression in the so-called Fairfield experiment, precipitated when the Govan firm passed into receivership in 1965, despite a recent '£5 million modernisation scheme' and an order book worth £30 million.[35] The Labour government co-ordinated a rescue of the yard, involving capital investment from the state, trade unions and private industry, and new leadership at Fairfield's, including businessmen from outside shipbuilding, most notably the Chairman, Sir Iain Stewart. It was proposed that the reconstituted firm would operate as a template for 'modernised' methods of working and industrial relations across the economy, with an emphasis on flexibility and partnership: the workers would relinquish their protective practices and the management would incorporate workforce representatives in planning production and developing the business. Jack Scamp, a Personnel Manager at GEC with a public reputation for industrial 'trouble-shooting', especially in the motor industry and the docks, was appointed to advise the board, which included Hugh Stenhouse, the insurance millionaire and future Tory Treasurer in Scotland, Lord Carron, President of the Amalgamated Engineering Union, and Andrew Cunningham, District Secretary of the General and Municipal Workers' Union.[36] Jack McGill – industrial correspondent, remember, of the *Scottish Daily Express* – belittled the experiment, ridiculing the involvement of businessmen with little or no experience in shipbuilding,[37] and from an entirely different perspective John Foster sees it as 'bizarre', and an important episode in the competition between Scotland's industrial 'modernisers' and 'traditionalists'. The former, including Thomson and STV, of which Stewart was Vice-Chairman, helped refinance the firm, and subsidised residential courses on industrial and employment relations that shop stewards attended. These involved some input from US management trainers, including associates of the Moral Rearmament movement, which emphasised the fundamental parity of interest between labour and capital and sought, throughout the period of the Cold War, to undermine working-class support for socialist critiques of capitalism.[38]

The 'traditionalists' despised the experiment, as might be surmised from McGill's hostile account. The rescue prevented a slackening of the Clyde's labour market, with Fairfield shop stewards 'outflanking' – Foster's word – the Labour government and their employer, quietly tolerating seminars on peaceful industrial relations while incrementally bargaining up wage rates that other Clyde firms were obliged to follow. This annoyed William Lithgow and the river's other potentates, Connell, Yarrow, Stephen and Scott. As third or even fourth-generation shipbuilders these figures resented sharing authority with the Fairfield executives who had little shipbuilding experience, and disliked even more strongly the interventionism of politicians, especially the 'socialist' politicians who Lithgow so pungently criticised in *The Times* in March 1968.[39] The UCS merger duly crushed the experiment in 1967, giving little leeway to the Fairfield executives in the new structure. In monitoring developments Tony Benn, the Minister of Technology, was conscious that older industrial attitudes prevailed, and was particularly scathing about Sir Charles Connell, UCS deputy chairman, who was seeking to 'punish' Fairfield's for its experiment and held fast to the 'idea of throwing men out of work to discipline them'.[40]

UCS managers were duly at odds with the government and the SIB throughout 1969, attempting to ratchet up state support by threatening imminent liquidation in February, May, June and November. This was designed to maximise pressure on the Labour government, with Wilson conceding eventually that the human and political costs of closure – a male unemployment rate of 8.5 per cent on the Clyde weighed against the electoral security of several Labour MPs in Glasgow – were unacceptable. He duly over-rode Benn's assessment that further government subsidy was unjustifiable on industrial grounds. Benn had been involving the STUC in dialogue about UCS and its future in the first half of 1969, although there was cross-party and cross-class support too that anticipated the broad basis of the 1971–72 work-in, with contacts between Benn and Betty Harvie Anderson, Tory MP for Renfrewshire East, who complained about the obdurate nature of the SIB in its negotiations with UCS. Meanwhile the Tory and SNP as well as Labour groups on the City Council, along with the Lord Provost, Sir Donald Liddle, participated in negotiations in June 1969 on an 'action plan' that would secure UCS. Liddle headed a Progressive group on the council, distinct from the Tories, although by tradition encompassing Tory or Unionist as well as Liberal sympathisers and aligned with small business interests.[41] By February 1970 the government had committed £7 million to this plan, reflecting Wilson's conclusion, supported by some SIB members, that the UCS was now a social rather than an economic question.[42] Heath's government in February 1972 would eventually reach the same assessment. In December 1969, however, the UCS lost Yarrow's, the only profitable member of the group, weakening considerably the combine's likelihood of improved future performance.[43]

Liquidation and the start of the work-in

The Yarrow's de-merger had been encouraged by Nicholas Ridley, the Conservative spokesman for shipbuilding, who in December 1969 – after talking to Sir Eric Yarrow – wrote his 'butcher' memorandum summarising UCS's debts and difficulties. This argued that a future Conservative government should publicly state its intention to commit no further public money to the company. While Yarrow's could align itself with the Scott-Lithgow group on the Lower Clyde, UCS should enter liquidation, with a government-appointed 'butcher' to dismember the firm and sell its assets cheaply to the Lower Clyde. Ridley's memo has been characterised as 'infamous', 'notorious' and conspiratorial, with its thrust sometimes related to his family's coal and steel interests in the north east of England.[44] Admittedly Ridley developed a habit for controversy. Following Heath's humbling by the NUM in 1972 and 1974 Ridley wrote another memorandum, this time outlining a strategy for a future Tory government to defeat the miners, involving coal stockpiles and new policing methods to subvert 'flying pickets'. When this memorandum appeared in *The Economist* in 1978 Ridley apologised to his party leader, Margaret Thatcher, but she was totally unabashed: the miners had to be defeated and there was no harm in publicising this fact.[45] Ridley in 1969 took the same reasonably open attitude to the UCS. His memo, while not officially Conservative Party policy, was certainly consistent with other policies being considered publicly by the Heath Shadow Cabinet,[46] and adopted at the famous Selsdon Park conference at the end of January 1970. This seemed to presage a decisive rightward shift, suggesting a Tory government committed to legislative controls on trade unionism, tax cuts, and 'tougher' measures on law and order and immigration.[47]

As a 'secret' document Ridley's memo also enjoyed unusually wide circulation. Copies were sent to Sir Keith Joseph, Tory spokesman on industry, Betty Harvie Anderson and Gordon Campbell,[48] and also reached Labour MPs. Tony Benn had one in his files, obtained from Eric Varley, Minister of State at the Ministry of Technology in 1969 and 1970, and this Benn passed to a friendly journalist, Mark Arnold-Foster of *The Guardian*, on Monday 14 June 1971.[49] Arnold-Foster's piece duly appeared on 15 June, and the 'conspiracy' element of the story developed in force. This annoyed Heath, however, who later wrote that the 'Ridley Report' had been falsely projected as 'evidence' of his government's class-confrontational instincts and aims.[50]

Benn released the Ridley paper when news developed over the weekend of 11–13 June 1971 that UCS was about to enter liquidation, the government refusing any further subsidy. Rumours of imminent closure had surfaced intermittently during the winter of 1970–71, notably in February, when one of the largest creditors to the UCS, the South of Scotland Electricity Board (SSEB), was complaining to the DTI that its monthly bill of about £40,000 had been unpaid since the beginning of September 1970.[51] Benn discussed the position with John Davies, Secretary of State for Industry,[52] who in the House of Commons confirmed that the government would not 'bail out' concerns unable to 'see their way through to viability'.[53] This gave ministers little room for manoeuvre in June, when it is generally agreed that UCS was roughly £28 million in debt.[54] Tony Hepper, UCS Chairman, met Davies in London on Wednesday 9 June,[55] and the Cabinet on Thursday 10 June agreed not to save the firm, with the likely loss of 8,500 jobs. The workforce heard this news on Friday, which was reported in the *Glasgow Herald* on Saturday.[56] The extent of the controversy emerged over the next few days and weeks as Ministers agreed to meet a variety of business and labour representatives. On Sunday 13 June Hepper told Davies, at the Minister's constituency home in Knutsford in Cheshire, that liquidation was inevitable without an immediate acquisition of £6 million, to pay suppliers and meet wages and other working expenses. Davies proceeded directly to Chequers for a conference with Heath, where liquidation was accepted as imminent fact.[57] Davies announced this the next day, in the House of Commons. Benn replied by positioning cash flow as the main problem, with the UCS unable to service creditors. Hence the government was partly responsible for the crisis, having withheld monies due to UCS under the Shipbuilding Industry Act that amounted to an income shortfall of £5 million between November 1970 and February 1971.[58] On this point Jack McGill, broadly critical of Benn and the Labour Party, notes that Tory ministers – Ridley especially – had indeed been less accommodating than UCS directors might reasonably have expected.[59]

As the liquidator, Robert Smith, set to work, meeting Davies on 17 June, the political difficulties of the position were summarised in a leader column in *The Times*, 'TRAGEDY OF THE CLYDE'. This argued that closure was fully justified on commercial grounds but that politically the crisis 'could hardly have come at a worse time', given the context of class and industrial tensions over the government's Industrial Relations Bill and the simultaneous growth of inflation and unemployment.[60] The job losses were especially important. Writing in the 1990s, after the Tory government had been re-elected three times despite the existence of unemployment in excess of two and three (and possibly even four) million, John Campbell, Heath's biographer, was keen to explain his subject's particular sensitivity to relatively smaller incidences of unemployment in the early 1970s. Heath, like several of his Cabinet colleagues, was schooled in the politics of the 1930s and 1940s, when mass unemployment across Europe stimulated the growth of fascism and hence the immense human catastrophes of the Second World War and the Holocaust. In the late 1950s, as Harold Macmillan's Chief Whip, Heath had learnt much about the inter-war difficulties of Stockton, Macmillan's constituency in the Durham coalfields, where unemployment had greatly disfigured economic and social development. For Heath and his colleagues, Campbell writes, the workless 'men in caps and mufflers were a real presence whom no amount of sophisticated rationalisation could explain away'.[61]

Heath's unease was not, of course, entirely a product of human sentiment. The material basis of industrial politics in the early 1970s was substantially different from the 1930s, when Sir James Lithgow had 'rationalised' the shipyards without encountering the type and scale of labour movement opposition facing the Conservative government over UCS.[62] The

Table 3.1   *Employment in UCS, by yard, on 19 July 1971*

Yard	Employment
John Brown's, Clydebank	3,111
Fairfield's, Govan	2,574
Stephen's, Linthouse	1,318
Connell's, Scotstoun	1,137
Total	8,140

Source: UCS Closure Contingency Planning, Note of Meeting at Scottish Office, 19 July 1971, SEP 4/3870, NAS.

labour movement's vigorous presence now made unemployment a pressing political problem as it rose steadily across the UK in 1971, before eventually passing the symbolic figure of one million on 20 January 1972. Ten years after Toothill the rate of Scottish unemployment, just under 6 per cent across 1971, was still roughly double the UK rate of just over 3 per cent,[63] and 'black spots' were still a powerful feature. With male unemployment on the Clyde at 9.3 per cent in June 1971, Benn observed that the closure of UCS 'would pitchfork Scotland into the deepest slump since the 1930s'.[64] Civil servants were duly detailed to calculate the potential losses, from the base level of employment in UCS during the period of provisional liquidation, between 14 June and 29 July, set out in Table 3.1.

Working on 'optimistic assumptions' about future employment growth at both Scott-Lithgow and Yarrow's, which was contingent on government support and naval orders, these officials – from the Scottish Office and the Departments of Trade and Industry, the Environment, Employment and Health and Social Security – concluded that at least 3,000 men would be looking for work outside shipbuilding, prompting hurried efforts to provide additional Department of Employment and Department of Health and Social Security office space in Clydebank.[65] Officials subsequently examined the likely losses of jobs in firms and sectors that supplied UCS. At a 'conservative estimate' the DTI predicted initially that these could range from 4,650 to 6,000,[66] but later upped this estimate to between 8,000 and 9,000, and observed – anticipating a contraction of operations at Govan and Linthouse and total closure at Clydebank and Scotstoun – that 6,000 jobs would be lost on the Upper Clyde.[67]

The scale of these direct and indirect losses explains the anger felt in the yards, in the labour movement, and on Clydeside and in Scotland more generally. It also explains the government's willingness to meet a sequence of labour delegations following Davies's statement to the House of Commons on 14 June. The STUC, led by James Jack, general secretary, announced its total opposition to the closure and obtained an immediate audience with Sir

John Eden, Minister of Industry at the DTI, who also met four UCS stewards, led by Sam Barr. Eden heard from both delegations that morale and productivity at UCS had been improving, and expressed his sympathy about the employment position in Clydeside while reaffirming the government's opposition to further public subsidy.[68] Paul Routledge, then at *The Times*, said the STUC delegates were 'bitterly disappointed' as they left Westminster, although a strategy for defending the yards had been agreed at a meeting with Benn, Willie Ross, Shadow Secretary of State for Scotland, and the four UCS stewards. This was to press for immediate nationalisation of UCS, framed in a Private Members' Bill by Benn who flew north to meet workers and stewards at Clydebank Town Hall and agreed to support their occupation of the yards.[69]

A larger Scottish presence arrived in Whitehall two days later, on 16 June, an overnight train from Glasgow bringing 400 workers, led by UCS stewards, who through Benn obtained an audience with the Prime Minister. This hour-long encounter was reported in *The Times* under the ominous headline, 'Upper Clyde workers say only force will get them out of the yards'. Jimmy Airlie, Chairman of the UCS joint shop stewards' committee, told reporters that the 'sympathy' offered by Heath was inadequate: the workers had come to London for something more 'concrete' and on their behalf Airlie promised a fight. 'If he [Heath] wants to get us out', Airlie said, 'he will have to come and try to get us out himself. This government will be moved far more quickly than the men of the Clyde.' This expression of determination to fight – along with an explicit challenge to the legitimacy of the government – was reinforced later that day. After a further tense meeting, this time with Gordon Campbell, Secretary of State for Scotland, the stewards told journalists at a press conference that the men were returning to Clydeside to occupy the yards. Jimmy Reid re-emphasised the cost to Glasgow – and even more so to Clydebank, where he worked in the yards and was a Councillor – of lost employment. Like Benn, Reid summoned the spectre of the 1930s, 'but this time', he added, 'there is one difference. We are not going to queue for the dole. We are going back to the yards and we are not leaving.'[70]

This popular militancy at the outset of the crisis is worth emphasising. The stewards' attacks on Heath, from a class perspective, and the declared intention that 'all the workers' and not just those in the shipyards would join the 'fight',[71] would become markedly less evident once the work-in was formally launched at the end of July. This followed the outcome of an inquiry into shipbuilding's future on the Clyde, established by the government on 13–14 June. The Prime Minister told the stewards that he hoped the industry would retain a significant presence on the river, and Davies appointed a trio of 'experts', the so-called 'wise men', to examine what shape this might take: Sir Alexander Glen, Director of Clarkson's, a shipbroker, David MacDonald, Director of Hill Samuel Bank, and Forbes McDonald, Chairman of Distillers.

It was suggested by Alasdair Buchan that Glen and MacDonald carried business interests that compromised their capacity to investigate UCS without prejudice: Clarkson's was the main broker for Scott-Lithgow on the Lower Clyde; MacDonald was on the board of a Wearside shipbuilder, Austin and Pickersgill.[72] 'To add a proletarian touch', as Stephen Johns impishly noted from a Trotskyist perspective, Lord Robens, the former Labour MP and head of the National Coal Board, 'the man who set an all-time record for pit closures', was brought on to the inquiry on 24 June.[73] In a meeting with a further deputation from the STUC, led by Jimmy Milne, Assistant General Secretary, on 21 June, Heath deflected all suggestions for immediate government action on the basis that he was waiting for the 'wise men' to conclude their investigation.[74]

The advisory quartet gathered evidence in Glasgow from employers and labour representatives and briefed Davies ahead of publication, who warned Heath on 19 July that the findings were 'not encouraging': while some part of UCS might be preserved 'viably' there were substantial obstacles to future profitability. Heath asked whether this was the time to abandon the Upper Clyde altogether, and shift operations to the deep water at Hunterston, where public investment would be altogether more attractive. Davis replied that this would merely compound the political and social difficulties of escalating unemployment in Glasgow. Heath, evidently summoning the thoughts of his Scottish Industrial Adviser, William Lithgow, referred to the *Oceanspan* debates by raising instead Hunterston's suitability as a site for a steel plant. Davies noted that from a commercial perspective it was 'as good a location as any other',[75] although this observation, as indicated in Chapter 2, was not reflected in the ultimate decision to place only an ore terminal there.

Heath's focus on Hunterston may also have been encouraged by contacts with Hugh Stenhouse, Treasurer of the Conservative Party in Scotland and Chairman of Hunterston Development Corporation, in which connection he was associated with *Oceanspan*. Through Stenhouse, or possibly Lithgow, Heath probably heard about the plans revealed to the media several days later by Robert Robertson, Chairman of Hutchison Engineering Group, to purchase UCS and move it to Hunterston, with a possible British Steel Corporation tie-in.[76] Such an intriguing prospect was overtaken, however, by the report of the 'wise men', published on 29 July. This concluded that UCS had been 'doomed' from the outset and recommended its immediate dissolution: a new company could be established, with reasonable hopes of profitability, at Govan/Linthouse, while Clydebank and Scotstoun should be 'disposed of' by the liquidator. This course of action – implying more than 4,000 redundancies – was immediately accepted by the government, and announced by Davies in the House of Commons.[77]

On the Clyde the UCS joint shop stewards – who had met Davies one day earlier – established a work-in to preserve all four yards and all 8,500 jobs.[78]

Work continued on ships that were already being prepared for delivery, some for the autumn of 1971 and others for early in 1972. These ships would become a matter of contention. The stewards' decision later to 'release' them to purchasers was criticised by some workers who saw this as surrendering important bargaining tools in the process of rescuing the yards, although the stewards and other workers argued that only by operating on conventional – 'respectable' – business lines could the work-in succeed.[79] This disagreement was part of a wider debate about the politics of the work-in, which encompassed nationalist as well as class discourses and so promoted legislative devolution as a means of arresting the pace of industrial change in Scotland.

The politics of the work-in: class

The politics of the work-in were complicated, and drew essentially on the occasionally parallel but frequently overlapping forces of class and nation. In organisational terms the work-in drew much strength from the institutions of the UK labour movement, and its broad opposition to the Heath government. This involved socialist politics and mobilised in general terms the class identities and interests of manual workers that government policy on industrial relations and 'lame ducks' was interpreted as transgressing. The government arguably demonstrated its own class feelings throughout the work-in, despite agreeing intermittently to meetings with workforce, labour and civic deputations. This can be read in an important sub-plot generated by the intentions of sixteen local authorities in Scotland to make monetary donations to the UCS stewards' fighting fund. Under the Local Government (Scotland) Act of 1947 these councils were obliged to obtain the permission of the Secretary of State. Gordon Campbell went against the advice of Scottish Office officials by refusing all sixteen requests, the largest of which – from Dumbarton County Council – was only for £1,000.[80]

While drawing on class politics, however, the work-in also mobilised a Scottish agenda, designed to maximise its support and increase the prospects of saving the yards. This de-emphasised the class interests involved, and cultivated further the idea – shared to an extent across class boundaries – that Scottish Home Rule could ameliorate industrial insecurity. John Foster argues that *Oceanspan*'s outcome was the eclipse of Scottish capital; this precipitated the UCS episode and facilitated the advance of the Scottish 'proletarian nation'. In fact *Oceanspan* and the work-in overlapped, and the 'proletarian' leaders – from Reid in the yards to James Jack at the STUC – carefully incorporated industrialists as well as local authorities, political parties and churches in the devolutionary movement that they came to lead but not dominate.

The blurring of class and devolutionist or nationalist imperatives within the Scottish labour movement since the 1970s has been usefully critiqued by, among others, Gregor Gall, who positions the work-in within a UK context encompassing working-class resistance to the Industrial Relations Act. Gall's discussion appeared in *Scottish Labour History* in 2003, with a cover photograph of the second of two Glasgow demonstrations in support of the work-in in 1971.[81] This illustration was important, for reasons that should become clear, and with consequences that Gall would possibly approve of, for the visual representation of the demonstrations in historical literature arguably provides some insight into the relative importance of the nationalist and class characteristics of the work-in.

The demonstrations took place on 23 June and 18 August; the second, attended by about 70–80,000, was roughly twice the size of the first. In August the rally involved three major figures in the British labour movement: Benn, Victor Feather, General Secretary of the TUC, and Hugh Scanlon, General Secretary of the Amalgamated Engineering Workers' Union. Scots who drew their position from the British labour movement were present too, with the platform including Willie Ross, shadow Secretary of State for Scotland, and Danny McGarvey, President of the Boilermakers' union, although the strongest speech of the day was reckoned by Benn to be Jimmy Reid's, while 'the Scottish Nationalist [William Wolfe, the party leader] was booed'.[82] It is this impressive cast that featured in the *Scottish Labour History* illustration of Gall's analysis, although without any explanatory caption. The same picture is in Bill Knox's *Industrial Nation*, although only Airlie, Reid and Benn are picked out in the caption, so there is some privileging here of the Scottish dimension to the second demonstration.[83] Meanwhile the first demonstration, although significantly smaller, appears in a larger number of other illustrated histories. This may be due to the unmistakable presence in the marching crowd, some ten or eleven ranks from the front, of Billy Connolly, probably the world's most famous former shipyard worker. But it also reflects the fact that Scottish personalities predominated in this march's front rank, especially the stewards Airlie and Reid. Only Benn of the British Labour establishment appears in this photograph, which is even presented in one account as a record of the larger August demonstration.[84]

The UCS developments encouraged Benn to continue his political journey, moving from Labour's centre to its left or even outside left. This journey reflected – in slightly exaggerated manner – the broader shift to the left within the British labour movement, driven by Wilson's incomes policies and *In Place of Strife*, and then Heath's no 'lame ducks' approach and the Industrial Relations Act. Shopfloor militancy resulted in increased support for the CPGB and other organisations, chiefly Trotskyist in character, to the left of Labour. In 1966 the CPGB established a Liaison Committee for Defence of Trade Unions to resist Wilson's wages and industrial relations policies, which mobilised or intersected with more general non-Communist labour opposition to the government. Hence the STUC criticism – examined in Chapter 1 –

of Wilson's government encompassed Communists, notably McGahey, ex-Communists, such as Daly, and mainstream Labour Party members, including Kitson. The Liaison Committee for Defence of Trade Unions duly tapped into wider labour movement opposition to Heath's Industrial Relations Bill, organising a one-day strike on 8 December 1970. This was observed by between 350,000 and 440,000 workers in the UK, including in Scotland engineers, miners, dockers and print workers.[85] The STUC organised a sequence of meetings and demonstrations in towns and cities across Scotland to mobilise opposition to the Bill in the months that followed, culminating in a rally attended by 15,000 in Glasgow on 7 March 1971.[86]

The Bill sought to 'modernise' industrial relations, overturning Britain's voluntarist collective bargaining traditions. Agreements between employers and unions would be legally binding, with unions conceived as corporate and hierarchical bodies: executives issued orders to and were duly accountable for their members. This conceptualisation, in the age of the unofficial strike and the decline of social deference, was highly problematic. Matters were further complicated by the Bill's inclusion of a National Industrial Relations Court, to impose penalties – including prison sentences – on parties or persons contravening legally binding agreements. Hence unions could be fined for the 'freelance' or unofficial actions of their members. The legislation was hurriedly brought forward and union leaders told that its principles were 'non-negotiable'. This approach encouraged the view across the UK that the government sought confrontation with the labour movement, and in Scotland nourished anxieties about the centralising tendencies of UK governance. It also reflected Heath's European ambitions, which were opposed by many in the Scottish as well as the British labour movement.[87] The opportunities of EEC membership had to be maximised and in industrial relations this meant curtailing unofficial strikes, inter-union disputes and other difficulties believed to lower productivity and generate inflationary economic pressures.[88]

The Bill became law in the spring of 1971 but in the twelve to eighteen months that followed its operation was resisted, initially by dockers who sought to protect their jobs by illegally picketing inland container depots where other workers processed cargoes.[89] Several pickets were arrested and imprisoned in June and July 1972, precipitating a major crisis that Heath's government defused by 'conjuring' up a hitherto obscure civil servant, the Official Solicitor, who released the men from jail and averted a one-day general strike across the UK. The 1971 Act incrementally fell into disrepute, union resistance built by the militancy of ordinary workers – on building sites and in engineering works as well as the docks – who compelled mainstream union officials to oppose the legislation in order to retain credible leadership of their organisations.[90]

This was the macro-class and industrial environment in which the UCS episode developed, with union and Labour Party leaders being pushed to the left by pressures from below. The start of the work-in coincided with the union conference season and this helped mobilise immediate support. Starting with the Engineering Workers, a number of unions passed conference resolutions condemning the government and restating the demand of nationalisation of the yards.[91] These included the NUM's Scottish Area, meeting in Leith on 11 August, and addressed by Reid and Airlie. A copy of this conference's UCS resolution was sent to Heath.[92] Privately, however, some union officials were less enthusiastic about the work-in. James Jack of the STUC told Sir John Eden's private secretary, Christopher Pollitt, that he disliked the practice of ministers meeting UCS stewards. This made it difficult for 'official union leaderships' to 'gain control of the union side of the situation' and Jack recommended that such contacts be avoided where possible.[93] This candid admission suggests that some union leaders were worried that the work-in was further shifting the influence within labour organisations from union office to shopfloor. In these terms Jack's support for the work-in resembled the pragmatic opposition of union leaders to the Industrial Relations Bill and Act; in Scotland the class characteristics of the crisis would be further softened by union officials, including Jack, relating the work-in to a devolutionist or nationalist agenda.

The UK leadership of the Labour Party, perhaps excepting Benn, shared this essentially pragmatic and conditional approach to the work-in. On Harold Wilson's death in 1995 Reid remembered the Labour Party leader's early visit to the work-in in Clydebank, on 4 August 1971. 'We had a discussion', Reid recalled. 'Now let me tell you: it was a discussion. He was talking to us. But he was listening to us.' Wilson toured the yards, spoke to workers in the canteen and then faced the press outside. 'He wasn't sitting on the fence. He wasn't hedging his bets. He wasn't adopting a kind of lofty above-the-struggle neutrality. He came out unequivocally in support of the workers. Oh that we were blessed with such a leader today',[94] Reid observed, a blunt reference to Tony Blair, leading the Labour Party for just ten months when Wilson died. This assertion of unambiguous support from Wilson sits uncomfortably with Alasdair Buchan's eye-witness report, which indicated in fact that he supported the men in what they were 'facing' rather than what they were 'doing'.[95] The ambivalence of Wilson's true position is further spelt out by his biographers, Philip Ziegler and Ben Pimlott, who concur that he stopped short of supporting the work-in because of its possible illegality. Wilson was keen, however, to maximise the government's political discomfort. He told Benn that he was considering arriving in Clydebank by boat, as a counterpoint to Heath's intended although eventually cancelled participation in yachting's Admiral's Cup.[96] Benn, perhaps missing a joke, was 'sickened' by this proposed gimmickry, but Wilson's public ambivalence at least provided other Labour figures – and their allies in the unions – with the 'room' to support the protest. Wilson certainly did not criticise Benn or anyone else who endorsed the occupation. This allowed Labour in Parliament to make substantial political capital of the crisis, and enabled the left to link the work-in with a new issue in British public life in the early 1970s: industrial democracy. This, claimed Benn, at the demonstration in Glasgow in August 1971, was being born in the work-in.[97]

Industrial democracy had its opponents in the labour movement. The chief concern was that trade union participation in industrial management might legitimise decisions – on closure, say, or reductions in investment – that damaged the interests of workers.[98] In these terms industrial democracy was perceived as a managerial trap, and an undesirably ambiguous diversion from the certainties of confrontational, across-the-table industrial bargaining.[99] This type of thinking had influenced the Donovan Commission in 1968, which characterised industrial democracy as potentially complicating the really important task of strengthening collective bargaining by improving the standing of trade unionism within work places, and so narrowing the perceived gap between the shopfloor and union office.[100] But in the early 1970s the mood in trade unions was shifting, in the context of industrial concentration, the increasing prevalence of multi-national firms and intensifying market pressures. These forces tended to produce the sort of problem encountered by the workers at UCS: a decision taken on narrow economic or business grounds about the future of a company, which jeopardised the employment of thousands and the health of several communities. Participation in management would enable trade unionists to apply broader social criteria to decision-making, and also extend the reach of their influence into areas of activity, within companies, that were outwith the scope of established collective bargaining, either at national or shopfloor level.[101] Industrial democracy also had an institutional focus in the Institute for Workers' Control, founded in 1968 and directed by Ken Coates and Tony Topham of Hull University. Topham was an associate of John Prescott, MP for Kingston-upon-Hull, whose maiden speech in the House of Commons in July 1970 emphasised the need for at least public – if not quite workers' – ownership and control of ports and shipping.[102] Dockers on the Humber, meanwhile, drew strength from the work-in on the Clyde. Walter Cunningham, a waterfront activist who risked jail by contravening the Industrial Relations Act, later linked the Hull men's establishment in 1972 of a successful collective stevedoring firm to the inspiration of the UCS action, and spoke about the financial aid that he and his work-mates had gladly given their comrades on the Clyde.[103]

The work-in was indeed reliant on the financial as well as moral support of the UK and wider international labour movement. Donations were collected by the stewards and disbursed in lieu of wages to the men nominally declared redundant by the liquidator. A bunch of red roses and cheques amounting to £1,000 came from Yoko Ono and John Lennon,[104] whose emerging involvement in British industrial politics – which intrigues at least one cultural discussant – was curtailed when the couple moved to New York City in July 1971.[105] John and Yoko provided welcome publicity, but while the liquidator, Robert Smith, was quietly locating funds to pay wages to a majority of UCS workers, there was a large minority of perhaps 800 men who were maintained by monies raised externally by the stewards.[106] Between £8,500 and £9,000 was being paid out weekly, so it was the cash – about £500,000 in total – of English, Welsh, and Irish as well as other Scottish workers that sustained the work-in.[107] But while encouraging workers and trade unionists to support the protest with hard-earned cash, and think about the fundamentals of industrial ownership, organisation and control,[108] the leaders of the work-in were incrementally retreating from the militant and class-conscious territory occupied in June 1971. The Institute of Workers' Control distributed 2,000 pamphlets in Glasgow between the liquidation of UCS and the start of the work-in,[109] but the stewards – along with the union officials involved – increasingly sought conventional relationships with private capital. Benn sensed this as the stewards gradually moved back from calling for the dissolution of the Heath government and the nationalisation of the yards, and articulated instead a desire to work with ministers to obtain a private purchaser for UCS. By February 1972, with the government about to sweeten such a transaction with fresh state subsidy, Reid and Airlie were telling Benn to stop criticising Davies, lest this scupper the establishment of the new business, Govan Shipbuilders. Several months on, as the stewards finalised a deal to build oil rigs at Clydebank with Marathon, a US corporation, Benn met Reid, Airlie and others at the Labour Party Conference in Blackpool. Airlie spotted a photographer and suggested a group picture but Reid objected, reminding colleagues that the stewards had a meeting scheduled for the next morning with Chris Chataway, DTI Minister of Industrial Development. It 'might be embarrassing', Reid said to Benn, 'if we were photographed with you'. Benn tried to laugh off the shift in politics that Reid's observation suggested: one year earlier he had worried about being seen with the militant stewards; now the respectable stewards were anxious about being seen with the militant politician. Reid and Airlie 'saw the point immediately', Benn wrote, 'and they laughed, and they got the photographer'.[110]

Trotskyist observers explained the stewards' emphasis on conventional industrial and political relationships in terms of the Communist – or rather the *Stalinist* – politics of Reid and Airlie. They were hopelessly compromised, from a revolutionary perspective, by their membership of the CPGB, which was incorporated 'into the structures and conventions of "responsible" collective bargaining'. The consequent requirement to build relationships with mainstream labour institutions, employers and government ministers and officials fundamentally inhibited the capacity of the stewards to pursue the class interests of the workers they represented.[111] Reid, Airlie and other

Communists at UCS vigorously refuted this analysis, arguing that the preservation of employment was in the class interests of the workers,[112] but in pursuing this aim there is little doubt that the linkages between the work-in and the wider class-informed set of campaigns, struggles and conflicts across the UK were consciously and deliberately down-played. These struggles and conflicts had been invoked at the outset of the campaign, perhaps to consolidate support in the yards and convey an attitude of determination to the government. Yet these were then overlain – to widen the basis of the campaign – with an emphasis on the Scottish component of the work-in. This brought under scrutiny the linkage between remote administration and industrial insecurity, and hence contributed to the growing debate about the desirability of political devolution for Scotland within the UK.

The politics of the work-in: nation

In May 1970 Jimmy Reid was one of three CPGB representatives who appeared before the Commission on the Constitution in Glasgow. The CPGB's written evidence indicated that legislative devolution could mitigate remote economic and business decision-making, where corporate direction in the key industries of electronics, oil refining, chemicals and motor manufacturing was shaped outside Scotland.[113] Giving oral evidence to the commissioners, including Lord Crowther, Reid emphasised that support for a devolved Scottish Parliament was a logical extension of the CPGB's commitment to decentralised and pluralist democratic politics. This position had roots in the Popular Front politics of the 1930s, when Communists sought alliances with all 'progressive' anti-fascist political forces, and a footing too in the post-Second World War Communist platform, *The British Road to Socialism*, which avowed that Britain's revolution would flower through pluralist electoral politics.[114] Lord Crowther was unaware of these earlier developments, or teasingly chose to ignore them, and instead articulated his assumption that the CPGB was a revolutionary organisation, which envisaged governing Scotland as a one-party state. This infuriated Reid, who characterised Crowther's interruption as 'facetious'. 'Our evidence is serious evidence', he said, in terms that would not have surprised Trotskyist critics of the CPGB. He then outlined a theme that would become familiar during the work-in: the loss of industrial activity, arising partly from remote administration of economic and political power, and the consequent trend to outward economic migration from Scotland, were an affront to Scottish 'national identity'.[115]

The work-in's developing emphasis on Scottish imperatives is the core of Foster and Woolfson's discussion of the 'languages' mobilised by Reid and other UCS figures in 1971–72. These languages were designed to maximise the political and social base of the campaign to save the yards. Business, Tory and local authority support was obtained on the Clyde and in Scotland more generally through a careful and deliberate rhetorical campaign that constructed a stark dichotomy between the defence of local communities and the regional economy on the one hand and support for Heath's government on the other hand. This approach also drew in support from the SNP although this was not entirely welcome in the labour movement, as the party's leader, William Wolfe, acknowledged in his discussion of the episode.[116] The CPGB approach to the Constitutional Commission was frequently reprised, with national sentiments invoked, along with the remote nature of industrial and political power. This was central to the growth of broader support in Scotland for legislative devolution. Reid talked of the 'faceless men' who wrote off the Clyde and its workers from distant rooms in Whitehall; there was much talk, meanwhile, of the interests and hopes of the 'community' and of 'Scotland' itself. Class frontiers were further transcended, and bridges built across the sectional barriers within the shipyards themselves, by organising the protest not around a 'strike' but a 'work-in'. This was a new term, 'a non-word' even, according to Foster and Woolfson, that Reid and others could fill with meanings of their own choosing, enabling the workforce to be cast – and this, in the context of industrial politics and protests was highly unusual – as the 'responsible' party, facing up to the 'irresponsible' government 'wreckers'.[117] The force of this sentiment was vividly expressed in Reid's memorable words to the Clydebank workers on the morning of 30 July 1971, as the work-in commenced:

> Everybody talks about rights. There's a basic elementary right here – that's our right to work. We're not strikers. We are responsible people and we will conduct ourselves with the dignity and discipline that we have all the time expressed over the last few weeks. And there will be no hooliganism. There will be no vandalism. There will be no bevvying, because the world is watching us, and it's our responsibility to conduct ourselves responsibly and with dignity and with maturity.[118]

'We are responsible people' with a 'responsibility' to behave 'responsibly': the retreat from class politics through the course of the work-in reflected these sentiments, although there was an echo too of Worsthorne's political and social 'stalemate'. When Davies came to Glasgow for a series of meetings on 3 August the UCS liquidator, Robert Smith, told him that the workforce generally had been very 'helpful' with the yards 'operating normally'. Managers were still managing, in other words, although the maintenance of conventional employment relations had been shaped by Smith's 'instructions that managers should avoid giving orders which would lead to a confrontation and the flouting of authority'.[119]

The delicate management of social relations was evident also beyond the yards, where a wider Scottish social and political network of support for UCS was constructed. Lord Clydesmuir invited Smith to a scheduled meeting of the

SCDI's Executive Committee in Edinburgh on 21 June. The liquidator expressed unhappiness about being drawn away from attending to business in Glasgow, but confirmed to the SCDI that UCS had 'neither the cash nor the credit' to continue. He was not entirely pessimistic about the situation; Davies and the DTI had guaranteed the continuation of shipbuilding activities and wages until 6 August – to cover the holiday period and allow the 'wise men' to complete their report – and Smith, who had met Davies on 17 June, interpreted this as evidence of the government's hope that shipbuilding would retain a presence on the Upper Clyde. But when asked about the prospects of small business creditors, owed just under £16 million, Smith was not optimistic. 'That the contractors would be hurt', he said, 'was a fact'. After Smith left the meeting the SCDI's Executive looked more broadly at unemployment across Scotland, which, it was agreed, was far more serious than the government appreciated. Liddle, preparing a civic delegation from Glasgow to meet Heath on 24 June, asked the SCDI to make immediate representation to the government, to communicate 'the very real concern in Scotland' about UCS and unemployment generally.[120]

Clydesmuir told reporters later on 21 June that the government's response to Scotland's economic difficulties was both tardy and inadequate, given 'the tragic mounting figures of unemployment', and put this criticism to Gordon Campbell on the telephone, requesting a meeting with John Davies and other ministers.[121] This took place in London on 7 July. At a press conference in Edinburgh two days later Clydesmuir said that he had spoken to ministers about the 'groundswell of feeling which is invading every part of Scotland at this moment', referring to 'the punishing effects of closures and cutbacks by well-established companies' and the 'growing army' of unemployed. It was high time, he added, for the government to 'turn on all the taps' of public investment in Scotland.[122]

The broad Scottish social and political constituency facing the government on UCS became clearly evident on 3 August when Davies came to Glasgow, accompanied by officials and Gordon Campbell, for meetings with civic and industrial representatives, including the stewards. This was the day before Wilson's Clydebank visit. Alasdair Buchan's account of 3 August dramatised its security angle,[123] with concerns about ministerial safety heightened following the damage to Davies's London home by an Angry Brigade bomb on 31 July.[124] The Angry Brigade was an extremely marginal terror organisation with absolutely no footing in or connections with the labour movement,[125] Clydeside or the shipyards. But the authorities were nervous nevertheless, the Secretary of State – in the words of a DTI official – being 'whisked off' on arrival at Glasgow airport 'with a strong police escort' to the City Chambers. Here various meetings took place, including a large conference of ministers, their officials and forty-seven business, labour and civic representatives, where Davies reiterated that 'subsidisation' of the yards was not 'realistic or suitable'. He added, responding to Clydesmuir's plea that 'all the taps' be turned on, that regional aid could not be increased and so 'assisted areas' would have to await 'an upsurge to the national economy' for additional stimulus. Replies from the floor revealed almost total opposition to the government, with criticism from Provost Liddle and his Progressive group, Hamish Grant of the CBI in Scotland, Robin MacLellan of the Glasgow Chamber of Commerce, Clydesmuir of the SCDI, various UCS creditors, Labour and Communist councillors – including Reid, present in this capacity – from Clydebank and Glasgow, the stewards, and STUC and other union officials. The workers' representatives walked out of the meeting before it ended, with the ministers returning to the airport, again under police guard, where they had a fairly tense dinner at the hotel with Liddle.[126]

For Foster and Woolfson the involvement on 3 August of the many creditors, whose difficulties were examined by the SCDI on 21 June, was especially significant. This was 'Local Capital in Crisis': the hundreds of small businesses that, between them, were owed many millions of pounds by UCS. The mobilisation by the stewards of this business insecurity and anger was central to the outcome of the work-in,[127] with the government also encountering criticism over UCS from Tory supporters in the north east of England, where shipbuilding was almost as precariously positioned as on the Clyde. Davies was forwarded a telex sent to Conservative Central Office from the Sunderland Conservative Association on 4 August, characterising the government's handling of UCS as gifting a 'wonderful platform' to the party's Labour and Communist opponents.[128] It should be noted, however, that non-labour and business support for the work-in was far from unconditional. Liddle, by trade a clothing manufacturer, strongly criticised the half-day strike observed by around 200,000 workers to coincide with the demonstration of 18 August.[129] This is a reminder of the delicate nature of the cross-class alliance, and the underlying tension between capital and labour in Scotland.

Nevertheless this national alliance increased the pressure on Heath in the winter of 1971–72, the crowning development here being the Scottish Assembly, convened by the STUC, and held in Edinburgh's Usher Hall on 14 February 1972. The STUC General Council had linked the problems on the Clyde with Scotland's wider economic, industrial and political position.[130] This gathering duly marked a clear linkage – or stepping stone – between McGahey's 1968 STUC initiative, discussed in Chapter 1, and the STUC's advocacy after 1974, with Labour back in government, of a 'meaningful' devolved Scottish Parliament with legislative powers.[131] The 1972 Assembly encompassed a very broad social and political base, with 92 per cent of the population 'virtually' represented through the presence of representatives from the four City, twenty-one County and 123 District Councils. There were also representatives of the CBI in Scotland and a number of Chambers of Commerce. The speakers included the Chairman of the Conservative Party,

Sir William McEwan Younger, and Teddy Taylor, Tory MP for Cathcart in Glasgow, along with Liddle, each of whom raised the linkage between rising unemployment and the remote administration of economic policy and regional development. None of these three dissented from the broad and apparently consensual view of the meeting, summarised by Chris Baur, industrial correspondent of *The Scotsman*, who wrote of Scotland's 'historic and irrevocable step to self-government'. While the Assembly might not have quite marked Scotland's 'Damascus Road', he added, there were nevertheless 'some astounding conversions', most notably John Boyd, prominent in the Amalgamated Engineering Workers' Union in Scotland, ex-Chairman of the Labour Party and 'arch-enemy' of the SNP who now spoke – 'as ears pricked up' – of his view 'that the only answer to Scotland's economic problems is Scottish government'.[132]

The many other speakers included David Steel, Liberal MP for Roxburgh, Selkirk and Peebles, Winnie Ewing, now SNP Vice-President, who earlier in the day had delivered the Scottish Covenant of 1947–49 – which had been located in a builder's yard in Rutherglen – by lorry to the National Library of Scotland,[133] and McGahey, but press coverage was dominated by the contributions of McEwen Younger and Liddle. McEwen Younger praised the STUC for convening the Assembly, and – with shades of his notes to Heath on regional policy that featured in Chapter 2 – spoke of his strong desire to move Scotland away from its position as the location of branch plants and branch offices only. Major public and private investment was needed, he said, to support 'natural resources' like Hunterston's deep water and the North Sea Oil potential. Liddle was more outspoken, characterising the volume of unemployment in Scotland – now around 150,000 and expected to top 160,000 by the end of February – as unacceptable, and an affront, borrowing the work-in's phrase, to the people's 'right to work'.[134] Foster and Woolfson emphasise, with very good reason, that the alignment of these Tory and business leaders in Scotland with the labour movement over unemployment and UCS was a very powerful 'indication of how far they believed fundamental changes were taking place in Scottish politics'. James Jack proclaimed at Edinburgh that the most desirable feature of a devolved Scottish parliament was that it would be 'a workers' parliament', committed to securing a path for economic and social development very largely on the labour movement's terms.[135]

Jack's rhetorical flourish was a further expression of the labour movement's political confidence; it also articulated what would become, certainly in the 1980s and perhaps even the 1990s, the dominant idea in Scotland about the potential of a Parliament, that it would be an instrument for redistributing economic and social resources in favour of the working class. Foster sees Jack's claim as central to the argument that the Scottish proletarian nation was entering maturity in the early 1970s.[136] Yet the presence of Tory and business figures plainly constrained the extent to which the Assembly could speak for 'the workers'. The class and national impulses were complicated: while the UCS crisis further promoted the idea of legislative devolution, in the short term it was pressure from the Scottish Tory and business constituency as well as the UK labour movement that encouraged the government to reconsider its position on subsidising and protecting employment on the Clyde. The SCDI's audience with Heath on 13 January 1972 was discussed in Chapter 2. It concluded with no firm commitment from the Prime Minister to *Oceanspan*, but Clydesmuir and Liddle, despite his public criticism of government policy at the Assembly on 14 February, told colleagues on the SCDI's Executive Committee on 21 February that the meeting had been positive. They looked forward in particular to the budget scheduled for 21 March, perhaps alerted to its likely assistance to industry.[137] Clydesmuir and Liddle perhaps also gathered intelligence that an about-turn on the Upper Clyde was imminent, the government unable to resist pressure from its natural business and political supporters in Scotland, troubled as they were by the damage to the regional economy incurred by the UCS liquidation.

The outcome of the work-in

In April 1971 David McNee succeeded Sir James Robertson as Glasgow's Chief Constable. With diminishing financial resources and an increasing workload he found the force's morale to be low, and recruitment and retention problematic.[138] It is within this structural context, perhaps, that the new Chief Constable's famous report on the supposed public order implications of the UCS work-in, delivered to the Cabinet via the Secretary of State for Scotland towards the end of 1971, should be read. McNee said he could not guarantee public safety if the yards were forcibly cleared and closed, adding that Glasgow might experience the type of violence that was developing in Northern Ireland unless he was equipped with an additional five thousand officers.[139]

Although McNee was probably exaggerating this aspect of the crisis to lever new resources for his force, Foster and Woolfson suggest that it would be 'unwise' to disconnect his report from the Cabinet's decision to announce major new subsidies for Upper Clyde shipbuilding late in February 1972.[140] Moreover, like McNee, one of the stewards who met Heath in June 1971, Willie McInnes, had offered another parallel between Scottish and Northern Irish developments, claiming that the government would have 'to get the soldiers from the Bogside to get us out of the Clydeside'.[141] On the other hand, it is worth emphasising that one of the earliest accounts to attribute the about-turn to public order concerns was written by Jock Bruce-Gardyne, MP for South Angus, whose 1974 book on the Heath government inflated

McNee's claim for additional resources from five to fifteen thousand officers.[142] Described as an 'eccentric monetarist' by John Campbell, Bruce-Gardyne was a confidante of Thatcher,[143] and often spoke about the violence and intimidation that he saw as central to labour organisation and protest. During a Scottish unemployment debate in the House of Commons, late in the evening of 27 July 1971, he claimed that stewards were threatening families of workers who were considering leaving the UCS yards to take jobs at Yarrow's or the Lower Clyde. These yards, he boasted, were 'crying out' for labour, and only intimidation was preventing a mass exodus and the collapse of the work-in.[144]

Worries about public order also pervaded – or clouded – the thinking of mainstream Conservative figures, including Douglas Hurd, Heath's private political secretary and part-time novelist, whose diaries and fictional offerings were both characterised by the threat of insurrectionist violence. John Mackie is the working-class and socialist-cum-nationalist anti-hero of *Scotch on the Rocks*, a novel co-authored by Hurd in 1971 with Andrew Osmond. During a general election campaign Mackie rallies a large, predominantly working-class and socialist crowd to nationalism in Glasgow Green while covertly planning a Soviet-financed Communist takeover of Scotland. Described as a black-haired and charismatic man in his late thirties, he strongly resembles Jimmy Reid.[145] Hurd the novelist here reveals much, perhaps, about British Tory neuroses and the imagined rather than actual public order implications of labour protest in the early 1970s. It is implausible, even risible, to suggest that the work-in threatened public disorder, given the recurrent emphasis placed by the stewards on 'responsibility' and 'discipline'. Reid's demand that there be no vandalism or hooliganism was broadly met. There was not much bevvying either. Early in 1972 Benn spoke to some of the stewards about their involvement in a recent edition of the *David Frost Programme* on television. Before the broadcast the hospitable producers had provided generous volumes of alcoholic drink that the stewards had regarded suspiciously, believing that it was designed to loosen tongues and tempers and so give rise to 'a punch-up on the air'. Airlie was said to have taken charge of the situation, making it clear that any steward consuming more than a single beer would not appear on the programme. 'Very impressive', noted the teetotal Benn.[146]

In any event, returning to the issue of public order, as Foster and Woolfson also indicate, the timing of events does not support the idea that McNee's report forced the about-turn, for moves were in hand from August 1971 onwards to reconstruct shipbuilding on the Upper Clyde, in line with hopes expressed by Heath and Davies in June and July, and with fairly heavy hints of government subsidy.[147] On 19 August Eden held a sequence of meetings in Glasgow, seeing, among others, the liquidator, Liddle, and a group of stewards. Eden, perhaps mindful of Jack's 'warning' about talking to stewards, told them that the government was sticking to the position of preserving only the yards at Govan and Linthouse. The stewards were still, in the words of a DTI official, 'trying to hold the line' that all four yards had to be saved, but a softening of their position was detected by the government: Reid especially, but also the others, were 'concerned not to close the door completely to any solution'.[148] A major step towards maintaining the Upper Clyde industry duly arrived in September, with the government overseeing the formation of Govan Shipbuilders under the Chairmanship of Hugh Stenhouse. This appointment was driven through by Heath, according to Jack McGill,[149] and despite the objection by Sir Douglas Haddow, Permanent Under Secretary of State at the Scottish Office, canvassed for an opinion by the DTI, that Stenhouse's 'political links with the Scottish Conservatives are probably too close and too public for him to qualify'.[150]

It will be remembered that the 'wise men' in July had envisaged a future for Govan Shipbuilders operating from the Govan and Linthouse yards. The UCS stewards resisted dealing with Stenhouse, seeking safeguards for all four yards, despite hints, widely circulated by early October, that the new firm could encompass Scotstoun also, but not Clydebank. These murmurs reached the press after Stenhouse visited Davies at his constituency headquarters on 1 October.[151] The government, moving incrementally towards its about-turn, initiated a further inquiry, this time by Hill Samuel, to consider the funding of a three-yard company.[152] By 20 December DTI officials were advising Davies that a three-yard Govan Shipbuilders could be viable if launched with £20m of government money.[153]

Stenhouse was killed in a car crash in Leicestershire on 25 November, and was succeeded at the beginning of 1972 by Lord Strathalmond, Chairman of British Petroleum (BP), and a personal friend of Davies.[154] Danny McGarvey, UK leader of the Boilermakers' union, was searching in the meantime for a backer for Clydebank, which had briefly been coveted by the local Clydeside entrepreneur, Archibald Kelly, in the summer of 1971. But Kelly, whose nicknames of 'Scrap Iron' and 'Cash Down' seemingly conveyed his limited business capacities and horizons, was not a serious bidder, at least not for all four yards, although he raised the possibility of building oil-rigs, along with car ferries, at Clydebank.[155] Against the inclination of its officials in Scotland, the DTI in London scotched any prospect of financial support for Kelly's proposals under the Local Employment Acts, given that he was seeking to develop an existing site rather than establishing a new one.[156] But the 1972 Industry Act, brought forward rapidly in March after an employment-raising expansionist budget, allowed government aid to extant enterprises, and this helped to facilitate the rescue of Clydebank that spring. McGarvey had pursued the oil-rigs idea to Houston, Texas, where he held talks in the second week of January 1972 with Wayne Harbin, president of the Marathon Manufacturing Corporation, the world's largest builder of deep-sea oil-rigs.[157] Foster and Woolfson suggest that this contact was probably established through the DTI, and this is likely given that Harbin met DTI officials and then Sir John Eden a fortnight later in London after first visiting Clydebank. With Britain on the cusp of exploring and exploiting the oil resources of the North Sea, this seemed a compelling fit, although Harbin argued that the 'terrible' facilities would require significant upgrading. Making the deal 'work' would require major financial incentives from the DTI and a four-year 'no strike' agreement from the workforce, which he was optimistic about obtaining, having met the stewards as well as McGarvey.[158]

The preliminary conclusions of the Hill Samuel report were passed to Strathalmond and the board of Govan Shipbuilders on 2 February. These reprised shipbuilding's importance to the Clyde in social and political rather than commercial terms,[159] a sentiment endorsed by Strathalmond,[160] and accepted by the Cabinet's Ministerial Committee on Economic Policy and then the Cabinet. Davies told the Cabinet on 24 February that the Committee on Economic Policy had agreed measures that would maintain three yards under the Govan Shipbuilders. This, he added, was neither a 'satisfactory' or an 'optimistic' position; the company 'might move' from deficit to surplus in three years, but only in the context of sluggish economic activity and continuing unemployment. Davies then noted that it would be politically valuable to announce the £35 million rescue package in a Commons debate on unemployment scheduled for the following week. The atmosphere around the Cabinet table was presumably sour, and the flattening tone of the official minutes cannot disguise the unmistakable sense of ministerial disappointment: 'a decision to provide Government finance on this scale would not be likely to commend itself to the Government's supporters'. The transparent nature of the government's defeat on the Clyde – following so quickly its loss to the miners, which culminated just five days earlier – was also explicitly regretted, with ministers bemoaning the probability that the public would interpret the change of policy on the UCS as the result of the work-in, which forced a reversal of the original decision to 'abandon' the company 'to its fate'.[161]

Davies endured a humiliating Commons debate the following week, contrasting the criticism of Benn and others in the Labour Party with the 'constantly constructive and helpful role' played by McGarvey, who had worked tirelessly 'to make this phoenix rise again'. He predicted that the new Govan grouping would safeguard 4,300 jobs, and a 'proportion' of the remaining 2,500 jobs at Clydebank would be encompassed in the American project.[162] Tory ministers continued to agonise over the outcome. A Cabinet colleague advised Davies in June that 'in Scotland Jimmy Reid is regarded as the victor and we the villains', with the government's efforts on the Clyde securing no political reward at all.[163]

A conclusion to the work-in at this point was still some way off: the deal involving Marathon and Clydebank was particularly complicated, and took several months to finalise. A sequence of contacts and meetings between

Marathon and the DTI, including three days of talks in Houston in the second week of March, eventually produced incentives amounting to a £6m loan plus £5½m in various grants.[164] The agreement was signed in September, from which point Govan Shipbuilders, comprising the three yards at Govan, Linthouse and Scotstoun, was also operational.[165]

The new firm seemed to be in a better position than UCS, starting with a 'clean sheet', its inherited debts cleared by roughly half of the government's £35 million. Murray wrote, optimistically perhaps, but before the first great 'Oil shock' at the end of 1973, of the 'prospect of a new era in labour relations' and talked up the stability of the industrial and employment position on the Clyde. Aggregate demand for labour was steady, although this position incorporated a gradual shift from the Upper to Lower reaches, with Scott-Lithgow now the biggest shipbuilder on the river.[166] Johnman and Murphy's history, of course, is able to reflect on the subsequent and disappointing history of the Clyde. The salient fact for them is that only about 19 per cent of the public money granted to Govan and UCS, roughly £65 million between 1967 and 1972, was devoted to capital investment. This encapsulated the enduring shortage of investment in the industry, a characteristic feature of the longer post-1945 environment and the most significant single source of shipbuilding's ultimate slide in the closing quarter of the twentieth century.[167]

It is partly this subsequent history that raises questions about whether the work-in was a 'success' or a 'victory'. It was clearly a remarkable event. A major departure in government policy was secured by the determined actions of the workers of the Clyde and their supporters. In the sense that substantial employment was preserved by this action, at least in the short term, it was a victory. But the power of remote administration, although questioned, was not dislodged: it was on the 'distant blackboards' of Whitehall and now Houston, the global headquarters of Marathon, that the Clyde's industrial future would continue to be sketched. Its more meaningful legacy, arguably, was the stimulus it gave to the quest for devolved forms of political as well as administrative control in Scotland, with the Assembly at Edinburgh in February 1972 clearly an important landmark in the incremental acceptance that devolution might offset industrial insecurity. Yet even this suggested fragile success for the workers, given the precarious nature of the cross-class alliance constructed during the work-in. The collapse of UCS had threatened a substantial body of the Conservative government's natural political and business support in Scotland, with small suppliers and contractors owed unsecured millions. This explains the presence in the Scottish Assembly of McEwen Younger, Liddle and Teddy Taylor, who supported the rescue of UCS but were anxious about some aspects of the work-in, notably the protest strikes and the perceived damage it had caused – witness McEwen Younger's lunch conversation with Heath and other ministers in January 1972 – to business confidence. The highly contingent nature of the Scottish national alliance established over UCS, and reflected in the Edinburgh Assembly, was more strongly observable in a related episode in the winter of 1971–72, the miners' strike. In the coalfields there was a further blurring of the imperatives of class and nation in ways that highlighted the limits rather than the extent of any cross-class devolutionary alliance. Popular support for the miners was evident, but this was mainly from other manual or union-organised workers; opposition, to an extent of a class nature, was mustered around ideas or stereotypes of industrial workers and protests as undemocratic threats to civil order.

Notes

1 Edwin Morgan, *Selected Poems* (Manchester, 1985), pp. 79–80.
2 Devine, *Scottish Nation*, pp. 584–5; for criticism of this see Christopher Harvie, *Mending Scotland: Essays in Economic Regionalism* (Argyll, 2004), p. 36.
3 Irene Maver, *Glasgow* (Edinburgh, 2000), pp. 213–15; Harvie, *No Gods*, pp. 158–9.
4 Johnman and Murphy, *Shipbuilding in Britain*, p. 190.
5 Alasdair Buchan, *The Right to Work: The Story of the Upper Clyde Confrontation* (London, 1972); Jack McGill, *Crisis on the Clyde* (London, 1973).
6 Frank Broadway, *Upper Clyde Shipbuilders: A Study of Government Intervention in Industry … the Way the Money Goes* (London, 1976), pp. 34–6, 51–2.
7 Willie Thompson and Finlay Hart, *The UCS Work-In* (London, 1972).
8 John Foster and Charles Woolfson, *The Politics of the UCS Work-In: Class Alliances and the Right to Work* (1986); Foster and Woolfson, 'Workers on the Clyde'; Foster, 'Twentieth Century', pp. 476–88; John Foster, 'A Proletarian Nation? Occupation and Class since 1914', in Dickson and Treble, *People and Society: Vol. III*, pp. 234–5.
9 Harvie, *No Gods*, p. 90.
10 Worsthorne, 'Class and Conflict in British Foreign Policy', pp. 421, 428.
11 Stephen Johns, *Reformism on the Clyde: The Story of the UCS* (London, 1973), *passim*.
12 Johnman and Murphy, *Shipbuilding in Britain*, pp. 94, 117–8.
13 Murray, *Scotland*, pp. 50–1, 61.
14 Andrew Patrizio and Frank Little, *Canvassing the Clyde: Stanley Spencer and the Shipyards* (Glasgow, 1994).
15 *Seawards the Great Ships*, produced by Templar Film Studios for the Clyde Shipbuilders' Association and Films of Scotland Committee, written by Clifford Hanley and directed by Hilary Harris, 1960.
16 Johnman and Murphy, *Shipbuilding in Britain*, pp. 109, 191.
17 Ministry of Labour, Monthly Report on the Main Features of the Employment Position in Scotland, April 1963, SEP 10/312, NAS.
18 Ibid., October and December 1964, SEP 10/312, NAS.
19 Johnman and Murphy, *Shipbuilding in Britain*, pp. 37, 41–3.
20 *Shipbuilding Inquiry Committee, 1965–1966. Report*, Cmnd 2937 (HMSO, 1966).
21 Johnman and Murphy, *Shipbuilding in Britain*, pp. 158–67, 176–7.
22 Wilson, *The Labour Government*, pp. 422–3.
23 *Glasgow Herald*, 21 September 1967.

24 Tony Benn, *Office Without Power: Diaries, 1968–72* (London, 1989), pp. 146, 156; *The Times*, 16 June 1971; McGill, *Crisis on the Clyde*, pp. 32–7.

25 Johnman and Murphy, *Shipbuilding in Britain*, p. 184.

26 Cmnd 2937, pp. 110–23.

27 McGill, *Crisis on the Clyde*, pp. 23–4.

28 Derek H. Aldcroft and Michael J. Oliver, *Trade Unions and the Economy: 1870–2000* (Aldershot, 2000), pp. 142–54.

29 Alan Booth, 'The Manufacturing Failure Hypothesis and the Performance of British Industry During the Long Boom', *Economic History Review*, 56 (2003), 1–33; and *The British Economy in the Twentieth Century* (Basingstoke, 2001), pp. 127, 145–50.

30 Jim Tomlinson, 'Inventing "Decline": The Falling Behind of the British Economy in the Post-War Years', *Economic History Review*, 49 (1996), 731–57, and *Politics of Decline, passim*.

31 David Edgerton, 'The Decline of Declinism', *Business History Review*, 71 (1997), 201–7.

32 Tim Claydon, 'Tales of Disorder: The Press and the Narrative Construction of Industrial Relations in the British Motor Industry, 1950–79', *Historical Studies in Industrial Relations*, 9 (2000), 1–37.

33 Theo Nichols, *The British Worker Question: A New Look at Workers and Productivity in Manufacturing* (London, 1986), pp. 33–4, 45–9, 101–6, 116–25, 138–9, 146.

34 Hyde, *Riding the Roller Coaster*, p. 200.

35 Johnman and Murphy, *Shipbuilding in Britain*, p. 163.

36 Buchan, *Right to Work*, pp. 25–7.

37 McGill, *Crisis on the Clyde*, p. 14.

38 Foster, 'Twentieth Century', pp. 473–4.

39 Johnman and Murphy, *Shipbuilding in Britain*, pp. 180–1.

40 Benn, *Office Without Power*, p. 155.

41 Maver, *Glasgow*, pp. 235, 240, 244; Foster and Woolfson, *Politics*, p. 122.

42 Benn, *Office Without Power*, pp. 147, 154–5, 158, 160, 165, 182–4, 189, 215, 235, 240.

43 Murray, *Scotland*, p. 62.

44 Thompson and Hart, *UCS*, p. 14; Foster and Woolfson, *Politics*, p. 179; Johnman and Murphy, *Shipbuilding in Britain*, pp. 185–6.

45 Paul Routledge, *Scargill: The Unauthorized Biography* (London, 1993), p. 129.

46 McGill, *Crisis on the Clyde*, pp. 60–3, 69–71.

47 Campbell, *Heath*, pp. 264–5.

48 Johns, *Reformism on the Clyde*, p. 113; Benn, *Office Without Power*, pp. 348–9.

49 Benn, *Office Without Power*, pp. 348–9.

50 Edward Heath, *The Course of My Life: My Autobiography* (London, 1998), pp. 347–8.

51 Lewis Allan, Chairman, SSEB, to P. Homan, DTI Scotland, 11 February 1971, SEP 4/3983, NAS.

52 Benn, *Office Without Power*, p. 329.

53 *Parliamentary Debates, Fifth Series, Commons*, 811, 811–12, 11 February 1971.

54 Johnman and Murphy, *Shipbuilding in Britain*, p. 187.

55 McGill, *Crisis on the Clyde*, p. 85.

56 Buchan, *Right to Work*, p. 53.

57 *The Times*, 14 June 1971; Buchan, *Right to Work*, p. 54.

58 *Parliamentary Debates, Fifth Series, Commons*, 819, 31–41, 14 June 1971.

59 McGill, *Crisis on the Clyde*, pp. 77–81.

60 *The Times*, 17 June 1971.

61 Campbell, *Heath*, pp. 409–10.

62 Slaven, 'Sir James Lithgow', pp. 224–5.

63 Murray, *Scotland*, p. 76.

64 *The Times*, 14 June 1971.

65 UCS Closure Contingency Planning, Note of Meeting at Scottish Office, 19 July 1971, SEP 4/3870, NAS.

66 E. J. D. Warne, DTI, Confidential Draft, undated but prepared for House of Commons Debate on 2 August 1971, SEP 4/3870, NAS.

67 DTI, Confidential Estimate, Job Losses, 11 August 1971, SEP 4/4423, NAS.

68 Notes of Minister of Industry's meetings with the STUC and UCS stewards, both 14 June 1971, SEP 3983, NAS.

69 *The Times*, 15 June 1971; Benn, *Office Without Power*, pp. 349–9, 520–1.

70 *The Times*, 17 June 1971.

71 Reid's words again; *The Times*, 17 June 1971.

72 Buchan, *Right to Work*, pp. 67–9.

73 Johns, *Reformism on the Clyde*, p. 33.

74 *The Times*, 22 June 1971.

75 P. L. Gregson, Note of Meeting between Prime Minister and Secretary of State for Trade and Industry, 19 July 1971, SEP 4/3870, NAS.

76 *Scottish Daily Express*, 26 July 1971, clipping in SEP 4/3870, NAS.

77 *Parliamentary Debates, Fifth Series, Commons*, 822, 791–801, 29 July 1971.

78 Benn, *Office Without Power*, pp. 362–4.

79 Johns, *Reformism on the Clyde*, pp. 69–71.

80 Note by R. D. M. Bell, 28 September 1971, SOE 6/1/1213, NAS.

81 Gregor Gall, 'Trade Unionism and Industrial Relations in Scotland since UCS', *Scottish Labour History*, 38 (2003), 51–74.

82 Benn, *Office Without Power*, p. 366; Wolfe claimed that his speech was actually well received, setting out the importance of Scotland moving beyond the position of a 'branch factory nation': Billy Wolfe, *Scotland Lives: The Quest for Independence* (Edinburgh, 1973), pp. 154–5.

83 Knox, *Industrial Nation*, final illustration, preceding p. 145.

84 Maver, *Glasgow*, p. 215.

85 John McIlroy, 'Notes on the Communist Party and Industrial Politics', in McIlroy, Fishman and Campbell, *British Trade Unions*, pp. 240–4.

86 STUC, *74th Annual Report, 1971*, pp. 163–4.

87 *Scottish Miner*, December 1971.

88 Taylor, 'The Heath Government and Industrial Relations', pp. 161–4.

89 Fred Lindop, 'The Dockers and the 1971 Industrial Relations Act, Part 1: Shop Stewards and Containerization', *Historical Studies in Industrial Relations*, 5 (1998), 33–72.

90 Fred Lindop, 'The Dockers and the 1971 Industrial Relations Act, Part 2: The Arrest and Release of the Pentonville Five', *Historical Studies in Industrial Relations*, 6 (1998), 65–100; Dave Lyddon and Ralph Hartington, *Glorious Summer: Class Struggle in Britain in 1972* (London, 2001), pp. 141–77.

91 *The Times*, 16 and 18 June 1971.

92 *Glasgow Herald*, 12 August 1971; William McLean, General Secretary, Scottish Area of the NUM, to the Prime Minister, 17 August 1971, SEP 4/4423, NAS.

93 C. J. Pollitt, Minute for Minister for Industry, 6 August 1971, SEP 4/3870, NAS.

94 BBC Radio Scotland, 24 May 1995; recording in author's possession.

95 Buchan, *Right to Work*, p. 89.

96 Philip Ziegler, *Wilson: The Authorised Life* (London, 1993), p. 377; Pimlott, *Harold Wilson*, p. 588.

97 Jad Adams, *Tony Benn* (London, 1992), pp. 319–21.

98 Michael Gold, 'Worker Mobilization in the 1970s: Revisiting Work-ins, Co-operatives and Alternative Corporate Plans', *Historical Studies in Industrial Relations*, 18 (2004), 65–106, pp. 51–4.

99 Colin Crouch, *The Politics of Industrial Relations* (Glasgow, 1979), pp. 107–9.

100 Cmnd 3623, pp. 258–60.

101 Michael Gold, 'Worker Directors in the UK and the Limits of Policy Transfer from Europe since the 1970s', *Historical Studies in Industrial Relations*, 20 (2005), 46.

102 *Parliamentary Debates, Fifth Series, Commons*, 803, 1387–91, 14 July 1970.

103 Transcript of interview between Fred Lindop and Walter Cunningham, Bevin House, Hull, 21 July 1981, MSS.371/QD7/Docks1/10, Modern Records Centre, University of Warwick. Warm thanks are extended to Fred Lindop for placing this and many other transcripts in the Modern Records Centre.

104 Buchan, *Right to Work*, p. 90.

105 Jon Wiener, *Come Together: John Lennon in His Time* (London, 1995), pp. 167–9.

106 Broadway, *Upper Clyde Shipbuilders*, pp. 46–7.

107 Thompson and Hart, *UCS*, pp. 60–1; Ken Coates, *Work-ins, Sit-ins and Industrial Democracy* (Nottingham, 1981), pp. 34–5.

108 Gold, 'Worker Directors in the UK', pp. 70, 80–1, 103.

109 Coates, *Work-ins*, p. 30.

110 Benn, *Office Without Power*, pp. 402, 456.

111 John McIlroy, '"Always Outnumbered, Always Outgunned": The Trotskyists and the Trade Unions', in McIlroy, Fishman and Campbell, *British Trade Unions*, pp. 259–64; Johns, *Reformism on the Clyde, passim*.

112 Foster and Woolfson, *Politics*, pp. 334–5.

113 *Royal Commission on the Constitution, Minutes of Evidence IV*, pp. 57–62.

114 Willie Thompson, *The Good Old Cause: British Communism, 1920–1991* (London, 1992), p. 89.

115 *Royal Commission on the Constitution, Minutes of Evidence IV*, pp. 65–71.

116 Wolfe, *Scotland Lives*, pp. 153–5.

117 Foster and Woolfson, 'Workers on the Clyde', pp. 306–10.

118 Foster and Woolfson, *Politics*, p. 200.

119 P. H. Twyman, 'Confidential Note for the Record. Shipbuilding on the Upper Clyde: The Secretary of State's visit to Glasgow on 3 August 1971', 4 August 1971, SEP 4/3870, NAS.

120 SCDI, EC, 21 June 1971, CH.

121 *The Times*, 22 June 1971.

122 Ibid., 9 July 1971.

123 Buchan, *Right to Work*, pp. 62, 85–6.

124 McGill, *Crisis on the Clyde*, p. 103.

125 Marwick, *The Sixties*, p. 751.

126 Twyman, 'Confidential Note', 4 August 1971, SEP 4/3870, NAS.

127 Foster and Woolfson, *Politics*, pp. 208–16.

128 Telex from Councillor Leishman, Sunderland Conservative Association, to Peter Thomas, Chairman of the Conservative Party, 4 August 1971, SEP 4/3870, NAS.

129 Buchan, *Right to Work*, p. 104.

130 STUC, *75th Annual Report, 1972*, pp. 258–61.

131 Aitken, *Bairns O' Adam*, pp. 226–30; Craigen, 'The Scottish TUC', p. 153.

132 *The Scotsman*, 15 February 1972.

133 Ewing, *Stop the World*, p. 160.

134 *Glasgow Herald*, 15 February 1972.

135 Foster and Woolfson, *Politics*, pp. 322–5.

136 Foster, 'Twentieth Century', p. 478.

137 SCDI, EC, 21 February 1972, CH.

138 'In a Playground of Violence', *The Times*, 4 December 1971.

139 Phillip Whitehead, *The Writing on the Wall: Britain in the Seventies* (London, 1985), p. 81; Campbell, *Heath*, p. 443.

140 Foster and Woolfson, *Politics*, p. 16.

141 *The Times*, 17 June 1971.

142 Jock Bruce-Gardyne, *Whatever Happened to the Quiet Revolution?* (London, 1974), p. 79.

143 John Campbell, *Margaret Thatcher: Volume One, The Grocer's Daughter* (London, 2001), p. 244.

144 *Parliamentary Debates, Fifth Series, Commons*, 822, 353, 27 July 1971.

145 Douglas Hurd and Andrew Osmond, *Scotch on the Rocks* (London, 1971), pp. 48–50.

146 Benn, *Office Without Power*, pp. 413–4.

147 Foster and Woolfson, *Politics*, p. 16.

148 Christopher Pollitt to Peter Gregson, 19 August 1971, and Note by L. R. Hinson, 25 August 1971, SEP 4/4423, NAS.

149 McGill, *Crisis on the Clyde*, p. 111.

150 Sir Douglas Haddow to Sir Robert Marshall, DTI, 10 August 1971, SEP 4/3870, NAS.

151 *Glasgow Herald*, 2 October 1971.

152 'The Crisis on Clydeside', *The Times,* 12 October 1971; Foster and Woolfson, *Politics*, p. 279.

153 E. V. Merchant to Davies, 20 December 1971, SEP 4/3984, NAS.

154 Ibid., 31 December 1971, SEP 4/3984, NAS; Johnman and Murphy, *Shipbuilding in Britain*, p. 188.

155 Note of meeting between the Minister for Industry and Mr Kelly, 20 August 1971, SEP 4/4423, NAS.

156 P. J. L. Homan, DTI Scotland, to P. le Cheminant, DTI London, 8 July 1971, and le Cheminant to Homan, 30 July 1971, SEP 4/4335, NAS.

157 *The Times*, 14 January 1972.

158 Note of meeting between the Minister of Industry and Marathon representatives, 28 January 1972, SEP 4/4500, NAS; Foster and Woolfson, *Politics*, pp. 241–5, 314–15; McGill, *Crisis on the Clyde*, p. 121.

159 Department of Trade and Industry, *Shipbuilding on the Clyde: Report of Hill Samuel & Co. Ltd.*, Cmnd 4918 (HMSO, March 1972), pp. 11, 18.

160 Foster and Woolfson, *Politics*, p. 325.

161 Cabinet Minutes and Conclusions, 24 February 1972, CAB 128, PRO.

162 *Parliamentary Debates, Fifth Series, Commons*, 832, 50–3, 28 February 1972.

163 Unidentifiable occupant of 12 Downing Street to John Davies, 22 June 1972; Gordon Campbell wrote to Davies on similar lines on 29 June 1972; both SEP 4/3984, NAS.

164 Report of visit of DTI officials to Marathon, 8–10 March 1972, 27 March 1972;
     Miss B. M. Eyles to Mr Cooper, both DTI, 22 May 1972; James Darragh, DTI
     Scotland, to Minister for Industrial Development, 2 August 1972; SEP 4/4500,
     NAS.
165 Foster and Woolfson, *Politics*, pp. 340–79.
166 Murray, *Scotland*, pp. 62–4.
167 Johnman and Murphy, *Shipbuilding in Britain*, p. 199.

4 Coal: mobbing and rioting, 1972

In November 1971 the NUM in Scotland held a large march and rally in Edinburgh, led by Michael McGahey, William McLean and Dave Bolton, respectively the union's Scottish President, General Secretary and Vice-President.[1] The centrality of coal and miners to the Scottish labour movement, seen in the STUC's industrial and devolution debates of the 1960s, was further evidenced here by the supportive presence of a broad spectrum of Labour MPs from mining constituencies: Alex Eadie of Midlothian, Chairman of the miners' group at Westminster, Adam Hunter of Dunfermline, a member of the NUM's Scottish Executive, Jim Sillars of South Ayrshire, Hugh McCartney of Dumbartonshire East (a former mining constituency), Harry Ewing, who had recently – although narrowly – defeated the SNP in a by-election in Falkirk, Stirling and Grangemouth Burghs, John Smith of Lanarkshire North and John Mackintosh of Berwick and East Lothian.

The rally at Edinburgh was dominated by the Scottish NUM's characteristically strong commitment to devolutionary politics, seen at various points earlier in this book, and especially in the STUC debates of 1967, 1968 and 1969. On McGahey's death in 1999 a later General Secretary of the STUC, Campbell Christie, would remember him – above all his notable industrial experiences – for mobilising trade union support in Scotland for Home Rule.[2] Sillars, of course, would leave Labour to establish the more aggressively nationalist Scottish Labour Party late in 1975, disappointed as he was by the limited character of devolution brought forward by Wilson's second government from 1974, before switching to the SNP after the 1979 referendum and the election of a Conservative government. Eadie, Ewing, Smith and Mackintosh, meanwhile, were or would become strongly associated with the devolution campaign;[3] Mackintosh was also well known as a principled supporter of EEC membership. Unfortunately for him opposition to the Heath government's move towards this end – the legislation was making its way through Parliament and would come to the decisive Second Reading in February 1972 – was one of the rally's main themes, along with unemployment and the NUM's wages claim, which would lead to the six-week strike that began on 9 January 1972. The audience duly booed Mackintosh when he spoke.

This was not a problem for Alex Kitson, the most senior labour movement figure present at the rally. Kitson, in the process of leading the Scottish Commercial Motormen's Union into a merger with the TGWU, was on the Labour Party's National Executive, where he was seeking to mobilise opposition to EEC membership,[4] and his brief speech was well received in Edinburgh. Yet the rally was dominated by Jimmy Reid, whose charisma, rhetorical skills and general leadership were contributing to the campaign that would climax about three months later with the Heath government's about-turn on UCS. His speech to the miners, like many others he was making during the work-in, criticised Heath's economic and industrial strategies from a Scottish devolutionist as well as a class perspective. It included a pungent attack on Lord Robens, linking the issues of employment insecurity and the pay campaign in the coalfields with the centralised direction of the industry from London. Robens was Chairman of the National Coal Board (NCB), and a fairly easy but nevertheless tempting target, as a former Labour MP and Cabinet Minister – in Attlee's 1945–51 governments – who had called for the replacement of Wilson's Labour government with a multi-party coalition 'of all the talents' in 1968.[5] He had recently also crossed Reid, it will be remembered, as one of Heath's 'wise men' on the Clyde. Robens was unpopular among miners because of his association with the large-scale closures of 'uneconomic' pits in the 1960s,[6] although this approach was shaped primarily by the Labour government's attachment to other energy forms, including nuclear power, favoured over coal by officials at the Treasury and the Ministry of Power. Despite the Labour Party's links with the NUM, successive Ministers of Power in Wilson's government endorsed the shift away from coal.[7] Hence the number of collieries in operation in the UK was reduced from 576 in 1963–64 to 289 in 1971–72 with the NCB's total average manpower falling in the same period from 517,000 to 281,500.[8] In Scotland employment in mining declined at roughly the same rate, from 50,800 in 1963–64 to 28,400 in 1971–72. The Toothill Report had anticipated these closures, and the Labour government encouraged them as the means of 'releasing' labour for utilisation in younger, high-growth enterprise, such as motor manufacturing and electronics assembly.[9]

These developments generated a great sense of unease among miners and arguably within the working class more generally, involving as they did increased degrees of foreign ownership and control, and changes in the character of work, with an accentuated emphasis on deskilled assembly processes. Hence they contributed to the leftward shift of the Scottish labour movement that John Foster has noted as an important characteristic of the early 1970s.[10] Reid and McGahey were important figures in the CPGB, serving together on the party's political committee in the late 1960s, with McGahey then joining the National Executive in 1971, and they were sometimes seen, especially by business and politically conservative critics or opponents of the labour movement, as driving this shift to the left. This would be particularly so with the miners in 1972. McGahey was portrayed in the business press and by the Prime Minister as one of the 'hard men', imposing the strike on the public, the government and even the unwitting – or unwilling – union membership.[11] In the previous chapter, however, an important characteristic of the UCS work-in was noted, namely the very large extent to which Reid and other stewards were operating *in response* to pressure from below. They articulated some of the grievances and aspirations of Scottish workers, but did not create or shape them. This was an example of an important characteristic of economic and social life that had emerged in the 1960s and was examined in Chapter 1, in connection with the unofficial strikes at Linwood, namely the powerful role of popular or rank-and-file agency in industrial politics.

Literature on the 1972 miners' strike tends to ignore this characteristic, and is dominated instead by 'top-down' accounts that privilege high politics, with developments engineered by government ministers and officials, 'peak level' business representatives and trade union executives.[12] There is some important work focusing on agency 'from below', with pressure from ordinary miners presented as the predominant historical contingency.[13] This chapter builds on this body of work, and utilises an earlier discussion of the 1972 strike, which examined its implications for the understanding of industrial politics in the UK by emphasising the decisive role of popular agency.[14] A similar approach is adopted here, in order to probe the strike's important Scottish dimensions, including its impact on debates about Home Rule, although the contextual importance of high politics is considered. The distinction between popular agency and high politics is significant, for the strike indirectly propelled the devolutionary campaign in Scotland, by giving further and vivid expression to working-class anxieties about the degree of employment insecurity that was thought to arise from the remote administration of political power. This was partly – but only partly – the function of the NUM's leadership. Most 'top-down' accounts of coalmining in this period emphasise the emergence in the late 1960s of 'militant' leadership on the NUM National Executive, 'militant' usually used to distinguish Communists and leftist Labourites from centrist or right-wing Labour Party figures, normally characterised as 'moderates'. McGahey and Lawrence Daly, leftist Labourite and NUM General Secretary, are usually identified here and depicted as out-flanking their moderate president, Joe Gormley, to force militancy on the union and a punitive settlement on the government.[15] This characterisation of the NUM and the 1972 strike is at odds with perspectives and evidence presented in this chapter, which points to substantial pressure from below on the NUM leadership to behave and negotiate militantly. It will be argued that McGahey was meeting the demands of his members for a militant policy in the coalfields, just as his advocacy of devolution – examined in Chapter 1 – was a response to devolutionist sentiments within Scotland generally and the Scottish labour movement specifically.

In November 1971 the NUM balloted its members on whether strike action should be pursued in support of a pay claim lodged with the NCB. Of those voting 41.2 per cent were opposed to a strike, but once underway the strike was observed more or less completely by all members of the union.[16] In the ballot support for the strike among Scottish miners was only marginally higher than among the NUM membership across the British coalfields, but the strike itself was conducted with particular vigour in Scotland. McGahey and the leadership were pushed into supporting a major blockade of the SSEB power station at Longannet, on the shore of the Firth of Forth in west Fife. This action – designed to speed up and maximise the scale of the miners' victory – was contrary to the official policy of the NUM. But, like other officials in many other sectors of the economy at this time, McGahey was obliged to respond to his members in Scotland in order to retain influence and credibility within his organisation.[17]

It is here that Eric Hobsbawm's maxim about the construction of nationalist movements from below – shaped by the 'assumptions, hopes, needs, longings and interests of ordinary people, which are not necessarily national and still less nationalist' – might be applied in conceptualising the Scottish road to devolution.[18] In taking their own path in the 1972 strike the Scottish miners were not consciously engaging in nationalist or even devolutionist politics. But their pressure for a militant policy – evident at Longannet and at other times in the strike – was derived from the structural insecurity of employment in the Scottish coalfields. This was a powerful reminder of the particular economic problems of Scotland, and contributed to debates about how these might be corrected through devolved forms of governance. In this indirect but nevertheless important manner industrial politics shaped the devolution movement from below in the early 1970s.

'Power in their hands': popular agency and militancy in the coalfields

An important expression of the trend towards militancy in the coalfields was the election of militant figures to official positions in the NUM. In 1966 McGahey was elected to the union's National Executive and in 1967 became President in Scotland, the union's third largest area after Yorkshire and South Wales, winning a straight contest with Alex Timpany of New Cumnock by 13,149 votes to 8,499. The turnout was solid, roughly 70 per cent of a potential electorate of 31,500, NCB Scotland's workforce.[19] Lawrence Daly, 'the militant miner', according to the *Glasgow Herald*'s John Fowler, became NUM national General Secretary in 1968, defeating Joe Gormley, 'right-wing' secretary of the NUM's north-west English miners and a member of the Labour Party's National Executive, by 115,531 votes to 105,501.[20] Daly's political trajectory was different from McGahey's. He left the CPGB in 1956, before the Soviet counter-revolution in Hungary, disaffected by the party's uncritical adoption of Moscow policy, and established the Fife Socialist League in 1957.[21] Daly joined the Labour Party in 1962, according to Willie Thompson, where he assumed a position on the left.[22] At the STUC he had been a strong critic of the Wilson government's economic and industrial relations policies; he advocated larger pay claims in negotiations with the NCB, to arrest the miners' relative decline against the wages of other manual workers; and he deprecated the NCB's programme of closures, which contributed to his victory over Gormley.[23] Yet Daly nevertheless insisted that the Labour Party was the best vehicle for the 'advance to a more just and humane society',[24] and this perhaps – along with his ex-Communism – under-pinned his rivalry with McGahey, although there was also a powerful regional dimension to this, between Fifer and Lanarkshire man. These differences, it should be noted, did not prevent the two from generally working closely together.

In Scotland the militancy of the miners was demonstrated by the outcome of two national ballots in the course of 1971: the UK presidential election in May and the national – i.e. UK-wide – vote on whether to support strike action in support of a pay claim in November. Gormley won the presidency in a contest with McGahey, taking 55.9 per cent of the 210,546 votes cast. But McGahey, using Scotland as a platform and in this personal contest presumably enjoying local support, took 80.6 per cent of the Scottish ballot. Significantly, however, McGahey also secured a large majority in South Wales, reflecting the weight, perhaps, of the region's substantial Communist tradition, but also the burden of pit closures, experienced there in the same disproportionate manner in the 1960s as in Scotland. McGahey also squeezed ahead in Yorkshire, just, with 50.9 per cent.[25] The linkage between militant voting and industrial insecurity was more visibly evident in the pay ballot, stripped of the personality component inherent in the presidential contest. On an 88 per cent poll in November this produced a majority vote of 58.8 per cent for strike action. Earlier attempts to stage official strikes had been stymied by a union rule requiring the support of two-thirds of members for national industrial action, but this high barrier to official action had given rise to major unofficial strikes in 1969 and 1970 and weakened the union's integrity.[26] A new minimum of 55 per cent had duly been established by a rule change at the NUM's annual conference held at Aberdeen in July 1971. This hurdle was passed in November 1971 chiefly through the 75 per cent strike vote in Yorkshire, the area with the largest number of NUM members, and the core of the 1969 and 1970 unofficial strikes that signalled the men's impatience with the closure of pits under the Labour government, and their dissatisfaction with the union leadership's toleration of the run down of the industry since nationalisation in 1947.[27] But there were also healthy majorities for strike action in the next two largest areas: Wales, with 65.5 per cent, and Scotland, with 59.5 per cent. These offset the more modest majorities in the fourth and fifth largest areas: 54 per cent in Nottingham and 54.75 per cent in Durham.[28]

The relative militancy of the Scottish miners was partly the consequence of the wider economic and social developments in Scotland that have featured at different points in this book, and were referred to briefly in the introduction to this chapter. Manual workers, particularly those who had been or still were engaged in heavy industry, were touched by worries about structural economic change, and concerned – as evidenced by the industrial relations difficulties at Linwood – about the changing character of work. The growth of multi-national enterprise, clustered around forms of assembly production that were characterised by enervation, stress and the low application of human skill, contributed to the atmosphere of insecurity and unbidden change, compounded by a sense more broadly of the increasingly remote nature of political and economic power.[29] These were general working-class concerns in Scotland in the early 1970s, but Scottish miners also had additional and specific worries that they shared – if perhaps in exaggerated form – with comrades in coalfields throughout the UK.

Miners had two principal grievances: employment insecurity and the falling value of their wages relative to earnings in other sectors. These sprung from the steady contraction of the industry since 1947, a process accelerated in the 1960s with the increased use of other energy forms, especially oil, although the move to greater nuclear power generation was also significant. Coal's share of energy supplied in Britain declined from 73.7 per cent in 1960 to 46.6 per cent in 1970, although this was a smaller share of an expanded aggregate. The according fall in the number of working miners has already been noted.[30] In the 1960s the NCB encouraged progress towards nationally uniform pay. This was designed to eliminate possible 'points of argument', but the diminution of local, regional and sectional differentials actually made large-scale industrial disputes more likely, mitigating the traditional rivalries and even divisions between miners in different localities and regions that had emerged and become entrenched over many generations in the fragmented and privately owned industry until nationalisation in 1947.[31] These divisions would resurface again in the national strike of 1984–85, amid a programme of selected closures, particularly between large bodies of Yorkshire and Nottinghamshire miners,[32] but in the early 1970s the trend was clearly towards inter-regional and industrial unity across the coalfields.[33] This became clear with the major unofficial strikes over wages of 1969 and 1970, in the latter case after a small majority had voted for an official strike, hence precipitating the demand for the lowering of the threshold that was secured in 1971. These stoppages revealed the accumulation of resentment in the coalfields over the process of contraction, and something of a generational shift too. Younger workers and activists tended to measure their position against other workers and their own future expectations. This made them more inclined to criticise the NUM and the NCB than older men whose comparative references tended to be the bitter experiences of the 1920s and 1930s, and who were perhaps reluctant consequently to criticise arrangements in the nationalised industry.[34] The unofficial disputes lifted the volume of working days 'lost' to strikes in the industry from 118,000 in 1966, 108,000 in 1967 and 57,000 in 1968 to 1,041,000 in 1969 and 1,092,000 in 1970,[35] and prepared the ground for official strikes by compelling the change of NUM rules at Aberdeen, the union leadership worried about the erosion of its authority in the face of continuing unofficial activity.

In the autumn of 1971 the NUM Executive submitted to the NCB a pay claim seeking to raise the basic underground weekly wage to £28, with £35 for those paid under the 1966 National Power Loading Agreement for mechanised pits. These proposed rises amounted to between 35 and 47 per cent, but were designed to improve the position of miners relative to workers in manufacturing industry. Here the comparison with car production was instructive, and made frequently by government officials and ministers. In February 1972, for instance, the Cabinet would discuss the manner in which the Chrysler Corporation settled a strike by its 6,500 workers at Linwood, who were seeking a significant raise – £8 per week – in continuing pursuit of parity with the firm's midlands employees. With a £20 million export order of Hillman Avengers for the USA under threat,[36] Chrysler made an offer of 20 per cent over eighteen months. This represented an annual increase of 14 per cent, bringing the basic weekly wage to £37, £9 *more* than the basic sought by the miners at the end of 1971. Cabinet Ministers were aware that this comparison decreased greatly the likelihood of the miners settling close to the NCB's terms.[37] But the NCB was boxed in by the government's unofficial counter-inflationary pay formula of 'n-1', stipulating that each pay increase should be smaller by 1 per cent than its predecessor. In coal this meant an intended settlement of no more than 7 per cent.[38] With no agreement possible, the NUM instituted an overtime ban, to minimise stockpiling, and held a strike ballot. This produced the majority vote of 58.8 per cent for strike action that has already been noted, above the revised 55 per cent threshold. On 9 December the National Executive agreed that a national strike – the first in coalmining since 1926 – would commence on Monday 9 January.

In taking this decision the union Executive was pushed by its members. This point has been overlooked amid the focus in much of the literature on the personalities and politics of the leadership. The relative inconsequence of personality can be illustrated by reflecting on the character of Joe Gormley's presidency, which belied his political moderation. Alastair Reid, who asserts that the strikes of 1972 and 1974 were less the result of 'popular insurgency' than the confrontational intransigence of the NCB and the government, nevertheless admits that Gormley presided over the NUM in the same essentially pragmatic character as his predecessors, and this meant responding to the militancy of the coalfields.[40] In a sense the personal politics of NUM leaders had a limited bearing on union policy: in office they operated at their members' calling. Such was true also of Daly's predecessors as General Secretary, the Welsh Communists Arthur Horner (1945–59) and Will Paynter (1959–68), who followed the logic of their positions as elected officials, and carried out the democratic will of their membership. Just as Horner and Paynter were compelled to act moderately however militantly they spoke, so Gormley, the rhetorical moderate, was – in different times – required to conduct a militant policy.[41]

To a large extent this development, of radicalised union members pushing their officials into positions of greater militancy, was a general phenomenon in industrial politics across the UK by the early 1970s. This was the product, observed in Chapter 1, of broad economic and social considerations, chiefly located in the impact of full employment – with the removal of unemployment as a disciplinary instrument – and the diminution of popular deference to various forms of public authority. From 1970 – as Chapter 3 examined – union militancy was additionally stimulated by the Conservative government's approach to industrial relations, and the proposed ending of public subsidies to 'lame duck' enterprises and sectors. The consequent and ongoing crisis on the Clyde had sharpened the animosity of trade unionists – in Scotland and the UK at large – towards the government. It had also encouraged the development of a culture of mutual support between workers across occupational and industrial barriers, and this was central to the miners' victory in 1972.[42]

The government was keenly aware of the dispute's broader industrial significance, and this strengthened its determination that the miners should be defeated. The Secretary of State for Employment, Robert Carr, conveyed his department's advice to Heath on 6 January, stating that the NCB's final offer 'went to the absolute limit. Any increase in it would ruin Government policy on the wages front.' The strike might last for six weeks, he noted, but the government could secure a valuable victory: if the miners were forced to accept the NCB's terms as well as the costs of a long strike, then the wage round 'next year' could be cut to 5–6 per cent. With growth at 4–5 per cent 'on the inflationary front the Government could achieve a 100 per cent success'. There were admittedly some 'serious risks', with claims outstanding in electricity, gas and the civil service, but these were 'worth taking'.[43] On 7

January Carr advised Reginald Maudling, Home Secretary, that Heath agreed with the Department of Employment's advice: 'The stakes are high and we must do everything we can to achieve our objective.'[44]

Despite worrying about these 'high stakes' and the prospect of a long strike, ministers and officials believed there would be little impact on domestic or business energy supplies. At a meeting at the DTI on 13 January, attended by Derek Ezra, who had recently succeeded Robens – who had retired – as NCB Chairman, it was noted that picketing of power stations would be ineffective, as coal stocks were 'mainly' within these stations already.[45] This view was shared in the business and daily press. The *Glasgow Herald*, leaning against the miners, advised them to measure the 'realities' of a strike without pay against their 'precarious position' in a 'declining industry'. Coal users, especially in electricity generation, were supposedly angered by the allegedly inflated nature of the pay claim, and already considering other forms of fuel. An early settlement was duly forecast,[46] but there were no immediate signs of the strike crumbling. By early February – partly because of a cold weather snap – power cuts were being anticipated, with industrial capacity already curtailed. In Scotland DTI officials noted the dates by which the coal stocks of large industrial users would be exhausted. These included British Leyland, at Bathgate, by 14 February; Scottish & Newcastle at Fountainbridge, Edinburgh and Chrysler/Rootes at Linwood by 21 February; and ICI at Grangemouth by 28 February.[47] Meanwhile the cuts were being experienced in other visible, public ways. On 5 February at Tannadice Park, Dundee, the first bank of floodlights had been switched off, to save energy, minutes before the end of a Scottish Cup tie between Dundee United and Aberdeen.[48]

On 8 February the government declared a State of Emergency, to ration electricity and maintain some order in industrial and domestic life. The following day Carr met NCB and NUM representatives separately, having seen them also on 21 January.[49] The government now saw that the miners' determination and organisational capacities had been greatly underestimated. Carr told John Davies and Anthony Barber, Chancellor of the Exchequer, that within days 'there would be real interference with supplies and the life of the community, particularly industry'. The miners realised this, Carr added: they 'were feeling their strength and had got power in their hands'.[50] This rank-and-file agency over events had been expressed chiefly through picketing which, in the absence of working miners, was geared to keeping pit deputies out of the collieries. The NUM executive had given a pre-strike undertaking to co-operate over maintenance and safety, and so unofficial action to the contrary was a plain sign that local NUM officials rather than national leaders were shaping the action. By the first week of February full safety cover was in place at just 31 of 289 mines.[51] Heath and Carr told Victor Feather, TUC General Secretary, on 15 February that they found this exasperating.

Feather observed that many miners would rather see the endangered pits close than continue being under-paid for a 'job which they and the public alike regarded as unpleasant and dangerous'.[52]

Picketing was made all the more effective by the support received by the miners – again, to the government's surprise – from unionised road transport and railway workers.[53] Miners needed only to offer token pickets to halt the departure of coal from the pits, allowing them to focus their efforts by the second week of the strike on power stations. This was the decisive action in the strike. 'It was on the gates of Longannet, Barking, Battersea and West Thurrock', wrote Malcolm Pitt, Kent miner, union activist and Communist, 'that the battle of the miners was won.'[54] Longannet was unusual in that the power station was integrated with coal workings on site, so the pickets' first aim was not to stop coal entering but leaving, principally to Cockenzie, the SSEB's second largest power station, east of Edinburgh. Members of the train drivers' union, ASLEF, cut this supply off, telling union officials once the strike had begun that they would carry no coal from Longannet or anywhere else. This, it should be emphasised, reinforces the importance of popular agency in the dispute. There were some initial road transfers of coal from Longannet but this was brought to an end by an NUM picket on 11 January and no further movements were attempted.[55]

The Longannet pickets also sought to prevent diesel for coal-handling equipment and flashing oil for starting up boilers from entering, although this action was not pursued with great vigour initially. On the night of 20–21 January, for example, a road tanker with diesel fuel entered Longannet unhindered, the two pickets, according to police reports to the Scottish Office, 'sheltering in [a] car from the snow'.[56] But a group led by Tam Coulter of Manor Powis in Clackmannan demonstrated more enterprise several days later. A breezy account of this incident was relayed in the *Scottish Miner*, the NUM Scotland paper established during the early days of McGahey's presidency. As a Danish tanker approached the Firth of Forth, heading towards Longannet with flashing oil, Coulter persuaded a trawler skipper by 'rustling a few notes' to 'take him and the lads out'. Three pressmen came on board too, agreeing to cover half of Coulter's costs. The *Scottish Miner* duly carried a picture of the huge tanker looming over the bows of the trawler, which, Scottish Office officials noted, failed in the unlikely and dangerous objective of halting the landing of the fuel.[57]

Physical confrontation periodically characterised more conventional forms of picketing, notably at NCB offices in Scotland and other parts of the UK when NUM members tried to prevent clerical staff from working. This further highlighted the NUM executive's limited influence. There were two clerical workers' organisations in the industry: the NUM's white-collar affiliate, the Colliery Officials' Staff Association (COSA), and the Clerical and Administrative Workers' Union (CAWU). Although instructed by the

NUM Executive to work, on 17 January COSA members pressed their officials to join the strike, while CAWU members stayed in. NUM pickets attempted that week to prevent CAWU members from entering NCB offices in Yorkshire and South Wales, against NUM official instructions to picket power stations instead.[58] At the NCB's Northern Scottish Area office in Alloa clerical staff were conveyed by seventy police officers through a picket of 400 miners, but not without injury: a young woman was treated for bruised ribs, several others treated for shock, and cars were damaged.[59] The socially conservative politics of *The Courier & Advertiser*, D. C. Thompson's daily paper published in Dundee but the regional title for much of central and eastern Scotland, including the mining counties of Fife and Clackmannan, were strongly evident in the language mobilised to condemn actions of the male pickets that were aimed at a largely female body of clerical staff. 'There can be no excuse for this kind of behaviour', the paper intoned. 'There was some measure of sympathy for the miners. But this disgraceful treatment of girls and women has destroyed it.'[60] A similar depiction of events appeared in the *Glasgow Herald*, now even more rigidly opposed to the miners, who had forfeited their hard-earned public esteem through the 'suicidal' strike and the thuggish picketing.[61] Similar action followed in South Wales and Durham, presented to *Courier* readers as 'More girls in picket trouble',[62] but at Alloa, according to C. T. Hole of the Scottish Office, advising Gordon Campbell, the picketing was now orderly, consisting of 'heckling only by varying numbers, sometimes large'. Hole characterised the picketing across Scotland as 'extensive', 'successful' and 'generally peaceful'.[63]

The coal strike, meanwhile, was being paralleled by a complicated dispute affecting power workers, which encompassed divisions within and between the four separate trade unions involved and some unofficial industrial action in the second half of January. On 7 February the electricity union negotiators accepted a pay offer on the casting vote of Frank Chapple, electricians' leader.[64] The importance of this dispute was felt at Longannet and especially Cockenzie, for Chapple's initiative was repudiated by a number of power workers in the Edinburgh area, directed by Councillor Ron Brown and Rab Jeffrey, respectively Chairman and Secretary of the SSEB Edinburgh Works Committee. Brown – future Labour MP for Leith – and Jeffrey criticised the official 'sell out' in a leaflet issued to Cockenzie workers on 16 February, and urged them to join the miners' picket lines and so further the 'fight of working class people against the illegal Tory government for decent wages and conditions'.[65]

The Cockenzie picket remained sparse, ranging from twelve to seventy on 16 February, and SSEB employees freely entered the power station with only two police officers present.[66] This reflected the Scottish NUM's concentration of effort at Longannet, which followed the intensification of picketing in other parts of the UK in the week beginning 7 February. In this connection the most dramatic development was the blockade by 7,000 miners and local engineering workers of the West Midlands Gas Board's coke depot at Saltley in Birmingham, led by Yorkshire miners and their full-time official, Arthur Scargill, operating independently of the NUM executive. This coincided with the declaration of a State of Emergency and climaxed on 10 February, when Maudling interrupted a Cabinet discussion about the law on picketing – this 'appeared to permit activities extending well beyond what could be regarded as tolerable' – to convey the news that Birmingham's Chief Constable had been obliged to 'request the closure' of the depot. The Cabinet concluded that this outcome, with the depot closed and no further stocks leaving, 'represented a victory for violence against the lawful activities of the Gas Board and the coal merchants'.[67] To Scargill and his followers Saltley illustrated the possibilities of working-class unity, but Margaret Thatcher, in the Cabinet confounded by the strike, interpreted it as evidence of the essentially undemocratic and repugnant character of trade union power that had to be challenged and then destroyed.[68] The blockade clearly had a large political impact, but its material bearing on the fuel crisis was actually insignificant. Saltley contained only a small fraction of the coal needed to supply the power stations that were already struggling to generate electricity. As Dennis Skinner, NUM-sponsored Labour MP for Bolsover in Derbyshire, would later put it, this episode's importance was really 'symbolic, it was psychological, and it helped to impress the establishment'.[69]

The picketing at Saltley and elsewhere, perhaps surprisingly, had little bearing on public opinion, which was broadly supportive of the miners, despite the power cuts, short-time working and jostling of 'girls'. This is worth noting, given the recurrent Tory emphasis on public disorder and 'extreme' left-wing political involvement. Private polling was conducted on behalf of the Conservative party by the Opinion Research Centre, and, contrary to government expectations, as the strike progressed this indicated a growth in support for the idea that the miners were right to strike for higher wages, from 54 per cent on 1 February to 66 per cent on 14 February.[70] So, the prisoner of public opinion as well as the miners' picketing, the government on 11 February appointed Lord Wilberforce, a High Court judge, to chair an inquiry into the miners' pay claim, with the assistance of John Garrett, Director of the Industrial Society, and Professor Lawrence Hunter of the University of Glasgow's Department of Economics.[71] This was a departure from the Department of Employment's earlier insistence that the strike had to be settled without reference to 'an outside agency which would be beyond our control', and was interpreted in the press as a significant defeat for the government.[72]

Longannet: 'get into them'

Ministers expected the supply position to be improved by Wilberforce's appointment, and on 14 February the NUM Executive decided to 'reduce pickets generally'.[73] Carr appeared on BBC's *Panorama* that evening, telling miners that the government would authorise any settlement recommended by Wilberforce if they went back to work immediately.[74] But the power of popular agency, and the likelihood that the NUM Executive would be disregarded, was alluded to in a conversation between Feather and Heath, with the Prime Minister warned that power stations especially would still be picketed,[75] and on 16 February the Home Office learnt that although the NUM executive believed 'they had won the battle', Gormley felt 'there would be no chance of getting the men off the picket lines'.[76] This was illustrated in dramatic terms at Longannet, where Scottish miners, led by their President, ignored the National Executive of their union and intensified a blockade that by Friday 11 February had grown to a thousand, with police officers just keeping the access road open.[77]

Events at Saltley have received much historical attention, but Longannet has been ignored – neglected even in Scottish historiography – even although it represented a more important practical target in terms of its energy generation. In September 2005 it appeared on a World Wildlife Fund 'Dirty 30' list of European carbon dioxide-emitting power plants,[78] but in February 1972 it was the acme of industrial modernism. Coal was delivered directly to the power station by an 8.8 kilometres-long underground conveyer belt from three large mines that had been opened to the north-west of the site,[79] where 1,803 NUM members were employed at the end of 1971.[80] Construction had begun in January 1964 and the first of the plant's four units for supplying electricity to the Scottish grid was completed in May 1968, along with the single, towering chimney, 183 metres high, visible from the Stirling to Larbert railway line to the west and the southern end of the Forth Rail bridge to the east. The final generating unit was finished in January 1973, at which point Longannet was the biggest power station in Britain,[81] responsible in normal conditions for producing roughly a third of the electricity generated by the SSEB and 27 per cent of the total electricity generated in Scotland.[82] During the strike only two of Longannet's three completed units were operating,[83] but even then its importance was increasing because it had ample coal on site, while other stations were running down non-replenishable stocks. By mid-February Longannet was probably supplying about 50 per cent of the SSEB's electricity generation. Of additional significance, however, is that 'normal' generation in Scotland exceeded local demand, so lost production there affected supply to other parts of the UK. This was what troubled the Cabinet's Official Committee on Emergencies when it learnt of the mass picket at Longannet; Cabinet Ministers were immediately advised, and would gratefully contrast the success of the police in keeping Longannet open with the 'inadequate' measures adopted elsewhere.[84]

The policing at Longannet was led by Robert Murison, Fife's Chief Constable, who over the weekend of 12–13 February learned that there would be over 2,000 pickets on Monday morning, with miners travelling from coalfields throughout Scotland. Murison obtained 300 reinforcements from other police forces and contacted W. K. Fraser of the Scottish Home and Health Department with this intelligence. At Dunfermline police station on the Sunday afternoon Murison and Fraser agreed that 400 police officers would be on duty from 5 a.m. on Monday. The power station's manager had told Murison that few of his staff would 'run the gauntlet' of a mass picket for long; Murison and Fraser discussed but rejected the manager's suggestion of using helicopters or boats to bring in specialist personnel, to be accommodated on site for the duration of the dispute without having to pass the picket each day. Murison was worried, however, about the scale of the Longannet site, and suggested using Group 4 security officers to safeguard the perimeter, but Fraser demurred, alluding to the occasionally murderous involvement of detectives in American industrial disputes with the adroit suggestion that 'the employment of private security forces in connection with strikes has unhappy connotations, even although these are mainly drawn from trade union history in the USA'.[85]

It will be remembered that on 14 February the STUC-organised Scottish Assembly, discussed in Chapter 3, was held in Edinburgh, outlining the case for devolved Scottish approaches to economic problems. The parallels between the high politics of the Edinburgh Assembly and the popular protest on the same morning at Longannet, where workers arguably exhibited an equally powerful sense of the importance of Scottish self-determination, should not be over-looked. The Longannet pickets, it should be emphasised, along with a large number of their Scottish officers, including McGahey, were acting in defiance of the UK-wide leadership of the union as well as the UK government. There were 2,000 miners and supporters at the power station by 6 a.m., despite the NUM Executive's directive from London that picketing be scaled down. Three coaches had come from Ayrshire, leaving Drongan at 2.15 a.m. and collecting supporters in Glasgow at 3.15. The *Scottish Miner*'s columnist, The Brusher, boarded one of the coaches at Glasgow and eagerly summarised the pleasures of the journey. 'From the back seat', he wrote, 'it was a pleasant sight to see the football tammies of Rangers, Celtic, Kilmarnock, and Ayr United mingling in a friendly atmosphere.' Half way to Longannet sandwiches 'like hauf loaves' were passed round, with the 'funnies flying fast and furious', most of which would have been 'unsuitable for soft ears. And Mr. Derek Ezra would not have been amused.' The Ayrshire contingent were joined by miners from Lanarkshire and Stirling & Clackmannan who joined their Fife comrades just before SSEB employees began arriving for work at the power station at around 6 a.m. Also present were a number of students, supporters of the miners, including a group from the University of Edinburgh.[86]

What *exactly* happened next is uncertain. The police kept the power station open, although a number of cars containing SSEB employees turned back. Murison's reports to the Scottish Office note the bald facts of arrests, criminal charges, numbers of pickets and his satisfaction that his operation kept the power station running. Press coverage varied. *The Scotsman*'s report was low-key, noting McGahey's complaints about police behaviour, and the probability that unofficial action by SSEB staff – encouraged by Ron Brown and the Edinburgh shop stewards – would not materialise. The *Glasgow Herald* was more expansive, recording the seriousness of the mobbing and rioting charge levied against thirteen pickets, and detailing the clashes and casualties, numbering three police officers, treated in hospital in Dunfermline, and McGahey too. According to the *Scottish Miner* he arrived home that evening with his leg in plaster and a £10 donation to the NUM strike fund from the doctor who treated him, having found time also to speak at the STUC Assembly at the Usher Hall.[87] The regional paper, *The Courier*, used characteristically colourful terms, describing how 'the pickets began to press forward and on several occasions men broke through the dark blue ranks to crowd in front of cars', and carried in full a statement from the SSEB condemning the 'intimidation' of its employees and the 'violent and vicious' behaviour of the pickets.[88]

The mobbing and rioting charges were unmistakably serious. It was alleged that the thirteen 'formed part of a riotous mob of evil disposed persons, acting of a common purpose, did conduct themselves in a violent, riotous and tumultuous manner to the great terror and alarm of the lieges and in breach of the public peace, and did shout, curse and swear, and utter threats of violence, and assault'. A further charge of assaulting six police officers was added before the trial in June.[89] These charges were of much greater severity, and carried significantly higher penalties, than the standard civil disorder of breach of the peace, as Ewen Cameron has shown when scrutinising the occasionally punitive legal treatment of land raiders in the Highlands in the late nineteenth and early twentieth centuries.[90] In the field of industrial relations mobbing and rioting charges were highly unusual, if not 'unknown', as a legal scholar, Peter Wallington, put it, although by 1972 some five decades had passed since the most celebrated – or notorious – case of this kind in an industrial dispute in Scotland. This had involved a group of seventeen striking miners in Ayrshire who, in 1921, as part of a wider pattern of disorder in connection with a national British dispute, compelled workers at a pumphouse at the Houldsworth colliery to abandon their station, resulting in the flooding of the workings.[91] By the early 1970s the mobbing and rioting charge was, in fact, only generally used against sizeable groups or gangs of men engaged in fighting, often on Scotland's new peripheral housing estates or outside pubs.[92]

The fairly specific association of mobbing and rioting with criminal violence in the 1970s must explain a large measure of the Scottish labour movement's revulsion at the charges. The miners and their supporters were further antagonised when, after the thirteen had been held overnight, James Douglas, Procurator Fiscal at Dunfermline Sheriff Court, successfully resisted their bail application. Douglas ordered police to clear 150 miners from outside the court and the accused were taken, handcuffed, to Edinburgh's Saughton prison.[93] McGahey, whose leg injury was the consequence, as he put it, of an 'accidental' kick from a policeman, offered a characteristically Marxist analysis of the position. The mobbing and rioting charges were 'scurrilous' but unsurprising, given the essentially anti-working-class character of laws used to control industrial protests in capitalist society: 'there is no such thing as neutrality in society and the law is not neutral', he advised reporters.[94] Feather and James Jack complained to Gordon Campbell about the arrests and the detention and handcuffing of the pickets, while Alex Eadie at Westminster described the situation as 'explosive',[95] and led a deputation of Scottish mining MPs to the Lord Advocate, Norman Wylie, the UK government's chief law officer in Scotland. Eadie and his colleagues urged Wylie to defuse the situation by obtaining the early release of the accused, which he did, after travelling to Edinburgh and holding meetings on 16 February with James Douglas, representatives of the Crown Office and Fife's Chief Constable, Robert Murison. This expedited matters with unusual rapidity. In normal circumstances the accused men would have been kept in prison on remand for a period of weeks, to allow evidence to be gathered prior to committal for trial. But instead the accused were returned to Dunfermline Sheriff Court only one day later, on 17 February, and granted bail at £20 each.[96] In the narrow High Street a thousand or so miners welcomed the thirteen with the victorious football cry, 'Easy, Easy'.[97] Meanwhile the picketing continued. 'We shall do a Birmingham on them', McGahey is said to have uttered on the night of 14 February, indicating an intention to emulate the Saltley blockade,[98] and a large presence was maintained until the national strike was provisionally settled early on 19 February, as Table 4.1 indicates.

The character of this picketing was further illuminated at the trial of the thirteen, which took place in June, with opening scenes in Dunfermline High Street that were reminiscent of those in February when the miners had first appeared in court. Several hundred miners stood outside, in 'silent vigil in protest', according to McGahey, at the continuance of the charges to trial.[99] Police witnesses, given the gravity of the charge, emphasised the unusually forceful methods being deployed by pickets on 14 February. The most experienced police witnesses were Chief Inspector Ian Walker, aged forty-five, and

Table 4.1 *Picketing at Longannet Power Station, 14–18 February 1972*

Date	Scale	Comments
Monday 14 February	'over' 2,000	thirteen arrests on charge of mobbing and rioting
Tuesday 15 February	2,000	two arrests on charge of breach of peace
Wednesday 16 February	500	'peaceful'; no arrests
Thursday 17 February	2,500	six arrests on charge of breach of peace; two of these charged also with assaulting the police
Friday 18 February	450	'no incidents'

Sources: Flaherty to Hole, 16 and 18 February 1972 and Chief Constable, Fife Constabulary, to Secretary of State for Scotland, 17 February 1972, HH 56/96, NAS.

Sergeant William Beveridge, fifty-one years old, both of Fife Constabulary, who contended that the 'action' that morning had been principally directed by nine NUM officials, including three of the accused, in the centre of the approach road. Beveridge emphasised the malicious atmosphere, pickets shouting 'Sieg Heil' and 'Fascists' in the faces of the police officers. Walker and Beveridge both attributed this sour atmosphere to the presence of men from outside Fife, McGahey and the other 'visitors' seemingly unaware of arrangements that had been agreed by police and local NUM officials, including the floodlighting of the approach road. When these lights were switched on one of McGahey's group shouted through a loudhailer, 'The police have five ——— minutes to put out these ——— lights!'[100] Walker said that the NUM officials, including McGahey, informed the crowd by loudhailer that nobody would enter the power station. At this point Walker, as the senior officer present, read these officials a prepared statement outlining the illegality of this action. Despite this warning, when the first car arrived, between 6 a.m. and 6.30 a.m., an NUM official shouted again, 'No more cars are to be allowed in'. The pickets, twenty deep in places, surged forward and stopped the car. Walker said that he gathered the officials around him a second time and indicated that 'serious consequences' would follow further attempts to block the traffic, but one of the accused, William Simpson, a union official from Cowdenbeath in Fife, immediately stood in front of another car and called to the pickets, 'This one is not going to stop, lads. You stop it.' At this point Walker arrested Simpson.[101]

A lull in the activities of the pickets followed: either cars stopped arriving or continued to pass with less hindrance. An interim report reached the Scottish Office to the effect that eight arrests had been made.[102] In any event, at 7.40 a.m., according to Beveridge, Graham Steel, the NUM's Northern Scottish area secretary and another of the accused, came forward and shouted, 'Come on boys, get into them'. This after Beveridge claimed to have heard Steel say, as many more cars entered Longannet than were turned back, 'We are not getting anywhere here. We shall have to do something.' Beveridge took hold of Steel and said he was being apprehended for 'inciting a mob to riot'. At this Steel struggled and was alleged to have shouted, 'I am being lifted for nothing', causing the pickets to 'swell forward'. Other arrests may have taken place at this point. With another sergeant Beveridge took Steel to Tulliallan, the police college close by, and charged him.[103] After Steel's arrest – or the arrests immediately following – Walker said the trouble ended and the crowd dispersed at roughly 9.30 a.m.

Steel and the pickets had failed in their main objective, with the power station still open. But a number of cars had turned back. Some of the occupants, perhaps, sympathised with the miners, although Beveridge spoke of how they were frightened or 'panicked' by the violence of the pickets.[104] The accused denied that violence or intimidation had taken place. One of them, William Sneddon, an NUM official from Larbert in Stirlingshire, said he was following the legally permissible practice of 'peacefully' persuading the Longannet people not to work: he was 'amazed' by his arrest. Evidence presented by SSEB employees was inconclusive, and may have contributed to the outcome of the trial. Robert Archibald, a twenty-one-year-old conveyor operator at Longannet from Oakley in Fife, was in a car that turned back because the occupants were frightened. Alexander Simpson, a forty-four-year-old mobile plant driver from Milnathort, just north of Kinross, said that on arriving at Longannet he was told by an NUM delegate that, 'These men are angry and I cannot guarantee your safety'. Simpson did not speak of fear or intimidation, but noted simply that he decided in the circumstances not go to work. Three young women employed at the power station, un-named in press reports, were in a car blockaded by the pickets, but 'none of them said she was particularly frightened at the time'.[105]

One of the final witnesses was Bailie John Simpson, brother of the accused William. Bailie Simpson, also of Cowdenbeath, was a teacher, and a former miner and NUM member. As such he was perhaps a partial witness, but having journeyed in life from pithead through union branch to school-house and council office his voice would carry considerable authority in West Fife, and his evidence apparently had a considerable bearing on the outcome of the trial. He had been at Longannet on 14 February with a group of his school pupils, he said, who were undertaking 'a project on strikes'. Bailie Simpson emphasised his experience of industrial conflict and his knowledge of the present temper of miners, and carefully explained that he would not have brought children to Longannet if trouble had been anticipated. Nor, he added, would he have kept them there if significant disorder had in fact materialised, before characterising the charges as 'grossly exaggerated': a 'riotous situation' had certainly not developed and no 'large-scale assaults' on the police had taken place.[106]

The accused were cleared of the charges. On Thursday 15 June Graham Walker, a miner from Ayr, was acquitted, the Procurator Fiscal, James Douglas, admitting that the evidence was insufficient for the charges to be sustained. On Friday 16 June it took the jury just twenty-three minutes to declare innocent, by majority verdict, eleven of the remaining twelve: Steel, Stewart Stobbs and Arnold Courtney, miners from Drongan, Colin Cameron, a socialist activist from Glenrothes in Fife, who was defended by Menzies Campbell, George Mitchell, a post-graduate chemistry student from Strathclyde University, Allan Currie, a miner from St Ninians in Stirlingshire, Alexander Keane and George Lennox, miners from Tullibody in Clackmannanshire, Robert Muir, an apprentice fitter from New Cumnock in Ayrshire, Simpson and Alexander McIlwain, a miner from Auchinleck, also in Ayrshire. The thirteenth, William Sneddon, was cleared unanimously. Victor Feather sent McGahey a telegram, expressing his delight at the verdict and offering 'Congratulations and best wishes to Scottish miners'. Outside the court McGahey said he would be raising with the miners' group of MPs the question of why these charges had been brought, and 'the competence of the men who raised the charges'. Steel complained about the cost of the trial to the NUM and the public purse, and added his question to McGahey's: why had the men been charged in this manner when 'we had a very amicable arrangement with the police'?[107]

Why, indeed? A certain degree of public and political pressure had been exerted in February on the government, mainly from Conservative Party members and supporters, to impel the police to take a tougher line with the pickets and end the blockades at power stations and fuel depots. John Davidson, Director of Information and Research at the Scottish Conservative and Unionist Central Office in Edinburgh, advised Gordon Campbell on the state of party feeling on the strike. Campbell was told of a resolution passed by the North Lanarkshire Conservative and Unionist Association which deplored the 'inaction' of the police at Alloa the previous week, when the NCB building had been picketed, and urged the Secretary of State to issue 'immediate instructions' to the police to prevent a recurrence of an incidence of this kind.[108] On the same issue, but from an entirely different perspective, in Parliament on 9 and 10 February Alex Eadie and Adam Hunter asked Campbell about instructions given to the police in relation to the arrest of pickets. Hunter was particularly concerned about the case of Peter Haggart, a miner from Steelend in Fife, who had been held overnight for an alleged picketing offence at Kincardine power station. Campbell replied that Haggart had been held at the instructions of the Procurator Fiscal and that generally no special instructions had been delivered to police officers, who were 'fully aware of their responsibilities in relation to any industrial dispute'.[109] It seems, perhaps, unlikely that a 'tougher' line had been enforced on Murison, who by the afternoon of 14 February was holding talks with NUM officials about how picketing should be conducted on the following and subsequent days.[110] But Murison and his officers were plainly conscious of the strategic importance of Longannet; they must have felt indirectly the pressure of the anti-strike strands of public opinion and were only too aware of the embarrassment to the authorities generally and the police in particular caused by the closure of Saltley the week before. In this sense no special instructions were necessary. The duty of the police officers was to keep the power station open and their actions, faced subsequently with a large and physically robust body of pickets, were logical, and certainly more logical than the vain attempt by the Procurator Fiscal to sustain the mobbing and rioting charges to trial.

The outcome of the strike

William Sneddon, at the trial of the thirteen, said that the Longannet pickets believed closing the power station would secure more rapid and pronounced victory in the strike, as a settlement – through the Wilberforce Inquiry – seemed to be imminent.[111] Longannet remained open but the picketing, jeopardising a key energy source, surely increased the pressure on the government to reach a quick settlement. Murison advised ministers that 10 per cent of total Scottish policing resources were concentrated on Longannet, and asked whether this was politically justifiable, given the implications for policing elsewhere, with more than 300 officers drawn from Dundee, Edinburgh and Glasgow. Alick Buchanan-Smith, Under Secretary of State at the Scottish Office, replied that Wilberforce's recommendations would be presented within days, implying that these would bring the strike to an immediate end and release the police officers from Longannet.[112] This eventuality materialised early on 19 February, with the conclusion of lengthy negotiations on the basis of Wilberforce's findings.

Wilberforce had gathered oral testimony on 15 and 16 February and written evidence from the NCB and the NUM, which was helped by Hugh Clegg, Professor of Industrial Relations at Oxford University, who had guided the 1968 Donovan Report's emphasis on voluntarism, Michael Meacher, Labour MP for Oldham North, and the Trade Union Research Unit of Ruskin College. The CBI submitted evidence, reproducing warnings about the inflationary implications of the miners' claim – including the likelihood that equally unwarranted claims would follow in other employment sectors – that were made by Campbell Adamson, Director General, on *Panorama* on 14 February.[113] On 18 February Wilberforce recommended a two-component rise: a 'normal periodic increase', adjacent to the government's maximum allowance of 8 per cent, and an 'adjustment factor', of 11–13 per cent, to increase the relative value of miners' wages.[114] Negotiations on these recommendations ensued from 10 a.m. on 18 February to 1 a.m. on 19 February at the Department of Employment and then at 10 Downing Street, and so obliged Heath to postpone a visit from President Pompidou of France that had been scheduled to help smooth Britain's coming membership of the EEC.[115] Heath initially negotiated with Victor Feather and Campbell Adamson, and then, along with Carr and Barber, met the NUM delegation and unsuccessfully encouraged them to accept Wilberforce's recommendations.[116] An improved package – involving 'non-wage benefits', including the methods of bonus payments – was agreed early in the morning of 19 February.[117] In the top-down or high politics accounts of the strike this settlement commonly appears as evidence of the 'left-wing' or 'militant' members of the NUM Executive extracting multiple and even arbitrary 'concessions' from the NCB and the government in order to maximise Heath's humiliation.[118] *The Economist*, very much in this manner, estimated that Wilberforce's terms comprised an extra £85m 'to the bill for coal', with the final settlement amounting to £116–117m, and mournfully observed that the 'moderate Mr Gormley now gives the impression of no longer being the man in charge'.[119]

The NUM executive was, however, operating within considerable practical constraints, obliged to procure terms that its members would accept. Daly told Heath that settling on the terms of Wilberforce alone would leave 50 per cent of the miners remaining on unofficial strike, and even the additional benefits would not prevent 'havoc in their ranks for a week or two', meaning some prolongation of picketing and strikes.[120] Longannet was free of pickets immediately, but some miners remained at Cockenzie on Saturday 19 February, one picketing the power station with a placard alluding to the Prime Minister's sailing hobby: 'We don't WANT a Yacht. We Don't Ask a Lot. Just a Living Wage.' And the sporadic 'havoc' forecast by Daly duly materialised in Scotland with a two-day unofficial strike at pits in West Lothian over the re-employment by the NCB of two men whose NUM membership had been withdrawn when they took other jobs during the strike.[121] These strikes followed a general relaxation of picketing that did materialise on Monday 21 February, allowing power stations to receive coal and oil freely by road and rail. The Cabinet's Official Emergencies Committee was thereby in a position to report, as Scotland's power generation approached pre-strike capacity, that 'Scottish' electricity was again being 'exported' to England.[122] The miners resumed work on Monday 28 February, following a national ballot that ratified the Downing Street agreement by an overwhelming 210,039 votes to 7,581.[123]

The evidence of the popular agency that underpinned the strike baffled Heath, as he admitted in his memoirs,[124] and in seeking to understand the miners' militancy he asked the Secret Service to explore the role of 'subversive organisations'.[125] This was a common enough Tory and business assumption, frequently reproduced in daily and financial newspapers as the chief explanation of industrial conflict. Some months after the strike, for example, *The*

Times carried a lengthy feature by Nigel Lawson, future Tory Energy Secretary and then Chancellor under Thatcher, but at this point a financial journalist and policy adviser for the Conservative Party. Lawson's piece, a top-down analysis characterised by very little insight, purported to dissect the 'Communist influence on industrial strife'. The CPGB was presented as the main agent of strikes generally, with McGahey 'behind' the miners' strike, while the UCS work-in was instigated and driven forward by Jimmy Reid with help from fellow Communists Jimmy Airlie and Sam Barr; the conspiratorial, malevolent and all-pervasive nature of this Communist activity was strongly emphasised.[126] But, at least as far as the miners' strike was concerned, the Secret Service advice to Heath did not support this analysis, revealing little in the way of grand conspiracy. 'For many years', Heath was told, 'the Scottish area [of the NUM] has been under Communist control.' This was a matter of public record, although the word 'control' was an over-statement: McGahey had become a member of the CPGB's National Executive in 1971, and William McLean, Scottish General Secretary, was also openly a Communist. The Communist identities of union officials and members in Yorkshire, South Wales and Kent that the intelligence officers drew attention to were also public knowledge. Nor should it have been a revelation to Heath that the CPGB supported the strike to advance its chief political aim, the defeat of the Conservative government.[127] The intelligence officers at least concluded on one sensible note: the NUM Executive, which contained a sizeable anti-Communist group guided by Gormley, was generally unanimous in its conduct of the strike, and it had not taken its lead from the CPGB.[128]

The evidence reviewed in this chapter shows, indeed, that the NUM executive was not guided in any conspiratorial sense by a group of activists but by the publicly stated requirements of its large body of members. Where the miners' leadership attempted to pull the miners back from militancy, as in Scotland over Longannet, it had been ignored. Dennis Barnes, Permanent Secretary at the Department of Employment, acknowledged this when asked by Heath to comment on the intelligence report. Barnes observed that the miners' militancy rested on broad industrial, social and political foundations. While the eight Communists on the NUM executive were 'wreckers' in the sense of being opposed to the 'existing political system generally', it was a 'reasonable assumption' that the twenty other executive members opposed the government and so were 'wreckers' too. The NUM was, moreover, supported in its aims and tactics by the political and industrial wings of the labour movement: 'what developed was a near wrecking consensus rather than any planned conspiracy'. Key to the formation of this consensus was the Labour party's support, in the country and at Westminster, for the NUM, and Feather's agreement that members of other TUC-affiliated unions should not cross the NUM picket lines. Barnes believed, with some legitimacy, that Feather was persuaded to accept this position by 'left wing' members of the

TUC General Council, especially Jack Jones, General Secretary of the TGWU, who themselves were guided by their increasingly militant members, in the context of rising unemployment and debates about the Industrial Relations Act.[129]

The 'wrecking consensus' identified by Barnes – although ignored by Lawson and others who preferred to emphasise the agency of Communist conspiracy – was perhaps most strongly in place in Scotland. The strike had been sustained by the solidarity of the labour movement in Scotland, which encompassed many species of labourist, social democratic and socialist orientation. The support for the miners – including the direct aid granted by unionised railway workers and lorry drivers, who refused to carry coal – drew upon the mobilisation of organised labour in Scotland that had developed in opposition to the UK government's pay and industrial relations policies of the later 1960s, and which was driven further forward by the UCS campaign from the summer of 1971. At the Edinburgh gathering of the Scottish Assembly on 14 February, the day that Longannet was almost closed by the Scottish NUM, acting against the wishes of the miners' British leadership, the possibility was raised of establishing a Scottish parliament with democratic powers of industrial intervention and public ownership. It will be remembered that James Jack of the STUC stated that this parliament would be 'a workers' parliament'.[130] The strike duly contributed to the further inter-meshing of class and national forces in Scotland, reinforcing the drive towards devolution, and strengthening the leadership by the labour movement – clustered around the STUC – of the campaign for Home Rule.[131]

Yet even in Scotland the 'wrecking consensus' was far from complete. The Assembly encompassed Tory and business voices – McEwen Younger, for instance, and Hamish Grant of the CBI in Scotland – that were opposed to the strike, and there were many other Scottish critics of the NUM. When Norman Wylie, the Lord Advocate, secured the release of the Longannet pickets on bail he was rebuked by a number of Scottish Tories who depicted the strike as a triumph for bullying and undemocratic trade unionism. Gary McLauchlan, a former Tory Parliamentary candidate for West Fife, described Wylie's intervention 'as an example of the Government weakening in the face of an unprecedented campaign of lawlessness by a small minority of people'. Meanwhile the 'Chairman' of the Scottish Conservative Women's Advisory Committee, Lucy Mardon, told a meeting of party activists in Carnoustie that '[what] we are experiencing today is an industrial civil war'. There was, Mardon claimed, 'a concerted effort in trying to overthrow the democratically-elected Government', driven by the 'definite evil elements' who had organised 'the recent picketing at power stations'.[132]

The Scottish daily press, ostensibly 'neutral', also amplified an increasingly vociferous critique of the miners and the labour movement as the strike progressed. The *Glasgow Herald* had made its position on 'violent' picketing clear enough following the incidents at NCB offices late in January. In the final week of the strike the paper was extremely frank about the extent and character of the social conflict that was developing. What was in train was a 'fight to the finish between the mineworkers and the community'; the dispute was no longer about the miners' pay claim but about the state of democracy and the need to resist the bullying minority. This produced a response from Harry McShane, the Marxist-humanist veteran of Red Clydeside, published by the paper, which compared Heath's 'war' on the miners with what he remembered as the fight against the miners and the working class by a previous Tory Prime Minister, Stanley Baldwin, in 1926.[133] Guided, perhaps, by Chris Baur, *The Scotsman*'s characterisation of developments was less intemperate than the *Glasgow Herald*'s, but still identified the existence of an 'industrial war', emphasised the need for 'responsible' trade union leaders to come forward and lower the social temperature, and asked whether the country was being run by the government or the miners.[134]

This relatively mainstream Tory and business criticism of the NUM and picket 'violence' was joined by something qualitatively different, however, with the strike arguably revealing the very strong existence in Scotland of radical conservatism, or what might be termed 'proto-Thatcherism'. Jock Bruce-Gardyne, hammer of the UCS work-in and perhaps the chief Scottish outrider for what became Thatcherite views on economic, industrial and social policy, drew early lessons from the outcome of the strike. This was an expression of labour's intemperate and militant character; it was also an embarrassing capitulation by Heath and his ministers. A government committed to a genuine change of direction would have to 'sit out the long months of its inheritance', he wrote, presciently, in 1974, and wait perhaps over a period of years for the 'consequences' of its 'economic choices' to be seen.[135]

Bruce-Gardyne was not alone in his thinking in Scotland in the early 1970s. To his name could be added Madson Pirie and Douglas Mason, the 'father of the poll tax', and others associated with Conservative students at the University of St Andrews and the Adam Smith Institute.[136] This phenomenon – Scottish radical conservatism – is extremely important and its emergence in the early 1970s represents at least a partial qualification to the model of Scotland's professional elites set out by David McCrone, who emphasises the development from the 1950s of a civic nationalism, neo-corporatist in nature, that dissented from the shift to 'market liberalism' in other parts of the UK from the 1970s.[137] McCrone's 'principled' elites were represented at the Usher Hall Assembly in February 1972, chiefly in the person perhaps of McEwen Younger, but it is important to emphasise that they vied for middle-class leadership with the radical right. This had a far more signif-icant presence in Scotland than is generally acknowledged, and rejected altogether the Assembly's conclusion that existing industrial structures could be preserved, modified and ultimately re-energised through devolved administration of economic management. The radical right lamented the particular position in Scotland, but only because this embodied in a more pronounced form than in the rest of the UK the range of economic and industrial features that it regarded as especially undesirable: publicly subsidised heavy industry, which was highly unionised and labour intensive, and industrial militancy. These were major obstacles to the desired – and related – outcomes of lower labour costs, industrial restructuring and inward investment, which required a determined revolution in economic management from Westminster and Whitehall rather than political devolution in Scotland. This process, Bruce-Gardyne noted, would be significantly assisted by the fundamental economic and political issue in Scotland from 1973 onwards: North Sea Oil.[138]

Notes

1 This account of the rally is based on reports in the NUM Scotland's monthly publication, *Scottish Miner*, December 1971.

2 'One of the Greats has Gone', *The Herald*, 1 February 1999.

3 Marr, *Battle for Scotland*, pp. 132–6, 146–8, 157.

4 Jack Jones, *Union Man: An Autobiography* (London, 1986), p. 242; Benn, *Office Without Power*, pp. 381–2.

5 Wilson, *Labour Government*, p. 493.

6 Tony Hall, *King Coal: Miners, Coal and Britain's Industrial Future* (Harmondsworth, 1981), pp. 165, 168.

7 Andrew Taylor, *The NUM and British Politics: Volume One, 1944–1968* (Aldershot, 2003), pp. 239–44.

8 W. Ashworth, *The History of the British Coal Industry: Volume 5, 1946–1982 – the Nationalised Industry* (Oxford, 1986), pp. 678–9.

9 Toothill, *Scottish Economy*, pp. 29–38, 106–7; Wilson, *Labour Government*, pp. 429–30.

10 Foster, 'Twentieth Century', pp. 476–9.

11 *The Economist*, 12 February 1972, p. 59; Heath, *My Life*, pp. 325–53.

12 Ashworth, *British Coal*, pp. 289–315; Campbell, *Edward Heath*, pp. 406–22; Heath, *My Life*, pp. 325–53; Kevin Jefferys, *Finest and Darkest Hours: The Decisive Events in British Politics from Churchill to Blair* (London, 2002), pp. 162–85; Morgan, *People's Peace*, pp. 325–56; Andrew Taylor, *The NUM and British Politics: Volume Two, 1968–1995* (Aldershot, 2005), pp. vii–viii, 50–72; Margaret Thatcher, *The Path to Power* (London, 1995), pp. 201–22.

13 Darlington and Lyddon, *Glorious Summer*, pp. 31–74; Hall, *King Coal*, pp. 166–96; Malcolm Pitt, *The World on our Backs: The Kent Miners and the 1972 Miners' Strike* (London, 1979).

14 Jim Phillips, 'The 1972 Miners' Strike: Popular Agency and Industrial Politics in Britain', *Contemporary British History*, 20 (2006), 187–207.

15 Ashworth, *British Coal*, p. 306; Heath, *My Life*, p. 353; Morgan, *People's Peace*, pp. 325, 328; Thatcher, *Path to Power*, pp. 215–8.

16 Taylor, *NUM and British Politics: Vol. Two*, pp. 53, 56–72.

17 Andrew Taylor, 'The "Stepping Stones" Programme: Conservative Party Thinking on Trade Unions, 1975–9', *Historical Studies in Industrial Relations*, 11

(2001), 109–25; John McIlroy and Alan Campbell, 'The Tide of Trade Unionism: Mapping Industrial Politics, 1964–79', in McIlroy, Fishman and Campbell, *British Trade Unions*, pp. 93–132; Taylor, *The Trade Union Question*, pp. 147–51; see also Jones, *Union Man*, pp. 246–53.

18 Hobsbawm, *Nations and Nationalism*, p. 10.

19 *Scottish Miner*, January 1968; Murray, *Scotland*, p. 59; some of the biographical information on McGahey here is taken from his obituaries in *The Times*, anonymously written by convention, and *The Guardian*, by Vic Allen, both 1 February 1999.

20 *Glasgow Herald*, 20 November 1968 and 2 December 1968.

21 William Thompson, 'The New Left in Scotland', in Ian MacDougall (ed.), *Essays in Scottish Labour History* (Edinburgh, 1978), pp. 208–9.

22 Thompson, *The Good Old Cause*, p. 134.

23 Taylor, *NUM and British Politics: Vol. One*, p. 238.

24 *Glasgow Herald*, 2 December 1968.

25 'Election, UK President, 1971', William McLean, Secretary, NUM Scotland, to Branch Secretaries and Delegates, 14 June 1971, Acc. 9805.217, National Library of Scotland (hereafter NLS); *Scottish Miner*, May 1971; John McIlroy, 'Notes on the Communist Party', p. 229.

26 Taylor, *NUM and British Politics: Vol. Two*, p. 42.

27 Routledge, *Scargill*, pp. 61–4; Hall, *King Coal*, pp. 149, 153–7; Taylor, *NUM and British Politics: Vol. Two*, pp. 1–48.

28 McLean to Branch Secretaries and Delegates, NUM Scotland, 3 December 1971, with result of ballot on National Strike Action, Acc. 9805.234, NLS.

29 Foster, 'Twentieth Century', pp. 476–8.

30 Ashworth, *British Coal*, pp. 38–9, 678–9.

31 Alan Campbell, *The Scottish Miners, 1874–1939: Volume One, Work, Industry and Community*; *Volume Two, Trade Unions and Politics* (Aldershot, 2000); John McIlroy and Alan Campbell, 'Beyond Betteshanger: Order 1305 in the Scottish Coalfields during the Second World War, Part 1: Politics, Prosecutions and Protest', *Historical Studies in Industrial Relations*, 15 (2003), 27–72, and 'Part 2: The Cardowan Story', *Historical Studies in Industrial Relations*, 16 (2003), 39–80; John Benson, 'Coalowners, Coalminers and Compulsion: Pit Clubs in England, 1860–1880', *Business History*, 44 (2002), 47–60; Roy Church and Quentin Outram, *Strikes and Solidarity: Coalfield Conflict in Britain* (Cambridge, 1998).

32 Martin Adeney and John Lloyd, *The Miners' Strike, 1984–5: Loss Without Limit* (London, 1986), pp. 91–128, 155–76, 257–77; Huw Beynon (ed.), *Digging Deeper: Issues in the Miners' Strike* (London, 1985), especially pp. 1–26; Chris Wrigley, 'The 1984–5 Miners' Strike', in Charlesworth et al., *Atlas of Industrial Unrest*, pp. 217–25; Taylor, *NUM and British Politics: Vol. Two*, pp. 173–280.

33 Ashworth, *British Coal*, pp. 289–301, 304.

34 Taylor, *NUM and British Politics: Vol. Two*, pp. 1–12.

35 *Department of Employment Gazette*, March 1972, p. 337; Hall, *King Coal*, pp. 149–65.

36 Murden, 'Demands for Fair Wages', pp. 15–16.

37 Cabinet Conclusions, 3 February 1972, CAB 128, PRO.

38 Campbell, *Heath*, pp. 412–3.

39 Hall, *King Coal*, pp. 170–2.

40 Reid, *United We Stand*, pp. xv, 307–8.

41 John Saville, 'Arthur Horner', in Joyce Bellamy and John Saville (eds), *Dictionary of Labour Biography: Volume V* (London, 1979), p. 116; Ashworth, *British Coal*, pp. 126–7, 241–2, 306.

42 Thompson and Hart, *UCS, passim.*

43 Carr to Heath, 6 January 1972, LAB 77/84, PRO.

44 Carr to Maudling, 7 January 1972, LAB 77/84, PRO.

45 Sir Dennis Barnes, Minute of Meeting at DTI, 13 January 1972, LAB 77/84, PRO.

46 *Glasgow Herald*, 13 January 1972; see also *The Economist*, 11 December 1971, p. 85 and 8 January 1972, p. 53.

47 J. W. Anderson, DTI Scotland, 4 February 1972, HH 56/95, NAS.

48 By this point the visitors had completed the scoring in a 4–0 victory; see *The Courier & Advertiser*, 7 February 1972.

49 Ashworth, *British Coal*, p. 309.

50 G. Holland, 'Note for the Record', 9 February 1972, LAB 77/84, PRO.

51 Ashworth, *British Coal*, p. 308.

52 Note of meeting between Prime Minister, Secretary of State for Employment and General Secretary, TUC, 15 February 1972, PREM 15/985, PRO.

53 Hall, *King Coal*, pp. 180–1.

54 Pitt, *World on our Backs*, p. 17.

55 A. J. Murray, 'Coal Strike: Effects on the Electricity Industry', 13 January 1972; Electricity Branch, Scottish Development Department (SDD), 'Coal Strike: Electricity Sitrep', 21 January 1972, HH 56/75, NAS.

56 Kelly, SDD, to C. T. Hole, Scottish Office, 13 January 1972; Electricity Branch, SDD, 'Coal Strike. Electricity Sitrep (situation report)', 21 January 1972; A. J. Murray, 'Confidential', to H. Robertson, 24 January 1972; HH 56/75, NAS.

57 'TAM AND HIS MERRY MEN TAKE TO THE SEA', *Scottish Miner*, March 1972; Electricity Branch, SDD, Sitreps, 24 and 27 January 1972, HH 56/95, and W. K. Fraser, 'Miners' Strike: Longannet Power Station', 14 February 1972, HH 56/96, NAS.

58 Darlington and Lyddon, *Glorious Summer*, pp. 40–2.

59 DTI Coal Strike Report, 24 January 1972, HH 56/75, NAS.

60 *The Courier & Advertiser*, 25 January 1972.

61 *Glasgow Herald*, 25 January 1972.

62 *The Scotsman*, 25 January 1972; *The Courier & Advertiser*, 27 January 1972.

63 C. T. Hole, note for the Secretary of State for Scotland for Ministerial Committee on Emergencies, 26 January 1972, HH 56/75, NAS.

64 Darlington and Lyddon, *Glorious Summer*, pp. 53–5.

65 Chief Constable, Lothian and Peebles Constabulary, to Chief Constable, Edinburgh City Police, 15 February, with copy of the Brown/Jeffrey leaflet, HH 56/96, NAS.

66 Flaherty, Scottish Home and Health Department (SHHD), to Hole, Scottish Office (Dover House), 16 February 1972; Chief Constable, Lothian and Peebles Constabulary, to Secretary, SHHD, 16 February 1972; HH 56/96, NAS.

67 Cabinet Conclusions, 10 February 1972, CAB 128, PRO.

68 Darlington and Lyddon, *Glorious Summer*, pp. 56–62; Thatcher, *Path to Power*, p. 218.

69 Routledge, *Scargill*, p. 75; Whitehead, *Writing on the Wall*, pp. 75–6.

70 James Douglas to Robert Carr, 16 February 1972, with enclosures, 'Snap Surveys on the Coal Strike', LAB 77/84, PRO.

71 Department of Employment Press Notice, 11 February 1972, LAB 77/84, PRO.

72 Carr to Heath, 6 January 1972, LAB 77/84, PRO; *The Economist*, 12 February 1972, p. 59.
73 DTI Report, 'Day 37', 15 February 1972, PREM 15/985, PRO.
74 *The Times*, 15 February 1972.
75 Note of meeting between Prime Minister, Secretary of State for Employment and General Secretary, TUC, 15 February 1972, PREM 15/985, PRO.
76 Home Office note on picketing, 16 February 1972, PREM 15/985, PRO.
77 Robert F. Murison, Chief Constable, Fife Constabulary, to James M. Dunlop, Clerk, Fife Police Joint Committee, 17 March 1972, HH 55/1392, and Murison to the Secretary, SHHD, 14 February 1972, HH 56/95, NAS.
78 http://news.bbc.co.uk/1/hi/Scotland/4306818.stm, accessed 4 October 2005.
79 Guthrie Hutton, *Fife – the Mining Kingdom* (Ochiltree, Ayrshire, 1999), pp. 6–8.
80 NUM Scottish Area, Notes on Branch Membership, October 1971, Acc. 9805.235, NLS.
81 South of Scotland Electricity Board, *Longannet Power Station* (London, undated, presumed 1974); copy in COAL 74/2205, PRO.
82 Murray, *Scotland*, p. 38.
83 Kelly to Hole, 13 January 1972, and A. H. M. Mitchell, Note on Energy position, 11 January 1972; both in HH 56/75, NAS.
84 Cabinet Official Emergencies Committee, 14 February 1972, HH 56/97, NAS; DTI, 'Day 36', noting 'Heavy picketing of Longannet Power Station', 14 February 1972, circulated to various Cabinet ministers, PREM 15/985, PRO; Cabinet Conclusions, 17 February 1972, CAB 128, PRO.
85 Murison to Dunlop, 17 March 1972, HH 55/1392; W. K. Fraser, 'Miners' Strike: Longannet Power Station', 14 February 1972, HH 56/96, NAS.
86 *Scottish Miner*, March 1972; Chief Constable, Fife Constabulary, to the Secretary, SHHD, 14 February 1972, HH 56/95, NAS.
87 *The Scotsman* and the *Glasgow Herald*, 15 February 1972; *Scottish Miner*, March 1972.
88 *The Courier & Advertiser*, 15 February 1972.
89 Ibid., 16 February 1972; *Glasgow Herald*, 8 June 1972.
90 Ewen A. Cameron, '"They Will Listen to no Remonstrance": Land Raids and Land Raiders in the Scottish Highlands, 1886 to 1914', *Scottish Economic and Social History*, 17 (1997), 43–64.
91 Campbell, *Scottish Miners: Vol. One*, pp 303–8.
92 Peter Wallington, 'The Case of the Longannet Miners and the Criminal Liability of Pickets', *Industrial Law Journal*, 1 (1972), 223.
93 *The Courier & Advertiser*, 15 February 1972.
94 *Glasgow Herald*, 22 and 23 February 1972.
95 *The Courier & Advertiser*, 16–17 February 1972.
96 Wallington, 'Longannet', pp. 220–1.
97 *The Scotsman*, 17 and 18 February 1972.
98 Duncan Dee, SHHD, 'Miners' Strike: Longannet Power Station, Further Minute', 14 February 1972, HH 56/96, NAS.
99 *The Times*, 7 June 1972.
100 The expletives were denoted with dashes in the *Glasgow Herald*, 8 June 1972.
101 *Glasgow Herald*, 7 and 8 June 1972.
102 Duncan Dee, 'Miners' Strike: Longannet Power Station', 14 February 1972, HH 56/96, NAS.
103 *Glasgow Herald*, 7 June 1972.
104 Ibid.

105 *The Times*, 10 June 1972, *Glasgow Herald*, 8 and 15 June 1972.

106 *Glasgow Herald*, 15 June 1972.

107 Ibid., 17 June 1972.

108 John Davidson to Gordon Campbell, 7 February 1972, HH 56/97, NAS.

109 *Parliamentary Debates, Fifth Series, Commons*, 830, 377, 435–7, 9 and 10 February 1972.

110 Duncan Dee, SHHD, 'Miners' Strike: Longannet Power Station, Further Minute', 14 February 1972, HH 56/96, NAS.

111 *Glasgow Herald*, 15 June 1972.

112 Duncan Dee, SHHD, 'Miners' Strike: Longannet Power Station', 14 February 1972, HH 56/96, and 'Further Minute', 14 February 1972, HH 56/96, NAS.

113 *The Times*, 15 February 1972.

114 Ashworth, *British Coal*, pp. 310–11.

115 Robert Armstrong, note, 21 February 1972, PREM 15/986, PRO.

116 Minute for Record, Prime Minister's 10.20 pm meeting with the NUM, 18 February 1972, LAB 77/84, PRO.

117 Taylor, *NUM and British Politics: Vol. Two*, pp. 71–2.

118 Campbell, *Heath*, pp. 418–9; Heath, *My Life*, p. 383; Morgan, *People's Peace*, pp. 327–8; Routledge, *Scargill*, pp. 80–1.

119 *The Economist*, 12 February 1972, p. 59, and 26 February 1972, pp. 15, 65–72.

120 Minute for the Record, Prime Minister's 10.20 p.m. meeting with the NUM, 18 February 1972, LAB 77/84; Note for the Record: Discussion, 10 Downing Street, Saturday 19 February 1972, PREM 15/986, PRO.

121 *Glasgow Herald*, 21 February 1972; *The Times*, 1 and 2 March 1972.

122 Cabinet Official Emergencies Committee, 21 February 1972, HH 56/97, NAS.

123 Telegram from Gormley, Schofield and Daly to McLean, 25 February 1972, Acc. 9805.235, NLS.

124 Heath, *My Life*, p. 350

125 Note by Robert Armstrong, 25 February 1972, PREM 15/986, PRO.

126 Nigel Lawson, 'Communist Influence on Industrial Strife: Assessing a Danger in Britain's Trade Union Movement', *The Times*, 24 May 1972.

127 McIlroy, 'Communist Party', pp. 228–9; Pitt, *World on our Backs*, pp. 90–1.

128 Secret Service, 'Influence of Subversive Organisations in the NUM and the Miners' Strike', 24 February 1972, PREM 15/986, PRO.

129 Sir Dennis Barnes to Robert Armstrong, 8 March 1972, PREM 15/986, PRO.

130 *The Scotsman*, 15 February 1972; *Glasgow Herald*, 15 February 1972.

131 Foster, 'Twentieth Century', pp. 477–8.

132 *The Courier & Advertiser*, 17 February 1972.

133 *Glasgow Herald*, 14, 16 and 17 February 1972.

134 *The Scotsman*, 11 January 1972 and 16 February 1972.

135 Bruce-Gardyne, *Quiet Revolution*, pp. 84–5.

136 Obituary of Douglas Mason, by Alex Singleton, *The Guardian*, 16 December 2004.

137 McCrone, 'Towards a Principled Elite', pp. 190–5.

138 Jock Bruce-Gardyne, *Scotland to 1980* (London, 1975), pp. 6–7, 54–5, 59–72.

5 Oil: the 'failed' road to devolution, 1973–79

'Oil has added a new dimension to British politics', recorded *The Economist* in July 1975. 'It has turned an increasing number of Scots against the British connection. Whether they will end it remains to be seen. In the meantime oil has brought the certainty of an assembly in Edinburgh.'[1] The author of these words was *The Economist*'s Scotland correspondent, Andrew Neil, then establishing his reputation as a business journalist with a pungent line in anti-statism, anti-socialism and indeed anti-nationalism. Neil was summarising what became and remains the fairly standard view of North Sea Oil, which was first piped onshore in the course of 1973. This, the familiar part of the story about industrial development and devolution, is that oil was the major economic factor – and indeed possibly the most important single factor of any kind – in advancing the case for Home Rule in Scotland. The extent of oil's abundance in UK offshore waters became clear in 1973 and 1974: by 1980 the UK would be self-sufficient and in the process of becoming a major net exporter. This transformed potentially the economic prospects of Scotland, within the historic territories of which it was often commonly understood that the bulk of the oil resources were located. This shifted the debate about Scotland's constitutional position, opening up the possibility of complete independence, with arguments about the economic 'viability' of a sovereign Scotland considerably strengthened by the added factor of oil. The SNP duly enjoyed major success in the general elections of February and October 1974, taking seven and then eleven seats in the House of Commons. The UK Labour Party, back in office under Harold Wilson, although with only a slender majority of five after the second of the 1974 elections, was obliged to respond to this Nationalist surge in two ways: managing oil in such a way that Scotland was seen to enjoy a particular share of its benefits; and legislating for a devolved Assembly that would meet some of the demands for Home Rule without breaking the Union of 1707, and hence preserving, it should be emphasised, the benefits to the UK Exchequer of the oil resource. This was consistent with internal Scottish trade union support for Home Rule since the late 1960s, short of 'separation', as Michael McGahey of the NUM characterised independence, although the move towards devolution was hampered by the arch-unionism of some Labour activists and officials in Scotland. In this connection class and national imperatives continued to overlap. Class interests and tensions certainly continued to inform at some level trade union and business approaches to Home Rule, seen as a possible means of alleviating in part the social and economic problems of industrial change. But class politics were also invoked by Labour opponents of devolution in Scotland, who emphasised instead the desirability of seeking the distribution of material resources in the interests of working people through the existing 'economic unity' of the UK.

In this chapter the impact of oil on devolution is discussed, encompassing the initial promise of the North Sea in 1973 together with the longer-running oil and devolutionary politics down to 1979, culminating in the referendum on the Labour government's Home Rule plans and the collapse subsequently of the Labour government, to which the SNP contributed in significant part. The broad received wisdom that oil 'advanced' devolution is accepted, although the emphasis here is on how oil tended to bring forward rather than actually initiate developments that – as the first four chapters of this book have demonstrated – had been in progress since the early 1960s and were well underway by the winter of 1971–72, with the UCS campaign, the miners' strike and the landmark Assembly in Edinburgh on 14 February 1972. The 'political' events from 1973 onwards – the SNP's by-election triumph at Govan in November 1973, the Labour government's handling of oil from 1974 and devolutionary legislation between 1975 and 1978, and the referendum of March 1979 – are presented as the products of these established economic and industrial forces. It is, for example, no coincidence that the particular safe Labour seat that fell to the SNP in 1973 was Govan, the centre along with Clydebank of the UCS work-in, and where so recently nationalist impulses had blurred with class and industrial politics to mobilise popular worries about the remote nature of economic and political power.

In supporting the broad thesis that oil advanced devolution, this chapter also takes little issue with the other standard view of the North Sea's political legacy, that of the 'wasted windfall', the central theme of Christopher Harvie's account.[2] The opportunity clearly was not taken in the UK to build an investment fund on oil revenues for the regeneration of economic and social infrastructure, as was broadly the case in Norway, the other major European beneficiary of the North Sea's riches. Instead revenues were dissipated, initially by the 1970–74 Tory and 1974–79 Labour governments and then even more so by Thatcher's Conservative governments, the monies expended on tax cuts and the maintenance of those cast adrift from employment during the economic and industrial restructuring that accelerated after

1979. This chapter notes – perhaps more directly than Harvie – how the 'wasted windfall' and the process of industrial change were very closely linked, with oil in fact tending to eliminate rather than promote employment in manufacturing. As John Foster and George Peden have separately observed, with the on-streaming of oil to the point of British self-sufficiency, sterling became a 'petro-currency', boosted greatly in relative value in international currency markets, and damaging those manufacturing jobs that were contingent on exports.[3]

The potential problem of oil-driven rapid economic restructuring was anticipated from an early date. Jock Bruce-Gardyne, who saw an opportunity to trim what he saw as the bullying and strangling power of trade unionism in Scotland, forecast in 1975 that oil would tilt the balance of the Scottish economy eastwards, away from Clydeside and heavy industry towards lighter industry, supplying the North Sea, and financial and other services.[4] Andrew Neil's view in 1975 was similar, although he worried that the Labour government would squander the possibilities of oil through the counter-productive direction of oil-related finance and initiatives to the allegedly 'inefficient' and union-controlled industrial districts of Clydeside.[5] Oil's impact on the currency – and the likely damage to manufacturing exports – was also predicted in the SNP, by Douglas Crawford, MP for Perth and Perthshire, at the party's conference in May 1975. Crawford's prediction was unpopular in the SNP, but Harvie suggests that it was not ignored, hinting that it influenced the less aggressive Nationalist campaigning on 'Scotland's Oil' in the second half of the 1970s.[6]

Within the apparatus of the UK government ideas about the potential paradox of oil were also circulating, summarised by Gavin McCrone, in a paper written for the Scottish Office's Economic Planning Department in February 1974, just before the general election that unseated Heath's Conservative government. This was released under the Freedom of Information Act in the autumn of 2005, after a request by the SNP's industrial spokesperson, Kenny MacAskill, who claimed that the UK government had buried McCrone's paper because it demonstrated that 'booming oil revenues' from the North Sea had made Scottish independence 'not only theoretically possibly but economically desirable'.[7] This was an accurate characterisation of some aspects of the McCrone paper, but MacAskill – who did not reprise Crawford's 1975 prediction either – said nothing about its important warning that a Scottish pound would appreciate in value, possibly attaining within two years of independence an exchange rate of '£1 Scots to 120p sterling', with the result that Scottish 'manufactured exports would be priced out of foreign markets and imports would become highly competitive at home'.[8] This paradox – that oil would undermine rather than regenerate established Scottish industrial enterprise – was perhaps the main economic legacy of the North Sea in Scotland. So the extent to which oil made Scottish independence more 'viable' in economic terms might be questioned, in the sense that it checked Scotland's potential as a major centre of indigenous and profitable productive enterprise, and would possibly have done so whatever the constitutional position. Yet in accelerating the process of industrial change, and exacerbating the already pronounced popular anxieties about remote administration and the related sense of human powerlessness, oil continued to keep Home Rule on the political agenda after 1979.

1973 and the promise of oil

Oil was central to economic development and fortunes across the globe in the second half of the twentieth century and continues to be so in the twenty-first. Cheap oil drove the long 'golden age' of economic growth; sudden price spikes – the consequence essentially of Arab-Israeli conflict – in 1973 and 1979 contributed to major slowdowns in all industrial economies and in the mid-2000s rising and then prolonged high prices revived anxieties, particularly in the west, about economic prospects.[9] Yet despite its core economic importance, oil has to a very large extent been hidden in the writing of Britain's recent political history. It seldom features in the memoirs and the biographies of the politicians who governed its development in the North Sea. An obvious example is the standard biography of Edward Heath, written by the University of Edinburgh-educated John Campbell, the index of which contains no references at all to the North Sea, and includes no discussion of Heath's involvement – in opposition or government – in debates about Scottish devolution.[10] Harvie points out that the Pimlott and Ziegler biographies of Harold Wilson ignore the North Sea altogether, despite the fact that the vital terms of state intervention and participation in oil production were established during his final stint in office from 1974 to 1976.[11] Morgan's biography of Wilson's successor in 1976, James Callaghan, acknowledges the issue, but only briefly. It notes that by the summer of 1977 the UK was on course for oil self-sufficiency by 1980, and then establishes that the Cabinet discussed the best way of utilising this major windfall from November 1977 to February 1978, before deciding – fatally, some might say – that oil revenues be incorporated in mainstream Treasury accounts instead of being ring-fenced, as Tony Benn, the Energy Secretary, recommended, for dedicated industrial and social development purposes.[12] Denis Healey, the Chancellor of the Exchequer who helped to block Benn on this issue, is only a little more forthcoming, noting the beneficial impact of oil on the UK balance of payments, and relating developments in the North Sea to the politics of devolution and nationalism in Scotland.[13] But most telling of all, according to Harvie, is Margaret Thatcher's memoir. The wife of an oil executive, whose governing strategy was contingent on oil revenues and the strengthening of sterling that arose from Britain's position as an oil exporter, she managed to write up her *Downing Street Years* with only four fleeting references to the North Sea.[14]

Harvie observes that Scottish politicians, by comparison, have had far more to say about oil and oil politics than the metropolitan elites roughly represented by Healey and the four Prime Ministers and/or their biographers.[15] Journalists and academics in Scotland have also, perhaps, been more open on this subject: Frank Frazer of *The Scotsman* merits mention here, along with Alex Kemp, the Schlumberger Professor of Petroleum Economics at the University of Aberdeen in the 2000s, engaged in writing the 'official' history of North Sea Oil. The greater profile of the North Sea in research conducted and literature produced in Scotland is, of course, related to the more central position of oil in Scottish politics from 1973 onwards, when, after seven or eight years of speculative exploration and development, the first output from the North Sea came on shore amid much political and media publicity. 'Striking it rich', ran a headline in *The Economist* that January, framing a lengthy feature that opened with the words, 'Scotland's Texas is taking shape'. At this point roughly 5,000 Scots enjoyed oil-related employment. Growth was particularly marked in the north-east, in and around Aberdeen and Peterhead especially, on the Cromarty Firth in the Highlands, and in Lerwick, capital of the Shetland Islands. The UK government reportedly predicted in 1973 that 7,500 additional jobs would be directly created in Scotland as a consequence of oil over the next five years; there were, meanwhile, a range of estimates about related or secondary employment, in services and industries supplying the North Sea. The North East Scotland Development Authority optimistically forecast a multiplier of one to one, but at this point economists at the University of Aberdeen reckoned on a lower ratio, forecasting the creation of roughly 17,000 new jobs in total by 1978.[16] This turned out to be a significant under-estimate, with oil-related jobs eventually increasing to some 58,000 by 1980.[17] This greatly exceeded in concrete terms the great hopes of the SCDI's *Oceanspan*, which made promising but ambiguous noises about the 'spin-offs' from the ore and cargo terminals and the steel works, but offered only a peak additional labour force of 10,000. Hence the SCDI was quick to encompass the North Sea in its thinking, publishing in October 1973 a new survey, *A Future for Scotland*, written by a committee chaired by Professor Ronald Nicoll of the University of Strathclyde's Urban and Regional Planning Department, with a preface by Clydesmuir. This reprised the essence of *Oceanspan*, emphasising once more the value of the conjunction at Hunterston of deep water and flat land, but now arguing that the central west-to-east corridor should be supplemented by growth within a 'new axis' from south-west to north-east, stretching up from Ayr through the central belt and along the east coast to Aberdeen.[18]

Nicoll and his committee were entirely optimistic about the direct economic impact of oil on Scotland's economy. Big operating companies would spend money on Scottish goods and thereby inflate employment; by the mid-1980s production in the North Sea would match oil consumption in the UK, so helping to 'eliminate' the balance of payments deficit and allowing for more economic growth. This prognosis ignored the impact on manufacturing exports as the relative value of sterling appreciated on the basis of revenues accruing to the UK government from North Sea operators.[19] The same optimism characterised George Murray's survey for Roy Thomson's Scottish Television (STV) in 1973, which depicted oil as the potential 'catalyst' for *Oceanspan*, with Hunterston perhaps hosting an oil refinery, and Aberdeen adjusting 'overnight' to its status as 'fledgling Houston of the north'. Murray presented this shift as unproblematic, for Aberdeen, Scotland and the UK as a whole, with the revenues plus savings in foreign exchange transforming the balance of payments position without any reported or potential difficulty for industrial production.[20]

These three business surveys in 1973 – from *The Economist*, the SCDI, and Murray for STV – all engaged with the politics as well as the economics of the North Sea. These politics were broadly defined, of course, by the SNP's 'It's Scotland's Oil' campaign, launched in March 1973.[21] The SCDI restated its attachment to devolution: centralised UK policy-making did not suit Scotland's needs, with industrial development tending to cluster around the seats of political power. A proposed 'powerful new Scottish executive agency' for industrial development, steered by an anticipated legislative Assembly, would operate on the basis of authority delegated by the UK Parliament, and the UK government would 'retain full reserve and supervisory controls'. There was no suggestion here that revenues from the North Sea would be diverted to Scotland.[22] After the SNP's success in the 1974 elections *The Economist* would become more emphatic in its denunciation of Scotland's 'claim' on the North Sea; in 1973 it briefly referred to the allegedly short-sighted aspirations of Scottish Nationalists, who were 'anxious' about immediately accessing revenue from oil instead of spotting the real potential benefit of equipping Scottish industry so that over the longer-term it could operate as a supplier of equipment to the offshore industry across the world.[23] Murray, meanwhile, was adamant that North Sea Oil was 'not Scotland's oil'; it would be 'dangerous' – presumably for the integrity of the United Kingdom – for revenues to be 'directly returned to the regions of origin'.[24]

Licensing arrangements for exploration and production – including the terms of the exploitation of gas, an additional significant North Sea resource – had been negotiated between the UK government and major oil firms from the mid-1960s, at first, tentatively, by Wilson's Labour administration, and then, in larger volume, by Heath's Tory administration. Prior to the Tory *Oceanspan* lunch of January 1972, it will be remembered, Heath was warned by his party's Scottish Chairman, McEwen Younger, about the political dangers in Scotland for the government were it to mishandle oil. 'I believe it is no exaggeration', McEwen Younger wrote, 'to say that if the Government permits North Sea Oil to be treated as a purely extractive industry, with no more than temporary benefit to North East Scotland, and very little benefit elsewhere in Scotland, and if the scale of public investment in Scotland is not substantially influenced by these circumstances, the consequences for the Tory party in Scotland will be disastrous.'[25] This is, in fact, more or less how oil was developed, and the result for the Tories was indeed disastrous, if not fully felt until the 1990s.

The manner in which Heath's government had given away this non-replenishable resource was exposed in the March 1973 report of the House of Commons Public Accounts Committee (PAC), chaired by Harold Lever, Wilson's Financial Secretary to the Treasury from 1967 to 1969 and then Paymaster General until 1970.[26] The PAC made two criticisms of the government's offshore policy. First, the tax regime was too liberal, allowing companies to offset losses in other trading areas against North Sea profits, a position that had benefited Shell and BP especially. Second, the terms under which companies were licensed to explore and exploit the North Sea were too generous. The PAC recommended two changes: North Sea profits should be isolated from other group activities for tax purposes, with tax yield to be further increased with a special revenue measure, such as a barrelage tax; and all future licenses should secure the Exchequer a greater share of the overall 'take'. In the budget speech that followed just a few days later Anthony Barber, Chancellor of the Exchequer, accepted the logic of the PAC criticisms, promising legislation in the following Parliamentary session that would effectively require North Sea profits to be isolated from other group activities for tax purposes. Richard Crossman, writing in *The Times*, rejoiced that 'the North Sea oil scandal' – with the DTI under the Tories 'deliberately concealing the vast profits it has conceded to the oil companies' – was now 'finally admitted to be true'.[27]

Yet the Westminster debate, while focusing on the UK Exchequer's take, still excluded the 'Scotland's oil' argument. This largely explains the growing success of the SNP. An early marker here was the Dundee East by-election in March 1973, where Labour retained the seat but with its majority more than halved to just over a thousand. Gordon Wilson, the SNP's candidate and future leader, attributed his strong showing to the 'rising tide' of national feeling in Scotland, 'topped up by the current oil issue'.[28] More remarkable still, of course, was the SNP's successful by-election campaign eight months later at Govan, with electors asked whether they preferred the projected status of 'rich Scots' – attainable through independence – over their alleged existing status of 'poor Britons'. Summoning the phrase 'poor Britons' in 1973 was important, encouraging Scots to reflect on the central 'Home Rule' economic lesson from the Toothill era through to the UCS episode, that Scotland was ill served by UK macro-economic management. This had recurrently choked off

Scottish development through counter-inflationary controls designed to temper over-expansion in the high growth regions of central and southern England. To this established concern in Scotland the SNP added oil, which undoubtedly provided great momentum to the party's advance, with the debate about the North Sea tax regime strengthening the argument that Whitehall and Westminster were negligent in protecting Scotland's economic interests. Importantly, this debate also helped the SNP by drawing attention to the possibility of expanded public revenue through a strengthened fiscal regime. Scottish control of this enhanced regime, the SNP could argue, would secure both improved social services and lower taxes.[29]

The Govan by-election was one of four held on 8 November 1973, the others being Edinburgh North, held by Alex Fletcher for the Tories from Labour, with William Wolfe in third place for the SNP, Hove, also held by the Tories, and Berwick-upon-Tweed, taken by Alan Beith for the Liberals from the Tories.[30] Six days earlier *The Times*' John Chartres confidently predicted a Labour win in Glasgow: the 'cloth cap', he wrote, was 'likely to fit Govan again'.[31] But Tony Benn, visiting Govan the previous weekend, encountered a hopeless Labour campaign, saw the impact of oil, and privately forecast a Labour defeat.[32] Chartres was aware of these aspects too, juxtaposing the vigour and glamour of the SNP candidate, Margo MacDonald, with the relentlessly forbidding character – as he saw it – of the constituency's derelict post-industrial landscape. MacDonald was 'the most attractive thing to look at during a grim autumn day in Govan', and the simplicity of her message, that 'all Scotland's and Govan's troubles could be overcome if Scotland had all the profits from North Sea oil', was infinitely more direct and appealing than the low-key campaigning of the Labour candidate, the 'bachelor hairdresser' Harry Selby.[33] On a 51.7 per cent poll MacDonald's majority was in fact numerically slight: she took 6,360 votes, just 571 more than Selby's 5,789,[34] and in the subsequent general election, just less than four months later, Labour regained the seat. But the result was nevertheless significant, suggesting at least a partial weakening of Labour's electoral and political domination of industrial Scotland. MacDonald's predecessor as MP for Govan was arguably an archetypal Clydeside Labour man, John Rankin. Born in 1890, Rankin joined the Labour Party in 1915, first became an MP in Attlee's 1945 landslide, and represented Govan from 1955 until his death in October 1973. He was, perhaps, one of the 'wee hard men' – Christopher Harvie's ambivalent phrase – who dominated Scottish labour politics after 1945.[35] His long life of public service through the Co-operative movement and the Labour Party assisted, arguably, in raising the living standards of his constituents, but the deprivation and squalor that Chartres observed in Govan could equally be presented as substance to the Nationalist argument that Labour in Scotland and the UK – particularly in the 1960s, under the Wilson governments – had been unable to transform the quality of life in older traditional areas.[36]

The outcome of Govan had been further encouraged by two immediate developments: the impact of the first great oil price spike of the 1970s, and the report of the Commission on the Constitution established by Wilson in 1969. The oil spike followed the Yom Kippur War that began on 6 October, with Israeli forces confronting Egyptian forces on the Suez frontier and Palestinian and Syrian troops to the north. The Israeli army could not repeat its rapid six-day victory of 1967, and it might even have been defeated had the US government not airlifted in a significant supply of arms. The war placed the conservative Arab states of Saudi Arabia and Kuwait in a dilemma: neutrality would encourage Israel but intervention would stimulate Arab militancy, weakening the grip of conservatives in the Arab world. The comp-romise, proposed by the Organisation of Petroleum Exporting Countries (OPEC) cartel, was to use oil as an instrument of diplomacy. Embargoes were placed against the United States and the Netherlands, Israel's closest western supporters; production was cut by 10 per cent; and all countries were subjected to an immediate four-fold price increase.[37] This added immensely to the longer-term potential value of North Sea Oil as an energy source that would not be exposed to the uncertainties of the Middle East conflict, and as a commodity that was rapidly appreciating in market value it represented an even more attractive revenue asset for any government – including, potentially, an independent Scottish government – that controlled it.[38]

The Commission on the Constitution reported on 31 October,[39] eight days before Govan, and further contributed to Home Rule momentum, although its two Chairmen, initially Lord Crowther and then, after his death, Lord Kilbrandon, were both strongly opposed to Scottish nationalism and independence. This was suggested to Henry Drucker and Gordon Brown by their sceptical and sometimes hostile questioning of Nationalist witnesses, and the Commission's conclusions themselves, which offered a type of devolutionary rather than independent settlement for Scotland that would protect the position of the Labour and Tory parties.[40] The Commission proposed a Scottish Assembly, possibly termed a 'Convention', a Scottish Cabinet and Prime Minister. The Assembly and Cabinet would control mainly those matters that had been under the jurisdiction of the Scottish Office, and so the position of the Secretary of State for Scotland would 'disappear', although Scotland – and Wales, for which there were parallel devolutionary arrangements in the offing – would have their interests represented by another member of the UK Cabinet. It was further proposed that the number of Scottish MPs at Westminster be reduced from seventy-two to fifty-nine.[41] But the intended boost to the Labour and Tory parties was not forthcoming, chiefly because of the oft-noted paradox that activists of these parties in Scotland – particularly, perhaps, those in Labour – were much less enthusiastic about the idea of devolution than their leaders in London.[42] This clearly reflected the weight in the Labour Party of the centralised unionist tradition passed down from the Tom Johnston years.[43] It owed something also, perhaps, to anti-Communism, with Home Rule opposed by some Labour figures in Scotland, apparently, because of its association with McGahey and other Communists.[44] These various currents were duly encapsulated in Labour's generous gift to the SNP, a pamphlet published on the very eve of the Commission's report, and so just a fortnight before Govan, 'Scotland and the UK', outlining its total opposition to devolution.[45] With MacDonald and the SNP talking about the importance of implementing Kilbrandon as soon as possible, as a significant step towards independence, a Labour Party official in Scotland had conceded further ground by telling the press that the Commission's report 'was totally unacceptable'.[46]

Energy and devolutionist-cum-nationalist politics continued to predominate, in Scotland and the UK, throughout the winter of 1973–74, which was punctuated also by the re-emergence of conflict in the coal industry, with the resulting national dispute leading to the 'Who Governs?' general election of February 1974. The coal dispute was caused, as in 1972, by wages and the position of miners' earnings in relation to those of other manual workers. In the inflationary environment of 1972 manual wages, particularly in manufacturing, had increased at twice the rate anticipated by the Wilberforce committee when it contributed to the settlement of the national coal strike earlier that year, in February. These inflationary and wage movements thus negated Wilberforce's attempted improvement of the miners' relative position. Heath and his government spent much of the autumn of 1972 trying to negotiate an agreement on counter-inflationary pay, price and profit measures with the TUC, but this was rendered difficult by the Prime Minister's insistence on retaining the Industrial Relations Act, the source of much industrial unrest in 1971 and 1972. Unable to come to terms with the TUC, Heath instead declared a statutory freeze on wages and prices, to operate in three stages: Stage 1 was an immediate three-month stop on wage and price movements; Stage 2, to run from January until November 1973, would allow a maximum increase of 4 per cent plus £1 extra per week; and Stage 3 would run for a further year from November 1973, on lines that would not be finalised and published until October of that year.[47]

The coal dispute of 1973–74 was directly the result of this conjunction of statutory pay policy and the miners' further relative earnings decline in 1972–73, but it was also the consequence of the shift in energy politics arising from the Yom Kippur war and the OPEC spike. This transformed the market position of the miners, and the government's attempts to construct Stage 3 of the wages policy to accommodate a significant portion of their aspirations were unsuccessful. The NCB offered the NUM a 7 per cent increase on 10 October 1973. This was refused. Towards the end of November, it might be noted, *The Economist* suggested that a cash offer of 13 per cent would probably resolve the dispute, but no significant advance on the basic 7 per cent was offered.[48] Various minor amendments were tried, involving bathing and unsocial hours or overtime payments, and direct contacts between ministers and union officials were stepped up, but no progress was made. Events ensued: on 25 October the NUM instituted an overtime ban; on 13 November the government declared a State of Emergency, largely to try to intimidate the miners into settling, and the press was reporting the possibility of an early general election; on 13 December Heath declared a three-day industrial working week, to conserve dwindling energy stocks as the overtime ban began to operate; on 9 January 1974 representatives of the TUC General Council – anxious, perhaps, to avoid a general election being fought on the issue of union power – advised the government that any offer to the NUM outwith the terms of Stage 3 would not be invoked by other unions in pursuit of their wage claims, but this was rejected, the government, advisedly perhaps, doubting the TUC's capacity to enforce the offer; and finally, on 31 January and 1 February, the NUM held a ballot on the question of strike action. This resulted in an overwhelming majority – 81 per cent of votes cast – for strike action, which commenced on 9 February.[49]

As with the strike of 1972 the written accounts of the 1973–74 dispute, by journalists, historians and government protagonists, including Heath, tend to emphasise the top-down nature of events, and the particular influence of 'militant' leadership at the top of the NUM. This is sometimes linked to the major shift between March 1973, when roughly 63 per cent of union members voted against a strike over Stage 2 of the incomes policy, and February 1974, with the massive endorsement of strike action against Stage 3. In this connection the meeting at Downing Street on 28 November 1973 between ministers and the union's executive, arranged to discuss the pay claim, is often cited. It was here that Michael McGahey, who had been elected to the position of NUM Vice-President at the union's annual conference that July,[50] apparently told Heath that he wished to see the demise of the Tory government. Heath and others subsequently took this to represent a measure of McGahey's ambition to drive the Tories from office by the illegitimate means of industrial action.[51] McGahey later insisted that he was referring to his hopes for a future general election,[52] yet in any case – as in 1972 – the 1973–74 dispute was generated not by the conspiratorial scheming of miners' leaders but by the anger and drive of the miners themselves, whose switch in sentiment in the course of 1973 can readily be explained by their further falling behind in pay relativities, and the apprehension that this position of disadvantage was especially iniquitous given the post-OPEC spike shift in energy politics. Why, it was commonly being asked, would the government not pay the miners more for coal in the same way that it was being required, after October 1973, to pay OPEC suppliers more for oil?[53]

In these developments Scottish miners played an important hand. The strike ballot in March 1973, for example, was the outcome of a process initiated at a delegate conference of Scottish miners in January, which unanimously supported industrial action in support of the union's pay claim.[54] In December 1973 Ronald Faux of *The Times* found that support for the overtime ban at Seafield, the largest of Fife's seven collieries, was stiffened by the progressive loss of employment in the industry and the deaths of seven miners at the pit in an accident earlier in the year, a scorching reminder of the arduous and dangerous nature of mining.[55] But anger was evident across the coalfields, and even in some of the more 'moderate' English regions, as *The Economist*'s correspondent discovered in the midlands, shortly before McGahey's exchange of views in Downing Street with Heath. Local union officials, 'moderate' in outlook, sensed their members moving towards 'militancy', disgusted by news of higher wages in adjacent industry. With the NUM looking for £40 a week for general underground workers, and £45 for those covered by the National Power Loading Agreement, Chrysler was offering a basic weekly sum of £52 for assembly workers and £45 'to sweep floors'. Miners were even leaving the pits to take jobs in shoe manufacturing, hitherto derided as '"women's work"'.[56]

While rooted in the same general issue as 1972, and clearly grounded in the same kind and degree of popular sentiment in the coalfields, the 1974 strike was conducted differently. This was the result of Heath finally deciding, on 7 February, two days before the start of the strike, to call a general election for 28 February. NUM members and supporters, including in Scotland, generally adhered to the pragmatic policy of limited picketing, without the mass pressure on coal stocks and power stations that had won the strike in 1972, but at the cost of generating the type of anti-union feeling which Heath and the Tories were seeking to cultivate with the 'Who Governs?' approach to the electorate. The general election's outcome was extremely close: Labour won the largest number of seats, but without an overall majority, and for a day or two Heath attempted to retain power, unsuccessfully negotiating the terms of a possible coalition with the Liberal leadership before resigning. Wilson took office, and his Secretary of State for Employment, Michael Foot, quickly brokered a settlement of the coal dispute on more generous terms than those permitted under Heath's Stage 3, but which were rationalised as allowing a restoration of the miners' relative position, and establishing a co-operative relationship between the new government and the NUM. Wilson then worked towards a second general election, held that October, which produced a narrow majority of five for his government.[57]

These marginal UK results were partly the consequence of developments in Scotland, where Labour had significantly fallen back: the loss of Govan proved to be no blip. In February the party took just 36.6 per cent of the votes in Scotland, down from 44.5 per cent in 1970; Govan was retaken, but there were now forty Labour MPs, four less than in 1970. One seat was gained in October, but with a marginally lower share – 36.3 per cent – of the vote. The Tories, meanwhile, moved down in both elections, to just 24.7 per cent of the vote and sixteen MPs in October. The losses of both parties reflected, of course, the emergence of the SNP, which carried forward the momentum from Govan, the continuing prominence of energy politics in the winter of 1973–74, and the ongoing constitutional debate. It secured seven MPs and polled 22.5 per cent of the votes in February, and in October gathered eleven MPs and 30.7 per cent of the votes. Most of these victories were from the Tories, but the SNP came second in thirty constituencies and so clearly threatened Labour also.[58] Looking at these results a few years later, Drucker and Brown recorded the significance, inevitably, of oil and Kilbrandon, but also noted the importance of underlying economic and social forces. Scotland's economic, social and political composition had shifted, they wrote, since the early 1960s,[59] amid the adjustments in industrial structure and the movements in industrial politics that have been examined in this book. One symptom of this shift, perhaps, was the further articulation of business support for nationalism, with the second Sir Hugh Fraser, chairman of the House of Fraser, joining the SNP after the February general election, and campaigning for the party in advance of the October general election.[60] In the years after 1974 the UK government was obliged to respond to these forces, in the first instance through the management of oil politics, and then through the development of devolved political structures.

The politics of oil, 1974–75

While cars, steel, ships and coal – the industrial essence of this book's opening four chapters – have slipped away from public and political debate in Scotland, if not quite completely in the case of ships, the politics of oil and the North Sea have remained live and contentious. In the autumn of 2005 and the winter that followed there was a vigorous debate – conducted through the Scottish Parliament, the daily press and other media – about the manner in which the UK government had managed the resource in the 1970s. Looking back, the SNP, and Margo MacDonald, now an independent Member of the Scottish Parliament (MSP) for the Lothians, argued that Wilson's Labour administration had 'deceived' Scots about the true value of oil in order to constrain electoral support for independence. This would have secured for Scotland a much greater share of the benefits of oil, generating increased living standards, substantially improved public services at lower cost to tax payers, and significant economic and industrial restructuring, with a renewed manufacturing base as well as enhanced financial services.[61]

The Nationalist position in 2005–06 was based on a reading of selected papers released in government files, partly under the Freedom of Information

Act, and partly through the normal operation of the 'Thirty Years Rule'. The central piece of evidence produced was the 'secret' memo written early in 1974 by Gavin McCrone, which conceded an economic 'case' for Scottish independence on the basis of the revenues from the North Sea. The significance of this was twofold. First, McCrone was an important figure within Scottish economic policy-making. He had been appointed to the Scottish Select Committee of MPs in 1969 as an 'expert adviser', and was interviewed by the Commission on the Constitution – the only Scottish witness not attached to a government department or particular party or interest group – in May 1970. Second, in this 'expert' capacity in 1969–70 McCrone had supported legislative devolution, to provide a 'democratic forum' for the management of regional policy, but not independence, which he saw as risky from an economic perspective. He was worried about the low rate of economic growth in Scotland and the possibility of a substantial Scottish trade deficit; he also believed that there existed in Scotland a public expenditure deficit, which made it likely that an independent Scottish government – shorn of Whitehall subventions – would be obliged to cut public spending, including on unemployment and other welfare benefits.[62]

So McCrone's change of tack in 1974, adopting a more receptive position on the positive economic case for independence, is important. It seemed for some Scottish Nationalists in 2005–06, including Sir Sean Connery, who discussed the matter on the BBC Radio 4 *Today* programme on 30 January 2006, to add to the sense that Scotland had been cheated by Wilson's government. This sentiment was further developed with the appearance of Treasury papers that included a discussion early in 1975 of the possibility of the government delaying devolution legislation in order to preserve full control over the North Sea and its revenues. The SNP industry spokesman in 2005–06, Kenny MacAskill, presented these documentary fragments as evidence of the perfidious nature of Wilson's UK Labour government, and the basis for the subsequent 'diddling' of Scotland by successive UK governments. 'The fact', he said, '[that] everyone across the whole of Scotland would have been 25 to 30 per cent better off every year since the 1970s is a scandal and shows Scotland has been robbed of billions.'[63]

There were, however, three important shortcomings in the Nationalist argument in 2005–06. Each of these reflected the complexities of oil politics and are worth examining in some detail: the question of how far the UK government accepted the McCrone analysis; the impact of oil on the wider economy, including the manufacturing industry; and the extent to which the 'true value' of oil was really hidden. First, there are plain dangers in taking any single voice, extracted in isolation from the reams of papers in government archives, as representative of broad opinion within the UK state bureaucracy. The discussions about economic development in the 1960s, examined in Chapter 1, illustrate all too well, for example, that in the cultivation of UK policy the Scottish Office was subservient to the Board of Trade/DTI and the Treasury. There might have been some sympathy in the Scottish Office for McCrone's adjusted position in 1974. Peregrine Worsthorne, visiting Edinburgh in 1977 for the *Sunday Telegraph*, found officials at St Andrew's House broadly supportive of devolution, and talking without sensation or anxiety about independence, although they did not openly support it.[64] This reinforces Douglas Young's earlier assertion, in 1972, that most Scottish Office bureaucrats were 'quasi-nationalists' with some kind of commitment to 'self-government'.[65] But the thinking of Scottish Office personnel, whether inclined to devolution or independence, was likely to have been outweighed by alternative views in the UK bureaucracy, and these encompassed a very assertive position that oil was definitely *not* a Scottish but a British resource. This being the case the question of whether oil made Scottish independence 'viable' was immaterial.

The second important issue overlooked by Nationalists is the likelihood that the rapid industrial restructuring arising from the on streaming of North Sea Oil in an independent Scotland would have come with considerable social costs. This was forecast by McCrone in sections of his 1974 memo that Nationalists chose not to publicise in 2005–06. McCrone predicted that with no change to the constitutional position manufacturing industry would be damaged by UK sterling's new status as an oil currency. An independent Scotland would make this matter worse: a Scottish pound would appreciate quickly, attaining the value perhaps of £1.20 sterling within two years of independence, and Scottish manufacturing exports would become comparatively less competitive. The consequent loss of manufacturing trade, he added, would accelerate the shrinkage of established industrial sectors.[66] This, essentially, was the position acknowledged in 1975 by Douglas Crawford, to the annoyance of many of his SNP colleagues, and perhaps contributed to a slight downgrading thereafter of the party's emphasis on 'Scotland's Oil'.[67] Jock Bruce-Gardyne envisaged similar restructuring, although he did so with relish, looking forward to the demise of the labour-intensive and allegedly union-dominated manufacturing industries of Clydeside especially.[68]

In 1973, of course, there had been the opposite hope, that oil would regenerate older manufacturing capacity. Signs of this were evident at Clydebank, where, in February 1973, the new owners of the former John Brown's and UCS yards, Marathon, pronounced themselves highly satisfied with progress on the construction of drilling platforms for use in the North Sea. Wayne Harbin, the firm's Chief Executive, told the DTI's man in Glasgow, James Darragh, that work being conducted on the first platform was of the 'highest order'. This view was shared by Marathon's customer, Penrod Drilling Company,[69] another American firm which was set to operate in the North Sea. The Penrod Drilling vessel was launched in September 1973, at which point 1,800 men were employed in the Marathon yard, and other oil-rig orders were in sight.[70] In 1974 three rigs were built at Clydebank, but this was only a fraction of the total of 119 produced around the world that year and, in Harvie's terms, matters did not improve thereafter.[71] Nevertheless, Marathon maintained its presence at Clydebank until the end of 1979, kept in business in 1976 with a government subsidy to construct a drilling rig for the state-owned British National Oil Corporation, which is discussed later in this chapter.[72] These additional six years of employment at Clydebank were valuable, and by 1978 economists at the University of Aberdeen, led by Professors Donald MacKay and M. Gaskin, in a study undertaken for the Scottish Office's Economic Planning Department, were able to point to considerable economic benefits to Scotland as a whole from the development phase of the North Sea. These arose from increased employment, incomes and industrial production, although were presented as short-term relief rather than long-term solutions to the 'problem of building a more efficient and prosperous economy'. The traditional industries were not, in fact, experiencing regeneration,[73] and would move from stagnation to steep decline after 1979 as the petro-currency effect became more acute.[74] It is difficult to see how this position could have been averted in an independent Scotland.

The third issue raised by the Nationalists' discussion in 2005–06 was the question of oil's true value, obscured, it was alleged, by the UK government in 1974. Alf Young, a Labour Party researcher in the 1970s, looked at this argument in his business column in *The Herald* in February 2006, emphasising McCrone's anxiety about the appreciation of the exchange rate 'to the obvious detriment of its [Scotland's] traditional exporting industries', before moving on to the 'real issue'. There had never been any doubt, Young wrote, about the immense riches of the North Sea: the question had been how this wealth should be utilised. The 'unionist left', with which Young of course identified, and which in Scotland was best represented in the mid-1970s by Gordon Brown and Robin Cook, respectively editor of and contributor to the famed *Red Paper on Scotland*,[75] had believed that it should be used to tackle poverty, extracting wealth from the oil multi-nationals to 'transform the lives of working class people, wherever they happened to be in the UK'. Class, Young concluded, had still been the main political contingency in Scotland and the UK in the mid-1970s; the SNP had not altered this and so had failed to 'break down' the UK.[76]

Young's analysis might be disputed, above all on the basis that it ignored the 'wasted windfall' problem, that successive UK governments from the 1960s to the 1980s, including Labour in the 1970s, squandered the oil. Harvie's comparison with the situation in Norway remains apposite: the resource from the North Sea's eastern shore was managed with an emphasis on slower development and depletion, and oil revenues were set aside in a dedicated fund for industrial diversification and social investment. Such a programme could have offset some of the damage inflicted on traditional industry by the oil-driven appreciation of the currency,[77] and such a programme could, of course, have been adopted in an independent Scotland, although in itself this would not have 'saved' Scottish shipbuilding and its older established engineering industries. Yet there was nothing particularly deceptive or underhand – as the Nationalists claimed in 2005–06 – in the 1974 Labour government's approach. In the event of a Labour victory at a general election in 1978 or 1979 it is possible that the oil revenues might have contributed indirectly to steadier management of the process of industrial adjustment, without the sharp rise in unemployment and the damaging industrial conflicts that characterised Thatcherite economic management in the 1980s.[78] The Labour government was certainly open about the prize that oil represented, producing a White Paper on the North Sea in July 1974 that emphasised its very rich potential resources,[79] and did not particularly obstruct the path to Home Rule, producing a discussion paper in June and then in September a full White Paper with initial proposals for devolution in Scotland and Wales.[80] The government also – and here, again, Young is approximately right – attempted to manage oil on social democratic principles, if not quite on class lines, seeking and securing a much expanded state revenue 'take' that fed into a broadly redistributive social policy. This stemmed from the 'Social Contract' between the Labour Party and the TUC that was designed to minimise wage inflationary pressures through the provision of subsidised goods and services, including fuel, food and housing.[81]

Labour's oil policy was, of course, shaped with Scottish electoral considerations in mind. This was evident in a number of ways, including the location in Glasgow of the headquarters of the state-owned British National Oil Corporation (BNOC). But outweighing the Scottish question was the government's dependence on US capital for exploration, development and extraction. If it was not, in fact, Scotland's Oil, then neither was it quite Britain's Oil, with major oil corporations pushing hard to minimise the ground they were obliged to concede to the new government from 1974 onwards. The White Paper of July 1974 outlined a policy of state participation in the North Sea, and a strengthened tax regime. 'We are not talking about confiscation; we are talking about negotiating a share of interests', said Eric Varley, the Energy Secretary.[82] The government's share was to be exercised through BNOC, which eventually began trading in January 1976. This was criticised by Andrew Neil, who noted with some justification that BNOC's Glasgow location was designed to shore up Labour's precarious position in west-central Scotland and outmanoeuvre the SNP: from a business perspective Aberdeen – or elsewhere on the east coast – would have provided more suitable headquarters.[83] The White Paper also promised a Scottish Development Agency (SDA), responsible to the Secretary of State for Scotland, to assume control, essentially, of regional policy, and answer the various criticisms – outlined in Chapters 1 and 2 of this book – that had been articulated over time about the remote administration of industrial development in Scotland from Whitehall. The SDA, set up in 1975, would receive powers in three areas: industrial investment, the establishment of publicly owned factories, and the clearance of derelict land for economic development; in 1977 it acquired the responsibility of promoting inward investment, in which capacity it partly superseded the SCDI.[84] Meanwhile BNOC concentrated initially on negotiating shares in existing oil finds with the major corporations, before playing an important longer term role in shaping new licenses, which were issued on the condition that it received an option to acquire ownership of a stated proportion of oil or profits after paying a share in exploration and development costs.

These plans for government participation were placed on a statutory footing in 1975 with the Petroleum and Submarine Pipelines Act, which was resisted by the majors, with US firms, supported by their government, particularly aggressive in their opposition. In June 1975 Varley switched Cabinet positions with Tony Benn, Industry Secretary. This was seen as a repudiation by Wilson of the socialist planning and radical wealth redistribution agenda with which Benn was associated, chiefly through his Industry Bill that included proposals for the potential nationalisation of 'profitable manufacturing industries'.[85] In his new office in August Benn met the US Ambassador, Elliot Richardson, to discuss the Petroleum and Submarine Pipelines Bill. Richardson complained about two matters: the extent of exploratory work being required and the implied slowing of development, and the question of whether pressure was being placed on US firms to use more British equipment. Both of these were central worries in Scotland, with concern – articulated by the SNP – about the danger of a rapid process of extraction that would exhaust reserves within fifteen years,[86] and lingering dissatisfaction within the DTI in Scotland about the special arrangements secured by Marathon in 1972 that allowed the firm to bring oil-rig construction materials to Clydebank from the USA without paying import duty.[87] 'It was a friendly discussion', Benn wrote of his meeting with Richardson, 'but having the American Ambassador come to me on behalf of the oil companies was a tremendous and vivid reminder of the power of the American Government and its prime concern – namely to defend its own giant multinationals'. He likened this 'warning shot across my bows – and across the Government's bows' to the type of US intervention in Latin American countries where governments – most notably, of course, Victor Allende's socialist administration in Chile that had been deposed with US assistance on 11 September 1973 – conflicted with 'American international commercial policy'.[88]

After participation the second plank of the government's oil policy, increasing government revenue in line with the 1973 PAC recommendations, was secured through two measures: ring-fencing North Sea operations to prevent producers from evading corporation tax by offsetting general international losses against British tax liability; and introducing a dedicated additional tax on North Sea profits, the Petroleum Revenue Tax. The details of the new tax were developed in the winter of 1974–75, and announced in the budget debate of February 1975. It was fixed at a rate of 45 per cent, which most oil businesses and the Conservative opposition accepted as 'realistic'. When set alongside royalties and corporation tax it would still allow a 20 per cent return on North Sea investment, which suggested to the Labour left in Parliament that the government had been drawn into the attempted 'appeasement' of the 'international oil industry'.[89] This reflected the government's reliance on the majors for development and extraction, and the strong hand consequently that the majors held in negotiations with the Department of Energy and BNOC in the course of 1976 and 1977 over the terms of state participation. These agreements ensured that by the beginning of 1977 the North Sea was moving decisively from the exploration and development phase to production; by 1980 self-sufficiency was indeed achieved. It was at this point, with monies rolling in from the North Sea, that the government, early in 1978, took the decision outlined earlier in this chapter, to absorb oil revenues into the general public expenditure, with no separate fund for capital investment. This was rationalised in terms of the supposed impracticality of ring-fencing oil from general revenue, and the observation that it would be wrong for the level of investment in particular projects to be determined by the volume of oil revenues.[90] But here, in any event, was a very significant staging post in the wasting of the oil windfall,[91] which remains a persuasive component, it should be acknowledged, of the Scottish Nationalist argument about the lost opportunities of the North Sea in the 1970s and subsequently. But oil, it should be reiterated, would not have saved heavy industry; and nor had the UK government deceived the Scottish people about its value or held back from Home Rule in order to safeguard the spoils of the North Sea for the UK. Where devolution foundered, as the following paragraphs indicate, it did so on the basis largely of internal Scottish opposition.

The politics of devolution, 1975–79

The first oil from the Forties Field was landed at Aberdeen on Monday 3 November 1975. The occasion was marked by an elaborate ceremony at the Dyce headquarters of the state-owned BP, attended by the Prime Minister, the Foreign Secretary, the Energy Secretary, the BP top brass, the Queen and the Duke of Edinburgh. Behind a fence, Benn recorded in his diary, there 'were about 500 Aberdonians waving Union Jacks, and the Queen and the Duke of Edinburgh walked in front of them as if they were animals in a zoo'. The situation, to Benn, seemed to represent the worst expression of class-ridden industrial politics that the Labour government was consolidating instead of challenging:

> All the old big-wigs are brought out into the open as if they were somehow
> responsible for a great industrial achievement, while the workers are presented as
> natives and barbarians who can be greeted but have to be kept at a distance. It is
> a disgrace that a Labour Government should allow this to continue. I know there
> is a security problem but there was no need for this. I also felt that this great
> Scottish occasion was just an opportunity for the London establishment to come
> up and lord it over the Scots.[92]

Benn's position here was shaped in the first instance by his class view of
politics, although his strong family links with Scotland must surely also have
been significant: his English father, William Wedgwood Benn, was the non-
coalition Liberal MP for Leith from 1918; his mother, Margaret Holmes, was
the daughter of Daniel Turner Holmes, another Liberal, who won a by-
election in Govan in 1911.[93] In any event Benn's sensitivity to the Scottish
question – recently heightened through his involvement in the UCS episode –
can also be seen in his participation in discussions of the Cabinet's Devolution
Committee. At Chequers on 16 June 1975 Denis Healey and Roy Jenkins,
Home Secretary until he became President of the European Commission in
1976, spoke against moving too quickly, lest devolution encourage
'separatism'. But this position was vigorously challenged by Willie Ross, who
remained Scottish Secretary of State until Wilson's resignation in March 1976,
when the new Prime Minister, James Callaghan, replaced him with Bruce
Millan. At Chequers in June 1975 Ross observed that support for independence would in fact be readily stimulated by an absence of devolutionary
progress, and Benn agreed, although he saw the issue partly also in terms of
the centralisation of governance, with the UK possessing one of the last
'colonial' administrations in the world.[94]

The combined Healey and Jenkins view – to slow down devolution, to
balk separatism, and entrench UK control of oil revenues – is consistent with
the Nationalist argument, expressed in 2005–06, that Scotland's progress to
independence was blocked chiefly by the resistance of the UK government. But
this overlooks a central feature of the politics of devolution from 1974,
namely the extent to which the project was actually being driven forward by
the Labour Party in the UK in the face of opposition from the Labour Party
in Scotland. The arch-unionism of the Labour Party in Scotland had been
signalled by its evidence to the Commission on the Constitution, presented by
representatives of the party's Scottish Council just before the 1970 general
election. They had argued that legislative devolution would have a 'divisive
effect' on the UK, and, when pressed, admitted a preference for Tory rule
within an unreconstructed UK to Labour or socialist governance of a separate
Scotland. 'It is essential', one of the representatives, J. D. Pollock, claimed, 'to
maintain the kind of system in which a Labour Government at Westminster
in the future is able to control the country in the interests of all the people in
the UK'. Where constitutional changes were desirable, according to Scottish

Labour in 1970, was in the sphere of local government, with 'larger and more powerful local authorities' seen as the means of securing significant economic and social improvement.[95] This was an allusion to the recommendations of the 1969 Royal Commission on Local Government in Scotland, which favoured the establishment of the seven regional councils that eventually came into force in 1974–75, and which operated as a substantial disincentive to devolution for many in the Labour Party in Scotland, particularly those with an interest in serving in expanded local authorities with powers on regional development, planning and transport that might have been curtailed by a Scottish Parliament.[96]

Opposition within Scottish Labour to devolution had been further articulated in its response – 'totally unacceptable' – to Kilbrandon's report in October 1973, just before the Govan by-election, and was then given infamous expression on 22 June 1974, when the executive of the Scottish Council of the Labour Party met to discuss the government's initial discussion paper on devolution. Only eleven of the executive's twenty-nine members were present, the meeting coinciding with Scotland's World Cup football match in West Germany against Yugoslavia. A vote of six to five was cast against each of the various alternatives proposed in the government paper, the opponents of devolution rationalising their position in terms of the potential Assembly's absence of control of economic development, including North Sea Oil, and its imposition between the new Regional Councils and the 'major legislature' at Westminster.[97] This decision was effectively annulled on 26 June by the UK Labour Party's National Executive, under the guidance of Alex Kitson of the TGWU and Judith Hart, MP for North Lanark, which ordered an emergency conference of the Labour Party in Scotland, scheduled for Glasgow on 16 August. In the interim period, with Wilson readying his party for another general election, a MORI private poll for Labour indicated that it would lose thirteen Scottish seats to the SNP if no steps towards devolution were taken. This, according to Drucker and Brown, 'persuaded' the Scottish party to make amends for 22 June, and the emergency conference recommended the institution of a legislative Assembly 'within the context of the political and economic integrity of the UK'.[98]

This prepared the ground for the White Paper, *Democracy and Devolution*, published in September on the day that the second general election of 1974 was called. The White Paper committed the government to a scheme encompassing legislative devolution, but also signalled the 'tactical blunder', perpetuated in the further White Paper that followed in November 1975, *Our Changing Democracy*, that would set the project of devolution back by roughly two years by bringing together in one package measures for Welsh as well as Scottish constitutional reform.[99] There was admittedly some logic in approaching the matter in this manner, for there were clear parallels between Scotland and Wales. Across the 1960s and into the 1970s similar economic and industrial processes were certainly evident. There was the same emphasis in Wales as in Scotland on the importance of regionally planned industrial diversification, and in Wales this was also accompanied by worries about the dangers of remote administration arising both from Whitehall-shaped economic policy and inward investment. There was too the suggestion of cultural difficulties associated with the shift from craft and bespoke production to standardised assembly. Of the traditional industries steel remained fairly buoyant in Wales, although this was balanced by the rapid contraction of the mining industry in South Wales. This was reflected – perhaps even more than in Scotland – in an increased degree of militancy among the miners, evident in the support among Welsh miners for McGahey in the 1972 NUM presidential election that was discussed in Chapter 4.[100]

In Wales there was also support from within the labour movement for legislative devolution, with the Wales TUC supporting the Royal Commission on the Constitution's recommendation of an Assembly in Cardiff as well as in Edinburgh. But, for a variety of cultural and political as well as economic and industrial reasons, the support for legislative devolution was not so pronounced in Wales as in Scotland,[101] and this may explain why the government felt tempted to 'smuggle' the Welsh measure through Parliament along with the Scottish measure. The much greater embeddedness of Welsh people and organisations in English institutions extended to the labour movement. This was partly the result of the integration of northern Wales and southern Wales into different cross-border regional economies, which undermined to some extent pan-Welsh labour solidarity and bolstered suspicion that devolution might harbour separatist tendencies.[102] Hence the Wales TUC was established only in 1974, and in the face of some considerable circumspection among many Welsh trade unionists, particularly in the north,[103] and in the course of the 1974–79 Parliament it became clear that opposition to devolution was even more strongly felt in the Welsh than the Scottish Labour Party.[104]

The question of economic power was at the heart of this opposition, in Scotland as in Wales. Support for devolution was essentially created by economic and industrial problems, yet the Labour government's eventual proposals made little provision for the transfer of economic responsibilities from Whitehall and Westminster to Edinburgh and Cardiff. The SDA, along with the Welsh Development Agency, came into operation in July 1975. The November 1975 White Paper, *Our Changing Democracy*, indicated that these agencies would not be accountable to the new Assemblies, but would remain the province of the Secretaries of State for Scotland and Wales, answerable to Westminster. It will be remembered that the Commission on the Constitution proposed the abolition of these Secretaries of State, but the government now planned to retain them, consolidating their powers of 'economic planning and industrial steering and participation'.[105] This indicated very strongly the prospect of the management of 'regional' economic policies in Scotland and

Wales that would be shaped in Whitehall without meaningful reference to the devolved Assemblies. The STUC General Council criticised these arrangements, noting that to be effective the Assembly would have to control the SDA and economic planning, and suggested that with his enhanced powers, which would be unaccountable in Scotland, the Secretary of State would be a 'Governor General type figure'.[106] This narrowing of the scope of Home Rule, according to Drucker and Brown, was the consequence of Whitehall civil servants capturing the devolutionary process from October 1974 onwards, dominating the agenda of the Prime Minister's Constitution Unit.[107] These democratically narrowed arrangements were incorporated in the Scotland and Wales Bill of 1976. Labour enthusiasts for devolution were duly discouraged, and it was in this period that some of their number established the Scottish Labour Party, including two MPs, Jim Sillars and John Robertson of Paisley.[108] Labour sceptics – keen on preserving the economic unity of Britain from the perspective of class solidarity – were strengthened in their view that devolution was an irrelevance; and the Nationalist case for independence was apparently enhanced. By the spring of 1977, with the Scotland and Wales Bill defeated and abandoned, the SNP's opinion poll rating had risen to 36 per cent.[109]

The SNP's arguments about the economic and financial weaknesses of the UK were amply served, of course, by the crisis of the late summer and autumn of 1976. After protracted currency difficulties, prompted by escalating price inflation and resulting in a large-scale flight from sterling, the UK Treasury was compelled to obtain a loan from the International Monetary Fund, which came at a price. The government's social spending commitments were significantly cut, effectively bringing the Social Contract with the trade unions to an end. This included also the effective ending of Labour's commitment to industrial democracy, a component of the Social Contract, and endorsed in January 1977 by the majority report of a government-appointed Committee of Inquiry. But anxious about the scale of business opposition to this committee's recommendation of worker directors on the boards of companies with 2,000 or more employees, the government eventually brought forward – sixteen months later – proposals for a much-diluted form of workers' participation in management, although no legislation was forthcoming.[110] Meanwhile the emphasis in economic management on controlling inflation stimulated a distinct rise in unemployment.[111] Joblessness reached a new post-1945 peak in the UK in January 1977 of 6.1 per cent, but in Scotland it was 7.4 per cent and rising faster than in Britain as a whole.[112] Industrial unrest would follow, sporadically across 1977 and then, fatally for the government, in 1978–79, as rigid counter-inflationary controls on wage movements were attempted by ministers and resisted by workers, particularly in the public sector. In Scotland the subsequent increase in industrial insecurity was exemplified in the escalating losses of Govan Shipbuilders on the Upper Clyde and Scott-Lithgow's on the Lower Clyde. These yards were incorporated into the government's rescue of the industry through nationalisation, with British Shipbuilders established in 1977.[113] This was an extension, perhaps, of the political attempt to preserve employment elsewhere in traditional industrial areas, including the Clyde. The Marathon yard at Clydebank, it will be remembered, was kept alive in 1976 when the government bankrolled the construction of a drilling rig for BNOC.[114]

To Nationalist critics of the government these economic and industrial insecurities highlighted the deficiencies of Whitehall and Westminster management. The controls on pay movements, meanwhile, and the very suggestion implied in wage controls that workers' pay was a significant cause of poor economic performance, were sharply criticised by the STUC, which pressed for further public enterprise as an antidote to the 'real' source of the economic crisis, namely long-term capital under-investment from within the private sector.[115] But, perhaps paradoxically, while promoting calls for enhanced devolutionary mechanisms, and indeed support for independence, these problems and insecurities also constrained support for the government's actual Home Rule proposals, particularly within the Labour Party and especially the Parliamentary Labour Party. This was because of the ameliorative efforts being made by the government to maintain and develop economic activity in Scotland. These seemed to re-emphasise the value of the economic unity of the UK. Alongside the rescue of shipbuilding through nationalisation, the government and its supporters could point to cars. At the Linwood plant, where more than 6,000 were still employed, industrial relations remained problematic and highly adversarial in the mid-1970s,[116] and the factory itself was in grave danger, along with the rest of Chrysler's UK operations. But these were safeguarded by a government subsidy of £162 million early in 1976, and Linwood was kept in business.[117] The government was also putting into operation its *Plan for Coal*, prepared in the summer and autumn of 1974, which seemed to offer a long-term opportunity for mining and the 20,000 or so miners in Scotland, arresting the decline of the industry that had contributed to the major industrial disputes of the Heath years.[118] Meanwhile the SDA was up and running, along with BNOC, which started operating at the beginning of 1976, and the view that Labour in the UK was helping to stabilise Scotland in the face of industrial flux and social difficulty was further supported in 1976 with the establishment of the Glasgow Eastern Area Renewal project. This involved the expenditure of central government money – a reported £120 million – on a variety of economic and social amenities, including advance factory units, with support from the SDA and the new Secretary of State for Scotland, Bruce Millan.[119]

These initiatives probably supported Labour's rally in the polls towards the end of 1977 and into 1978, when the party won by-elections in April in Glasgow Garscadden, taken by Donald Dewar, and in May in Hamilton, the scene of Winnie Ewing's triumph in 1967, with George Robertson comfortably defeating Margo MacDonald, the victor at Govan in 1973.[120] Further evidence of Labour's apparent electoral health followed in October 1978, with John Home Robertson's victory at the by-election in Berwick and East Lothian that followed the death of John Mackintosh in July. The SNP had high hopes here, given Mackintosh's strong advocacy of Home Rule, but it finished a distant third with a lost deposit.[121] Dewar and Robertson, it might be noted, were on the losing pro-devolution side at the Labour Party meeting in Glasgow on 22 June 1974, and Dewar in particular now helped to lead the campaign for Home Rule.[122] The government had published separate Scotland and Wales Bills in November 1977. To meet criticisms mounted against the previous combined Scotland and Wales Bills, including from the Labour benches, and notably, of course, from Tam Dalyell, MP for West Lothian, who saw devolution as inevitably leading to undesirable 'separatist' ends, these included provision for referenda, where the electorates would be asked whether the legislation, once enacted, should be put into force. Labour anti-devolutionists exploited this aspect of the legislation. On 25 January 1978, Burns Night, as Vernon Bognador and Tom Devine both point out, George Cunningham, a Scot, and Labour MP for Islington South and Finsbury, inserted by amendment the fatal '40 per cent' proviso into the Scotland Bill: if less than 40 per cent of the total electorate voted 'Yes' to devolution in the referendum then the Secretary of State for Scotland would be obliged to place an Order in Council before the Parliament inviting members to vote for the repeal of the Scotland Act. The same proviso was attached to the Wales Bill.[123]

The government, and Labour devolutionist MPs, including Dennis Canavan, sought to reverse or even modify this position: there was talk of 40 per cent being revised down to 35 or 33 per cent, but no changes to the Cunningham amendment resulted. On 14 February representatives of the STUC General Council met Michael Foot, now Leader of the House of Commons, and John Smith, Minister of State at the Privy Council Office, who were responsible for piloting the devolution legislation. The trade unionists bemoaned the 40 per cent clause as a complete and unwarranted departure from the normal conduct of ballots by simple majorities of voters in the UK, but in spite of this disappointment, and its continued misgivings about the narrow scope of devolution, the STUC resolved at its annual gathering in Aberdeen in April 1978 to put its full support behind the 'Yes' vote at the coming referendum.[124]

1979: the 'debâcle'?

The outcome of the referenda in Wales and Scotland on the devolution legislation, held on 1 March 1979, is well known. In Wales 11.8 per cent of the electorate voted 'Yes', 46.5 per cent voted 'No', and 41.7 per cent did not vote; in Scotland 32.5 per cent voted 'Yes', 30.4 per cent 'No' and 37.1 per cent did not vote.[125] This result is normally presented in the literature on modern Scotland as an unambiguous defeat for devolution: Tom Devine writes of a 'debâcle', for instance, and Richard Finlay depicts a 'fiasco'.[126] It might be possible, however, to think about the result in different terms, as a victory of sorts, in fact, for the process of devolution. For what should be emphasised is that the Scottish majority of votes for 'Yes' was recorded in highly unpropitious political circumstances. Each of the main parties – Labour, Tory, Liberals and the SNP – was in a significant way divided on the issue. The 'Labour Says Yes' campaign, for instance, was hampered by the 'Labour Vote No' group, guided by Dalyell along with two future Labour ministers, Robin Cook and Brian Wilson. Some Tories and Liberals joined Labour folk in a cross-party 'Alliance for Assembly', and the 'Yes' campaign was supported by social democratic-leaning SNP figures, but the Nationalists' 'reactionaries' – this is the Drucker and Brown characterisation – were less involved, encapsulating the awkward position facing sincere advocates of independence when presented with a measure that was explicitly designed as a bulwark against 'separatism'.[127]

In revising the 'debâcle' interpretation of the referendum, it should also be noted that there may be some doubts about the integrity of the result, revolving around the accuracy of the electoral register, which was vital, given the 40 per cent proviso. The register records persons legally eligible rather than those who in practical terms are able to vote. Vernon Bognador notes that the government discounted about 90,000 voters from the Scottish register prior to the referendum, but sees this as a significant under-estimate of those who were not in a position to vote because they were sick, incapacitated, in hospital and so on. He suggests that as many as an additional 500,000 could have been discounted, in which case the 40 per cent target would have been reduced from 1,498,845 to 1,284,754, only 31,252 more than the number of Yes votes recorded in the referendum. Had such a narrow result materialised, Bognador adds, then it is highly likely that the measure would not have 'failed' at all, for Parliament might well have voted against the repeal order lain before it by the Secretary of State for Scotland. The devolution legislation would therefore have remained on the statue book.[128]

In these circumstances – with an ambiguous or at least an 'inconclusive' outcome, as James Mitchell puts it,[129] combined with the absence of clear political leadership – the Yes vote was a fairly impressive expression of support for devolution. Some of the credit here perhaps belongs to the STUC, the position of which was united, and consistent with its approach to the constitutional question since 1968. Business thinking on Home Rule, by comparison, remained ambivalent. After the February 1974 general election the SCDI had revived and even extended its devolutionary campaigning to political matters, developing the position set out in the 1973 *Future for Scotland* report. Further administrative and economic autonomy, through transferring the Department of Energy and other industrial agencies to Scotland, was to be strengthened by a Scottish 'assembly with discretionary control of taxation'. This would create 'a secondary centre of industrial, political and administrative power' to 'break the present London monopoly'.[130] Such might be interpreted as an attempt – like *Oceanspan* early in 1970 – to place free enterprise brakes on a Labour government elected with manifesto plans for selected nationalisation of industry and redistribution of wealth from capital to labour.[131] But with the SNP showing strongly in the polls, and the Scotland and Wales Bill making its uncomfortable progress through Parliament, in November 1976 John Toothill moved in the opposite direction from the SCDI, helping to launch 'Scotland is British', an anti-devolutionary campaign. This was endorsed by a few trade unionists and retired Labour MPs, according to Drucker and Brown, but mainly drew on business support, including that of Douglas Hardie, Chairman of the CBI in Scotland, and the opposition of industrialists to devolution undoubtedly weakened the position of the Home Rule Tories and duly contributed to the outcome of the referendum.[132]

The outcome of the referendum, while often characterised as calamitous, is also usually linked in historical literature to the Labour government's crumbling esteem in the 'Winter of Discontent',[133] the commonly used shorthand for a sequence of industrial disputes from October 1978 to March 1979. These were represented at the time and have been continually characterised since by critics and opponents of the labour movement as the embodiment of obstructive and paralysing trade union 'power'.[134] Different groups and interests were involved in these disputes. But each was broadly characterised by the reluctance of manual workers, especially in the public sector, to accept the fetters of the government's anti-inflationary wage controls which, in allowing for a flat rate increase of 5 per cent in 1978–79, appeared to discriminate against the low paid.[135] Seeing these strikes as a 'cause' of the referendum's 'failure' is problematic, partly because the very concept of 'failure' here needs to be measured against the ambiguous party political positioning on devolution. Labour's performance in the general election of May 1979, where it picked up seats in Scotland, further qualifies the notion that the government was 'punished' in the referendum for its conduct of industrial relations in the preceding winter. But the ultimate outcome of the referendum, the collapse of the Callaghan government, certainly was related to the strikes, with the SNP combining forces with Margaret Thatcher's Tories and other opposition parties to defeat Labour in a vote of confidence on 28 March 1979.

After the referendum the government had initially approached Scottish and Welsh Nationalist MPs to discuss possible ways of reviving devolution once the Home Rule legislation had been repealed. The Prime Minister ratio-nalised these efforts by gamely observing in the House of Commons that a majority of those voting in Scotland had favoured the Assembly in Scotland, setting aside Dalyell's objection that those not voting had been, in effect, consciously siding with the No campaign.[136] The SNP broke off the talks with the government, its MPs instructed to do so by the party's National Council,[137] and the opposition motion of no confidence followed in the House of Commons. Thatcher spoke vividly in this debate about the government's various alleged failings, including its incapacity to avert economic decline, and inability to avert the collapse, as she put it, of law and order, which she characterised as not just a matter of escalating criminality and violence, but encompassing also the increasing refusal of people to accept authority and orders, including in the workplace.[138] This partial view of economic perform-ance and social and industrial relations, shaped as it arguably was by fairly pungent anti-working class prejudices, was opposed from the Labour benches. Some Scottish Labour MPs, in defending the record of the govern-ment, notably Norman Buchan, combined their class perspectives on Thatcher's position with attacks on the Nationalists who had abandoned devolution and provided the Tories with their opportunity. This was an echo of a line offered by Callaghan, earlier in the debate, about Nationalist 'turkeys' voting 'for Christmas'. So it came to pass, after the government fell by a single vote.[139] Only two of the SNP's eleven MPs would be returned at the subsequent general election, and the party's share of the vote fell by around a half. The new Conservative government oversaw the repeal of the Scotland Act by Order on 26 July 1979.[140]

It was noted in Chapter 3 that Foster sees the 1979 election as a victory for Labour in Scotland, with the party's standing – in vote share and seats won – increasing, chiefly at the expense of the Nationalists.[141] This might indeed be seen as an achievement, given Labour's internal divisions over the referendum, and the various problems arising from economic management, the wages policy and the strikes of 1978–79. But it was not a victory. In Scotland the Tories, it should be remembered, also made gains on 1974, again both in vote share and seats taken,[142] and this contributed to the UK outcome, the election of a Tory government intent on dismantling the main economic, industrial and social pillars of the labour movement across Britain. In office from 1979 Thatcher's government would profit from oil, the resource that had accelerated support for independence, and persuaded the Labour government from 1974 to bring forward devolution as a means of restraining the Nationalist advance. Devolution had deep economic and industrial roots, shaped, as this book has shown, in debates about regional policy and the search for a solution – articulated within the labour movement by the STUC – to the problem of the remote administration of economic and social policy. But devolution also had shallow political roots, with the Labour Party coming to adopt it essentially on opportunistic rather than principled grounds, and unable to shake the principled resistance that existed within its Scottish ranks to incursions on the integrity – or 'economic unity' – of the UK. The politics would gradually change after 1979, as the concluding chapter of this book indicates, but as they did so the central paradox of oil would become apparent. While abundant supplies of oil in the North Sea had offered impetus to devolution and the prospect of stimulating industrial growth, the terms of the extraction of the resource – rapid and relatively unregulated – accelerated the decline of established manufacturing industries and strengthened the centralised hand of Whitehall governance.

Notes

1 *The Economist*, 26 July 1975, p. 50.

2 Harvie, *Fool's Gold*.

3 Foster, 'Twentieth Century', pp. 479–81; Peden, 'Managed Economy', p. 261.

4 Bruce-Gardyne, *Scotland to 1980*, pp. 89–90.

5 *The Economist*, 26 July 1975.

6 Harvie, *Fool's Gold*, pp. 250–1.

7 'Secret Whitehall Dossier', http://www.snp.org/wealthhidden, accessed 15 September 2005.

8 Gavin McCrone, 'The Economics of Nationalism Re-examined', February 1974, pp. 8–10, http://www.snp.org/wealthhidden, accessed 15 September 2005.

9 See, for example, William Keegan, 'Pouring Oil on Troubled Economists', *The Observer*, 10 October 2004.

10 Campbell, *Edward Heath*.

11 Harvie, *Fool's Gold*, p. 8; Pimlott, *Wilson*; Ziegler, *Wilson*.

12 Kenneth O. Morgan, *Callaghan: A Life* (Oxford, 1997), pp. 563, 577–8.

13 Denis Healey, *The Time of My Life* (London, 1989), pp. 412, 459–61.

14 Harvie, *Fool's Gold*, pp. 8, 368; Margaret Thatcher, *The Downing Street Years* (London, 1993).

15 Harvie, *Fool's Gold*, pp. 10–11.

16 *The Economist*, 20 January 1973.

17 Peden, 'Managed Economy', pp. 260–1.

18 Scottish Council (Development and Industry), *A Future for Scotland* (Edinburgh, 1973); see Clydesmuir's preface, and pp. 6, 66–7.

19 SCDI, *Future for Scotland*, pp. 66–7.

20 Murray, *Scotland*, pp. 98–106.

21 Whitehead, *Writing on the Wall*, p. 292.

22 SCDI, *Future for Scotland*, pp. 50–1.

23 *The Economist*, 20 January 1973 and 26 July 1975.

24 Murray, *Scotland*, pp. 104–5.

25 'Regional Policy: Scotland', 8 December 1971, PREM 15/1190, PRO.

26 *The Times*, 17 July 1970.

27 Ibid., 7 March 1973.

28 Ibid., 3 March 1973.

29 Whitehead, *Writing on the Wall*, p. 292.

30 *The Times*, 9 November 1973.

31 Ibid., 2 November 1973.

32 Tony Benn, *Against the Tide: Diaries, 1973–76* (London, 1989), p. 73.

33 *The Times*, 2 November 1973.

34 Ibid., 9 November 1973.

35 Harvie, *No Gods*, p. 106.

36 Obituary, John Rankin, *The Times*, 9 October 1973.

37 Ahron Bregman and Jihan El-Tahri, *The Fifty Years War: Israel and the Arabs* (London, 1998), pp. 121–6; Harvie, *Fool's Gold*, pp. 95–6; *The Economist*, 20 October 1973.

38 Whitehead, *Writing on the Wall*, p. 292.

39 *The Times*, 1 November 1973.

40 Drucker and Brown, *Politics of Nationalism*, pp. 55–6, 63–4.

41 *Royal Commission on the Constitution: Volume I, Report*, Cmnd 5460 (HMSO, 1973), pp. 335–44.

42 Drucker and Brown, *Politics of Nationalism*, p. 81.

43 Knox and McKinlay, 'Re-Making of Scottish Labour', pp. 174–93.

44 Aitken, *Bairns O' Adam*, p. 231.

45 Marr, *Battle for Scotland*, p. 137.

46 *The Times*, 1 November 1973.

47 Taylor, *NUM and British Politics: Vol. Two*, pp. 79–87.

48 *The Economist*, 24 November 1973.

49 Taylor, *NUM and British Politics: Vol. Two*, pp. 88–94.

50 *The Times*, 4 July 1973.

51 Campbell, *Edward Heath*, pp. 574–97; Jefferys, *Finest and Darkest Hours*, pp. 168–78; Morgan, *People's Peace*, pp. 346–9; Routledge, *Scargill*, pp. 90–5.

52 Obituary, Michael McGahey, by Vic Allen, *The Guardian*, 1 February 1999.

53 Whitehead, *Writing on the Wall*, p. 104.

54 *The Times*, 23 January 1973.

55 Ibid., 14 December 1973.

56 *The Economist*, 24 November 1973.

57 Whitehead, *Writing on the Wall*, pp. 110–15, 123–33.

58 Harvie, *No Gods*, p. 90.

59 Drucker and Brown, *Politics of Nationalism*, pp. 80–1.

60 Ewing, *Stop the World*, pp. 148–9.

61 'Secret Whitehall Dossier'; Margo MacDonald, 'The Truth Finally Comes Out – But 30 Years Too Late', *The Scotsman*, 2 January 2006.

62 *Royal Commission on the Constitution, Minutes of Evidence II*, pp. 23, 99–105.

63 *The Courier & Advertiser*, 31 January 2006.

64 Peregrine Worsthorne, *Peregrinations* (London, 1980), pp. 226–7.

65 Young, *Scotland*, p. 166.

66 McCrone, 'Economics of Nationalism Re-examined', pp. 8–10

67 Harvie, *Fool's Gold*, pp. 250–1.

68 Bruce-Gardyne, *Scotland to 1980*, pp. 89–90.

69 Note by James Darragh of meeting with Wayne Harbin, 22 February 1973, SEP 4/4500, NAS.

70 *The Times*, 28 September 1973.

71 Harvie, *Fool's Gold*, p. 73.

72 *The Times*, 16 January 1976, 14 September 1978 and 29 November 1979.

73 *The Economic Impact of North Sea Oil on Scotland: Final Report to the Scottish Economic Planning Department in a Study Conducted Within the Department of*

Political Economy, the University of Aberdeen, 1973–77 (Edinburgh, HMSO, 1978), pp. 30–4, 100–1.

74 Foster, 'Twentieth Century', pp. 479–81.

75 Gordon Brown (ed.), *The Red Paper on Scotland* (Edinburgh, 1975), pp. 7–21, 334–43.

76 Alf Young, 'Scots Were Never Deceived Over the True Value of Oil', *The Herald*, 3 February 2006.

77 Harvie, *Fool's Gold*, pp. 324–9.

78 Morgan, *Callaghan*, pp. 626–52.

79 *United Kingdom Offshore Oil and Gas Policy*, Cmnd 5696 (HMSO, July 1974); *Parliamentary Debates, Fifth Series, Commons*, 876, 1558–9, 11 July 1974.

80 *Devolution within the UK: Some Alternatives for Discussion* (HMSO, June 1974); *Democracy and Devolution: Proposals for Scotland and Wales*, Cmnd 5732 (HMSO, September 1974).

81 Thorpe, 'The Labour Party and the Trade Unions', pp. 140–5.

82 *The Times*, 12 July 1974.

83 *The Economist*, 26 July 1975.

84 Peter Payne, 'Scottish Development Agency', in Lynch, *Oxford Companion*, pp. 575–6.

85 Benn, *Against the Tide*, pp. 315–17, 393.

86 *The Economist*, 13 July 1975.

87 James Darragh, DTI Scotland, to Wayne Harbin, 7 February 1972, SEP 4/4500, NAS.

88 Benn, *Against the Tide*, pp. 427–9.

89 *The Times*, 26 February 1975.

90 *The Challenge of North Sea Oil*, Cmnd 7143 (HMSO, March 1978), pp. 15–16.

91 Harvie, *Fool's Gold*, pp. 209–13.

92 Benn, *Against the Tide*, pp. 453–4.

93 Adams, *Tony Benn*, pp. 4–5.

94 Benn, *Against the Tide*, pp. 401–2.

95 *Royal Commission on the Constitution, Minutes of Evidence IV*, pp. 23–39.

96 Whitehead, *Writing on the Wall*, p. 291.

97 *The Times*, 24 June 1974.

98 Drucker and Brown, *Politics of Nationalism*, pp. 90–4.

99 Whitehead, *Writing on the Wall*, pp. 295–6.

100 Joe England, *The Wales TUC, 1974–2004: Devolution and Industrial Politics* (Cardiff, 2004), pp. 1–16.

101 Morgan, *People's Peace*, pp. 368–9.

102 Keith Gildart, 'Thomas Jones', in Keith Gildart, David Howell and Neville Kirk (eds), *Dictionary of Labour Biography: Volume XI* (Basingstoke, 2003), pp. 159–66.

103 England, *Wales TUC*, pp. 17–36.

104 Drucker and Brown, *Politics of Nationalism*, pp. 120–1.

105 *Our Changing Democracy: Devolution to Scotland and Wales*, Cmnd 6438 (HMSO, November 1975), pp. 28–9, 55–6.

106 STUC, *79th Annual Report, 1976*, pp. 200–1.

107 Drucker and Brown, *Politics of Nationalism*, pp. 99–106.

108 Aitken, *Bairns O' Adam*, p. 247.

109 Whitehead, *Writing on the Wall*, p. 296.

110 *Report of the Committee of Inquiry on Industrial Democracy*, Cmnd 6706 (HMSO, January 1977); *Industrial Democracy*, Cmnd 7231 (HMSO, May 1978);

see also Jones, *Union Man*, pp. 312–14; Tony Benn, *Conflicts of Interest: Diaries, 1977–80* (London, 1990), pp. 11–12, 142–3, 266–7.

111 Alec Cairncross, *The British Economy since 1945* (Oxford, 1992), pp. 210–20.

112 *The Times*, 26 January 1977.

113 Johnman and Murphy, *Shipbuilding in Britain*, pp. 208–10.

114 *The Times*, 16 January 1976, 14 September 1978 and 29 November 1979.

115 STUC, *80th Annual Report, 1977*, pp. 573–82.

116 Alison Gilmour, 'The Trouble with Linwood: Compliance and Coercion in the Car Plant, 1963–1981', *Journal of Scottish Historical Studies*, 27 (2007), 75–93.

117 *The Times*, 5 and 30 January 1976.

118 Taylor, *NUM and British Politics: Vol. Two*, pp. 113–7.

119 *The Times*, 31 August 1977; Gavin McCrone and R. J. Randall, 'The Scottish Development Agency', in Saville, *Economic Development of Modern Scotland*, pp. 233–44; Maver, *Glasgow*, pp. 220, 268.

120 *The Times*, 15 April and 1 June 1978.

121 *The Times*, 31 July, 17 and 28 October 1978.

122 Drucker and Brown, *Politics of Nationalism*, pp. 92, 122.

123 Vernon Bognador, *Devolution in the United Kingdom* (Oxford, 1999), pp. 186–7; Devine, *Scottish Nation*, p. 387; Drucker and Brown, *Politics of Nationalism*, p. 117; for the Parliamentary phrasing see *The Times*, 26 January 1978.

124 STUC, *81st Annual Report, 1978*, pp. 254–9.

125 Drucker and Brown, *Politics of Nationalism*, pp. 120–1.

126 Devine, *Scottish Nation*, p. 591; Finlay, *Modern Scotland*, p. 340.

127 Aitken, *Bairns O' Adam*, pp. 257–9; Drucker and Brown, *Politics of Nationalism*, p. 123.

128 Bognador, *Devolution*, pp. 188–91.

129 Mitchell, *Conservatives and the Union*, pp. 94–5.

130 'Scottish Plea for More Say in Industrial Decisions', *The Times*, 4 July 1974.

131 Pimlott, *Wilson*, pp. 618–25, 634–47.

132 Drucker and Brown, *Politics of Nationalism*, pp. 111–12.

133 Devine, *Scottish Nation*, p. 589; Finlay, *Modern Scotland*, p. 340; Marr, *Battle for Scotland*, pp. 159, 161.

134 Morgan, *People's Peace*, pp. 417–21, 437; Jefferys, *Finest and Darkest Hours*, pp. 186–207; Paul Smith and Gary Morton, 'The Conservative Governments' Reform of Employment Law, 1979–97: "Stepping Stones" and the "New Right" Agenda', *Historical Studies in Industrial Relations*, 12 (2001), 134–8.

135 Taylor, *Trade Union Question*, pp. 250–62.

136 *Parliamentary Debates, Fifth Series, Commons*, 964, 1692–7, 22 March 1979.

137 Ewing, *Stop the World*, pp. 163–4.

138 *Parliamentary Debates, Fifth Series, Commons*, 965, 463–9, 28 March 1979.

139 Ibid., 965, 471, 501–6, 28 March 1979.

140 *Scotland's Parliament*, Cm 3658 (HMSO, 1997), p. 1.

141 Foster, 'Twentieth Century', pp. 476–88.

142 Harvie, *No Gods*, p. 90.

6 Conclusion: the politics of devolution

The politics of devolution in Scotland changed after 1979. Arguments emerged about the 'democratic deficit' within the UK, particularly after the 1987 general election, when the Tories won just ten seats in Scotland, down from twenty-two in 1979 and twenty-one in 1983, but then proceeded in any case to pioneer in Scotland – one year before its adoption elsewhere in the UK – the deeply unpopular reform of local government financing, the Community Charge, or Poll Tax, as it was generally characterised.[1] In Scotland, as in other parts of the UK, the Poll Tax was seen as socially regressive, with the flat-rate charges absorbing a greater proportion of low incomes, and seemed to symbolise the widening inequalities that had materialised since 1979 as a deliberate consequence of the Tory government's fiscal, economic and social policies.[2]

A variety of Home Rule-cum-nationalist initiatives and developments followed. The Campaign for a Scottish Assembly, a cross-party pressure group established within months of the referendum of 1979, and supported throughout the 1980s by the STUC, helped early in 1988 to set up the Scottish Constitutional Convention, to draft a 'blueprint' for an Assembly. This emerged as The Claim of Right, which drew – at the Constitutional Convention's gathering in Edinburgh in March 1989 – a range of political, industrial and religious adherents that strongly resembled the Edinburgh Assembly of February 1972, except now there was no significant Tory presence. The SNP, meanwhile, appeared a renewed force, winning – again – a Westminster by-election at Govan in November 1988, which strengthened the more vigorous Home Rule current in the Labour Party, organised around Scottish Labour Action, established in April 1988. These various currents contributed, eventually, to a strongly devolutionary feel to the 1992 general election won by the Tories, who increased their representation in Scotland by one, against expectations of further losses, to eleven seats.[3] This further concentrated Home Rule minds, and possibly the anti-Conservative minds of the electors who, in the 1997 general election, voted with some apparent tactical acumen, to eliminate the Tory presence altogether from Scotland in the context of Tony Blair's Labour landslide in the UK. The new government, with Donald Dewar as Secretary of State for Scotland, rapidly brought forward a White Paper, *Scotland's Parliament*, setting out the powers of the proposed legislature and Scottish Executive, and a programme of action,[4] which included a double-question referendum, held on 11 September 1997. This asked electors whether there should be a Scottish Parliament, and whether a Scottish Parliament, if established, should be empowered to vary the rate of income tax by plus or minus 3 per cent. There were strong majorities in favour of both propositions: roughly three to one for a Parliament, and just more than three to two for the tax-varying powers. The first elections were held – in full accordance with the timetable set out in the 1997 White Paper – and the Scottish Parliament and Scottish Executive were duly established in 1999.[5]

Attempts have occasionally been made to relate these changed politics to the personality and impact of the Tory Prime Minister from 1979 to 1990. 'The key reason', writes Lindsay Paterson, explaining the emergence in the 1980s of more broad-ranging electoral support in Scotland for political devolution than had been evident in 1979, 'was Margaret Thatcher'.[6] There was some basis to this, notably, perhaps, in the Prime Minister's grossly miscalculated address to the General Assembly of the Church of Scotland in 1988. This included a narrow and self-justifying interpretation of the words, 'If a man will not work he shall not eat', from St Paul's letter to the Thessalonians, which many present understood to apply to those who were denied work not by personal inclination – the Prime Minister's meaning – but by incapacity or lack of opportunity.[7] Thatcher also represented the parable of the Good Samaritan as an illustration of the importance of wealth creation and individual initiative: the Samaritan could only be Good because first he was Rich. Both readings greatly offended her audience, and consolidated its support both for the redistribution of material resources through progressive economic and social policy, and the nascent Scottish Constitutional Convention.[8]

Yet distaste for Thatcher and Conservatism in Scotland, and the related development of support for Home Rule, was also more broadly grounded in public anxiety about the economic and social costs arising from the post-1979 governments' emphasis on rapid industrial restructuring. These costs – industrial closures, redundancies, large-scale and long-term unemployment and related low incomes and poor health – seemed to be borne disproportionately in Scotland. The impact of what Christopher Harvie called 'instant post-industrialisation' was certainly experienced far more severely in Scotland as a whole than in England as a whole, where Thatcher's policies probably assisted the growth of the financial and service sectors, which in the south especially were more robust than those in Scotland.[9] Anti-inflationary fiscal mechanisms, designed by Thatcher's Chancellors to dampen roaring growth in the south, were experienced as crudely deflationary instruments in industrial Scotland, further speeding the contraction of primary production.

Pressure on manufacturing industry was partly the result, as noted in the previous chapter, of the government's management of North Sea Oil. The continued emphasis on rapid extraction after 1979 accelerated the accretion of revenues and royalties to the Exchequer, and further stimulated the appreciation of the value of sterling, reducing the international competitiveness of manufacturing exports. Conservative ministers, of course, saw as desirable this linkage between 'deindustrialisation' and oil, relishing – as Jock Bruce-Gardyne had in the mid-1970s – the prospect of running down unionised sectors of industry, and so 'liberating' business and the labour market from the perceived strangling influence of trade unionism. By 1983 Britain was a net importer of manufactured goods.[10] Revenues from the North Sea subsidised what otherwise would have been an even more painful process of economic and social change for those who lost their jobs in the sectors that shrunk or collapsed altogether. In 1984, Theo Nichols noted, the costs of maintaining the unemployed – which had more than trebled since 1979 across the UK to somewhere in the region of four million – were roughly equivalent to government receipts from oil. 'This', he wrote, 'more or less, is where the revenue from North Sea Oil has *gone*'.[11]

As manufacturing exports fell, Scotland remained a net exporter of people. Here it is worth reflecting on the demographic projections of *Oceanspan* in 1970, which envisaged a regional city in North Ayrshire, linking Kilmarnock and Irvine, of 250,000. The 1991 census recorded a population for this area of just over 100,000. In the Falkirk to Grangemouth conurbation, where *Oceanspan* had hoped for 230,000 by the 1980s, there were about 98,000 in 1991; and Greater Livingston's population in 1991, just under 104,000, was well short of the projected 185,000.[12] Within the generalised pattern of economic and social instability there were a number of high-profile industrial casualties. One of these was shipbuilding, stricken also by the major oil spike of 1979, which followed the Iranian revolution and considerably reduced global demand for new ships. Thatcher's government targeted British Shipbuilders for privatisation upon taking office in 1979, keen to end state subsidy of an industry that seemed to embody the allegedly widespread problems in 'sunset' industry of trade union privilege and weak management, although the sell off was delayed until after the 1983 general election. Within the subsequent incremental privatisation, Scott-Lithgow's was sold to Trafalgar House in 1984, and Govan to Kvaerner in 1988. Both transactions involved major redundancies – in Govan's case five hundred jobs were lost immediately – and considerable state sweeteners to the purchaser.[13]

At Linwood the car plant closed in February 1981, with the loss of 4,800 jobs.[14] There had been another change in ownership, with Chrysler UK acquired in 1978 by Peugeot, which was thought, rightly as it turned out, to be really interested only in the dealerships, with little commitment to manufacturing operations in Britain. When Linwood closed further pressure was placed on the rolling steel mill at Ravenscraig, which had lost its major Scottish customer.[15] It remained open in the 1980s largely because the Tory government, despite its broader approach to economic and industrial management, was unwilling to accept the high political cost of allowing this still nationalised resource to close. But following the privatisation of British Steel in December 1988 the government could no longer claim a stake in its survival, and operations ceased at Ravenscraig on 24 June 1992, with the closure of the terminal at Hunterston closely following.[16]

Ravenscraig's precarious position in the 1980s had also been contingent on developments in coal mining. Here the Tory government's Coal Industry Act of 1980 had superseded the Labour government's expansionist *Plan For Coal*. The new approach projected the dismantling of state subsidies by 1983–84, a task that could only be accomplished by closing dozens of pits and making redundant thousands of miners.[17] Facing a coal strike over the cuts early in 1981, the government staged a 'strategic' and temporary retreat, announcing further subsidy but at the same time placing a new emphasis on stockpiling coal and additionally preparing for future confrontation by planning the replacement of Derek Ezra as head of the NCB with Ian MacGregor who, as chairman of British Steel, was earning a reputation among Thatcherites for the 'butchering' of unionised state enterprise.[18] Ezra was forced out early in 1982, and replaced temporarily by his deputy, Norman Siddall, who then gave way to MacGregor in September 1983.[19]

In 1982 the new President of the NUM, Arthur Scargill, produced a 'hit list' of pits that he claimed – rightly, as it turned out – had been identified for closure by the NCB, and a ballot for strike action against these cuts and the annual pay offer was held at the end of October. Across the coalfields only 39 per cent of those voting supported a strike, but in Scotland the mood was evidently more determinedly militant, with 69 per cent in favour. This reflected the preponderance of job losses in Scotland since 1974, the highest along with the north-east of England among the NCB regions, although, when it came to the major dispute of 1984–85, there would be no simple or automatic relationship between a regional membership's rate of redundancy and its strike propensity. There would be more fragmentation among Scottish than Yorkshire miners, for example, where job losses had been in the mid-range since the 1970s, and were offset by the establishment of 'super' collieries, notably Selby, which were not present in Scotland, and which possibly gave the Yorkshire men a greater incentive to fight.[20] Scottish losses continued to accelerate, with 5,000 jobs going between 1981 and the start of the national strike in March 1984, at which point 12,000 men were still employed in Scotland's coalfields.[21] Many of these men were prepared to fight and did so from 1983, when the NCB's Scottish Chairman, Albert Wheeler, who has been characterised as 'pioneering' MacGregor-style aggressive management in the coalfields,[22] announced a series of closures. This began at Cardowan at Lanarkshire, where 1,100 men worked, and where Wheeler was kicked and punched by infuriated miners after making the closure announcement.[23] Divisions in Scotland ahead of the national dispute were, however, signalled in February 1984 at a Scottish delegate conference that opposed national strike action. This commenced in March, the NUM national leadership utilising provisions in the union rulebook that allowed regional groupings to come out on strike without a ballot of members, and then call for the support of other regions, where necessary through picketing of mines in those other regions.[24]

The subsequent activities of striking miners in Scotland centred on Ravenscraig, which exerted a major strain on relations between miners and steel workers and their unions,[25] and Hunterston, envisaged in *Oceanspan*, of course, as the core of Scotland's industrial regeneration, but now, arguably, a hub of deindustrialisation, as high-volume coal imports – substituting for Scottish and other British produce – passed through its terminal. In May 1984 there were major pickets at both Ravenscraig – including Michael McGahey and Eric Clarke, the NUM's Scottish Secretary – and Hunterston, with the NUM attempting to prevent coal from entering the steel plant and leaving the port, but these were resisted by large-scale policing operations, rivalling Longannet in 1972 in terms of officer deployment, with 1,500 in attendance at Hunterston, including mounted personnel.[26] The success of the policing operation, in Scotland and across the English and Welsh coalfields, along with stockpiling and the scheduling of heavy quantities of imported coal, were instrumental to the outcome of the strike, which eventually was called off across the coalfields in March 1985. There had been mounting tension between supporters and opponents of the strike within the Scottish NUM, partly owing to the loss of ten of Scotland's thirty-three production faces during the dispute. These included Frances and Seafield in Fife, abandoned in February 1985 after a lengthy fire,[27] and the strike ended with much bitterness. McGahey, who had private misgivings about the conduct of the strike that he did not express publicly,[28] was jostled outside the meeting in Edinburgh where Scottish miners agreed to resume working. On the following evening he was attacked – in a grisly echo of his 1972 injury at Longannet – by two men near his home in the south of the city, sustaining black eyes and other facial injuries,[29] but he retained a broad body of sympathy and support, which extended beyond the labour movement. Jock Stein, it might be noted, football manager and a former comrade in the Lanarkshire mines, made no secret of his admiration of McGahey, and his corresponding contempt for Scargill,[30] and when McGahey died in 1999 a range of commentators would emphasise his substantial contribution to Scottish public life. This included, of course, engineering the STUC's lasting conversion to Home Rule in 1968.[31]

The government's preparations for the miners' strike had been set out in the notorious 'Ridley memorandum', leaked to *The Economist* in May 1978. Drafted by the same hand as the 1969 'butcher' plans for the UCS, this outlined a strategy for defeating the miners on the basis of substantial coal stocks at power stations, reinforced by imports, which could be moved through picket lines by non-union lorry drivers with the support of large-scale mobile police units.[32] These plans emerged, of course, in the more general context of Tory rethinking after 1974, encompassing the 'Stepping Stones' approach to industrial relations and employment 'reforms', which proposed chipping away at the privileges and powers of unionised workers as an alternative to the grand but doomed single venture attempted by Heath with his Industrial Relations Act of 1971.[33] Events in Scotland were important to this process. Thatcher wrote in her 1995 memoirs of being 'deeply troubled' by the 'commercially unjustified rescue' on the Upper Clyde in 1972, which she discussed extensively with Bruce-Gardyne,[34] who shared her arguably intemperate and anti-working-class attitude to industrial protest. The voluble and radical conservatism of Scots like Bruce-Gardyne, along with Madson Pirie and Douglas Mason, was noted in Chapter 4 as an under-estimated feature of Scottish intellectual and political life in the 1970s. This helped to sustain the growth and incremental mainstreaming of Thatcherite discourses on such linked matters as economic performance, social policy, trade unions and industrial relations. The Scottish roots of these discourses – nourished, perhaps, by the greater preponderance of declining and state-subsidised heavy industry, and the related presence of labour intensive and unionised production – should be emphasised, not least as a corrective to the notion, articulated by David McCrone, that Scotland resisted Thatcherism in ways that other parts of the UK did not.[35] Bruce-Gardyne and other acolytes fed Thatcher's determination to seek revenge for the various humiliations of the early 1970s that the labour movement visited on the Heath government. The Prime Minister duly relished her triumph over the miners in 1985, enjoying especially the defeat of Scargill, who was characterised as the chief villain – along with McGahey – of 1972 and 1973–74. But it will also be remembered from Chapter 4 that the Heath government was not defeated by 'destroyers' at the head of the NUM, but by ordinary miners, like Tam Coulter of Manor Powis in Clackmannan, who enterprisingly commissioned a trawler in a quixotic attempt to halt a giant Danish tanker – laden with oil for use at the power station – as it progressed up the Firth of Forth. From this perspective Thatcher's subsequent 'revenge' assumes an unambiguously anti-working-class character: it was aimed not only at Scargill and McGahey and other union leaders, but also at the manual working class as a whole.

In Scotland there were, it should be reiterated, some misgivings within the NUM and the labour movement more broadly about the strike in 1984–85. But the twin imperatives of class and nation still characterised industrial politics in Scotland, as they had in the 1960s and 1970s, and the miners' defeat – devised and executed by the UK government with a limited Scottish electoral mandate – was duly and broadly received as further evidence of the damaging consequences of remote administration from Whitehall.[36] In this respect the strike and the Thatcher years more generally reinforced in Scotland the industrial and political trends of the 1960s and 1970s that have been examined in this book. The debates about regional policy in the 1960s, explored in Chapter 1, indicated a very strong sense among industrialists and trade unionists that Scotland's relatively slow rate of economic growth – in UK terms – was the consequence of the remote administration of macro-economic and industrial development policy. The Toothill report emphasised in the early 1960s that in Scotland there was room for greater expansion, but that this was checked by UK macro-economic management. This phenomenon remained evident across the 1960s, with the 'stop' element of the stop-go cycle of economic management, designed to restrain inflationary pressures in the economically and demographically congested regions of England, tending to choke off growth in Scotland. In this respect the Toothill debates were to an extent consistent with Michael Hechter's emphasis on 'internal colonialism', with the Scottish 'periphery' being dominated by the Whitehall/Westminster 'core', and the desire for greater autonomy within the UK – expressed particularly by Scottish industrial leaders in the 1960s – shaped the growth of support for the development of administrative devolution.

But regional policy, and support for devolution, was also generated by class relationships and pressures, within the UK and within Scotland. Manual workers, their expectations raised by post-war economic growth and the increased numerical strength and political status of the labour movement, were not prepared to tolerate unemployment in the 1950s, 1960s and 1970s. This was most notably evident in Scotland in the UCS episode, examined in Chapter 3, but clear in the Toothill debates also, with the STUC pressing for the establishment of motor manufacturing as a means of raising economic growth and eliminating joblessness. These class pressures and processes were, however, fairly subtle, reflecting the relatively even balance of social forces – between manual workers and employers, labour and capital – that prevailed in the context of continuous growth from the late 1940s to the early 1970s. Regional policy, and then devolution, were utilised by UK governments, and supported by employers and trade unionists, partly because they seemed to offer the means of ameliorating economic and social problems – chiefly revolving around relatively low working-class incomes – without raising awkward questions about the competing or indeed conflicting class interests that arguably sustained these problems. Yet the practice of regional policy sometimes drew fairly frank attention to these class interests. This was evident at Linwood, where the Tory government pushed Rootes against its will. The firm expected the workforce to be 'grateful', to accept wages that were lower than those available in car plants in the midlands, and to adjust to diminished autonomy at work and the rigid discipline of standardised assembly. The subsequent go-slows, strikes and other forms of industrial protest, characterised by the firm as illegitimate troublemaking, were logical responses by workers in pursuit of their separate and particular material interests, encouraged by the shift in working culture experienced perhaps by those moving into the car plant from shipyards and engineering works, where skill and autonomy on the job had been more pronounced characteristics of employment.

Devolution, it should be emphasised, also emerged from but sought to de-emphasise class differences. This was true of business advocacy of enhanced administrative devolution, articulated chiefly by the SCDI, which hoped to control or certainly very strongly influence the Scottish Office, and so sought the expansion of the latter's industrial and economic powers of intervention. It was also true of the political or legislative devolution brought forward by the Labour governments of Wilson and then Callaghan after 1974. This, as Chapter 5 indicated, was imposed as a devolved political or constitutional 'solution' to a set of economic and social problems that were arguably more the consequence of class tensions and inequalities. Hence the value of using Eric Hobsbawm's analysis of nationalism to conceptualise the evolving process of devolution in Scotland, which was both constructed – or perhaps even 'invented' – from above, by policy makers, but also shaped – through industrial politics – from below.

The complex inter-meshing of class and national imperatives was particularly evident in the episodes examined in Chapters 3 and 4 of this book, the 1971–72 UCS work-in and the 1972 miners' strike. These, it will be remembered, were regarded or have been regarded as victories for the workers involved, but they actually encompassed fairly ambiguous outcomes. On the Clyde, for instance, the workers 'won' only as a consequence of the construction and maintenance of alliances with two groups: Scottish capital, and workers mustered in the organs of the UK labour movement. Neither of these groups survived the 1970s in vigorous health, and both the absence of muscular indigenous Scottish industry and the fragmentation of the UK labour movement would isolate Scottish labour in the 1980s. The limits rather than the extent of any cross-class devolutionary alliance were also evident in the coalfields. There was popular support for the miners, but this was mainly from other manual or union-organised workers. Opposition, to some extent of a class nature, was mustered around stereotypes of industrial protests as undemocratic threats to civil order. So the miners' strike, while generating in

Scotland further impetus towards devolution, embodied in the Assembly that sat on 14 February 1972, the very day that the pickets almost closed Longannet, also brought into the open radical conservative views on economic, industrial and social matters. These views, given policy substance by Thatcher's UK government in the 1980s, would, in turn, push majority opinion in Scotland further towards devolution.

In the 1970s, of course, as the examination of oil and devolution in Chapter 5 indicated, class politics constrained the shift to Home Rule. The Labour Party in Scotland was divided over devolution, with a powerful strand of arch-unionist opposition that sought to protect the 'economic unity' of the UK. This, it was argued, was the better guarantor of improved working living standards, chiefly through redistributing resources from the wealthier southern regions of England to northern England, Wales and Scotland via progressive economic management and social policy from Westminster and Whitehall. This type of thinking was incrementally eroded in Scottish Labour as the 1980s and 1990s progressed, although it was never entirely abandoned. After the establishment of the Scottish Parliament in 1999 there remained important tensions within Scottish Labour between those who operated through Edinburgh, and those with a footing – particularly with New Labour in a prolonged period of office in the UK – at Westminster and in Whitehall.

Class and nation blurred in another important way from the 1970s onwards, with class a powerful element in the development and expression of a separate or at least a particular Scottish identity within the UK. Lindsay Paterson, Frank Bechhofer and David McCrone recently emphasised the curious phenomenon of an increasing proportion of Scots identifying themselves as working class during a period, roughly from 1980 to 2001, when the relative size of the manual working class was actually decreasing.[37] Gregor Gall has made a similar observation, relating this apparent paradox to the longer 'red thread' running through Scottish politics in the twentieth century.[38] John Foster also raises the longer twentieth-century history of economic, social and political development when explaining the peculiarity of the politics of the Scottish working class, relative to its English equivalent. In Scotland, he notes, occupational and economic structures were not dissimilar from England (and Wales), but labour markets were more localised and in the staple industries there was a more pronounced role for family-owned business. In the first half of the twentieth century these matters constrained the emergence and electoral strength of the Labour Party, but nevertheless slowly contributed to the shaping of a powerful working-class consciousness that became a prominent feature of the second half of the century. This survived industrial restructuring and rehousing – Scotland's economic and social 'modernisation' – from the 1950s onwards. If anything, reinvigorated by developments in industrial relations that were opened up by the presence of US firms and transplanted UK firms, notably Rootes at Linwood, this working-class consciousness became even more substantial in the second half of the century, amplified by workers' collective resistance to low wages and anti-union employer agendum.[39]

In these terms the industrial politics of the 1960s and 1970s were extremely important in shaping contemporary Scotland's identity. While business and labour in Scotland placed a common emphasis on the dangers and limitations of remote administration, the former sought to advance devolution initially in discrete terms, through the Scottish Office, without expanding the democratic remit. The Scottish labour movement took a different path, with the STUC from 1968 favouring an unambiguously democratic approach to devolution. It was this, perhaps, that enabled Scottish trade unionism to assume a leading position in the Home Rule movement, a development that probably helped to develop the association in Scotland between class and industrial politics on the one hand and national identity on the other hand.[40] This association was further strengthened by the various industrial episodes, crises and struggles that have made up the contents of this book. Each of these involved in some important respect a suggested general fusion of the politics of class and nation, contributing in particular to the apparently widespread conflation of working-class and Scottish identities. In this context the central class paradox of contemporary Scottish national identity – more Scots identifying themselves as working class while less Scots objectively are working class – becomes more understandable. This paradox, along with devolution, is the particular legacy of Linwood, *Oceanspan*, the UCS work-in, Longannet and North Sea Oil.

Notes

1 Mitchell, *Conservatives and the Union*, p. 117.
2 Marr, *Battle For Scotland*, pp. 176–80.
3 Aitken, *Bairns O' Adam*, pp. 269–70, 294, 303–6.
4 *Scotland's Parliament*, Cm 3658, pp. 3–9, 34.
5 Bognador, *Devolution*, p. 199; Devine, *Scottish Nation*, pp. 616–7.
6 Paterson, *Diverse Assembly*, p. 143.
7 Mitchell, *Conservatives and the Union*, pp. 119–21.
8 Obituary, 'The Very Rev. James Whyte', by Brian Wilson, *The Guardian*, 28 July 2005.
9 Harvie, *No Gods*, pp. 164–73.
10 William Keegan, *Britain Without Oil* (Harmondsworth, 1985), pp. 31–4, 108–110.
11 Nichols, *British Worker Question*, p. 237.
12 The North Ayrshire city here comprises Kilmarnock, Irvine, Dreghorn, Crosshouse, Kilmaurs, Hurlford, Kilwinning, Stevenston, Saltcoats and Ardrossan; Falkirk-Grangemouth includes Polmont, Stenhousemuir, Bo'ness, Carron, Denny and Bonnybridge; Greater Livingston encompasses Bathgate, Broxburn, East and West Calder, Whitburn, Armadale and Blackburn; General Register Office, *Scotland, 1991, Census: Key Statistics for Localities in Scotland* (Edinburgh, 1995).

13 Johnman and Murphy, *British Shipbuilding*, pp. 215, 234.
14 Aitken, *Bairns O' Adam*, p. 269.
15 Lee, *Scotland*, pp. 183–4.
16 Peter L. Payne, 'The End of Steelmaking in Scotland, c. 1967–1993', *Scottish Economic and Social History*, 15 (1995), 66–84, pp. 72–77.
17 Routledge, *Scargill*, pp. 103–5.
18 Taylor, *NUM and British Politics: Vol. Two*, pp. 155–62.
19 Adeney and Lloyd, *Loss Without Limit*, pp. 23–6.
20 Taylor, *NUM and British Politics: Vol. Two*, pp. 175–6, 189.
21 Adeney and Lloyd, *Loss Without Limit*, p. 85.
22 Taylor, *NUM and British Politics: Vol. Two*, p. 184.
23 *The Times*, 14 May and 21 June 1983.
24 Taylor, *NUM and British Politics: Vol. Two*, pp. 186–9.
25 Aitken, *Bairns O' Adam*, pp. 274–5.
26 *The Times*, 4, 8 and 9 May 1984.
27 Ibid., 4 and 7 February 1985.
28 Adeney and Lloyd, *Loss Without Limit*, pp. 49, 51–2, 270–6; Obituary, 'Michael McGahey', by Vic Allen, *The Guardian*, 1 February 1999.
29 *The Times*, 7 and 12 March 1985.
30 Archie Macpherson, *Jock Stein: The Definitive Biography* (Newbury, 2004), p. 27.
31 *The Herald*, 1 February 1999.
32 Adeney and Lloyd, *Loss Without Limit*, p. 73.
33 Smith and Morton, 'Conservative Governments' Reform of Employment Law', pp. 131–47.
34 Thatcher, *Path to Power*, pp. 201–22; Campbell, *Grocer's Daughter*, p. 244.
35 McCrone, 'Towards a Principled Elite', pp. 190–5.
36 Christopher Harvie, 'Scotland after 1978', p. 503.
37 Lindsay Paterson, Frank Bechhofer and David McCrone, *Living in Scotland: Social and Economic Change since 1980* (Edinburgh, 2004), pp. 80–104.
38 Gall, *Political Economy of Scotland, passim*.
39 Foster, 'Proletarian Nation?', pp. 201–40.
40 Aitken, *Bairns O' Adam*, pp. 215–19, 227–30, 277–9, 309–10.

Bibliography

Primary sources

Government papers

National Archives of Scotland, Edinburgh
HH 55   Scottish Home and Health Department, Police Services.
HH 56   Scottish Home and Health Department, Civil Emergencies.
SEP 4   Department of Trade and Industry in Scotland, Papers.
SEP 5   Department of Trade and Industry in Scotland, Papers.
SEP 10   Scottish Development Department, Papers.
SOE 6   Secretary of State for Scotland, Papers.

The National Archives: Public Record Office, Kew
CAB 128   Cabinet Conclusions.
COAL 74   National Coal Board, Publications.
DK 1   National Ports Council, Port Development Series.
HO 221   Royal Commission on the Constitution, Papers and Evidence.
LAB 77   Department of Employment, Coal Mining Disputes.
PREM 11   Prime Minister's Private Office Papers.
PREM 15   Prime Minister's Private Office Papers.

Business and labour archives

Modern Records Centre, University of Warwick
MSS. 371   Fred Lindop, transcribed interviews with figures from port transport.

National Library of Scotland, Edinburgh
Acc. 9805   National Union of Mineworkers, Scotland, Papers and Correspondence.

Scottish Council for Development and Industry, Campsie House, Glasgow
Scottish Council for Development and Industry, Executive Committee, Minutes and
        Papers, 1960–74.

Official publications

Boyd Orr, John, *Food, Health and Income: Report on a Survey of Adequacy of Diet in Relation to Income* (HMSO, 1936).

Central Scotland: Programme for Development and Growth, Cmnd 2188 (HMSO, 1963).

The Challenge of North Sea Oil, Cmnd 7143 (HMSO, March 1978).

Democracy and Devolution: Proposals for Scotland and Wales, Cmnd 5732 (HMSO, September 1974).

Department of Employment Gazette (HMSO, various years).

Department of Trade and Industry, *Shipbuilding on the Clyde: Report of Hill Samuel & Co. Ltd.*, Cmnd 4918 (HMSO, March 1972).

Devolution within the UK: Some Alternatives for Discussion (HMSO, June 1974).

The Economic Impact of North Sea Oil on Scotland: Final Report to the Scottish Economic Planning Department in a Study Conducted Within the Department of Political Economy, the University of Aberdeen, 1973–77 (Edinburgh, HMSO, 1978).

Fox, Alan, *Industrial Sociology and Industrial Relations: Royal Commission on Trade Unions and Employers' Associations, Research Papers, 3* (HMSO, 1966).

General Register Office, *Scotland, 1991, Census: Key Statistics for Localities in Scotland* (Edinburgh, 1995).

In Place of Strife: A Policy for Industrial Relations, Cmnd 3888 (HMSO, January 1969).

Industrial Democracy, Cmnd 7231 (HMSO, May 1978).

Ministry of Transport, *The Reorganisation of the Ports*, Cmnd 3903 (HMSO, January 1969).

National Ports Council, *Transshipment in the Seventies: A Study of Container Transport. Report prepared by Arthur D. Little* (London, June 1969).

Our Changing Democracy: Devolution to Scotland and Wales, Cmnd 6438 (HMSO, November 1975).

Parliamentary Debates, Fifth Series, Commons and *Lords.*

Report of the Committee of Inquiry on Industrial Democracy, Cmnd 6706 (HMSO, January 1977).

Report into the Major Ports of Great Britain, Cmnd 1824 (HMSO, 1962).

Royal Commission on the Constitution. Minutes of Evidence: II Scotland (HMSO, 1970).

Royal Commission on the Constitution. Minutes of Evidence: IV Scotland (HMSO, 1970).

Royal Commission on the Constitution: Volume I, Report, Cmnd 5460 (HMSO, 1973).

Royal Commission on Trades Unions and Employers' Associations, 1965–1968, Cmnd 3623 (HMSO, 1968).

Scotland's Parliament, Cm 3658 (HMSO, 1997).

The Scottish Economy, 1965 to 1970: A Plan for Expansion, Cmnd 2864 (HMSO, 1966).

Select Committee on Scottish Affairs, *Minutes of Evidence*, 23 April–16 July 1969 (HMSO, 1969).

Shipbuilding Inquiry Committee, 1965–1966: Report, Cmnd 2937 (HMSO, 1966).

United Kingdom Offshore Oil and Gas Policy, Cmnd 5696 (HMSO, July 1974).

Business and labour publications

Committee of Inquiry appointed by the Scottish Council (Development and Industry) under the Chairmanship of J. N. Toothill, *Report on the Scottish Economy* (Edinburgh, 1961).

Scottish Council for Development and Industry, *Unemployment in Scotland* (Edinburgh, November 1967).

Scottish Council for Development and Industry, *Oceanspan: A Maritime-Based Development Strategy for a European Scotland, 1970–2000* (Edinburgh, 1970).

Scottish Council for Development and Industry, *Oceanspan 2. Eurospan: A Study of Port and Industrial Development in Western Europe* (Edinburgh, 1971).

Scottish Council for Development and Industry, *A Future for Scotland* (Edinburgh, 1973).

Scottish Miner.

Scottish Trades Union Congress (STUC), *Annual Reports, 1967–72*.

Newspapers

The Courier & Advertiser
The Economist
Glasgow Herald and *The Herald*
The Guardian
Morning Star
The Observer
The Scotsman
The Times

Secondary sources

Adams, Jad, *Tony Benn* (London, 1992).

Adeney, Martin, and John Lloyd, *The Miners' Strike, 1984–5: Loss Without Limit* (London, 1986).

Aitken, Keith, *The Bairns O' Adam: The Story of the STUC* (Edinburgh, 1997).

Aldcroft, Derek H. and Michael J. Oliver, *Trade Unions and the Economy: 1870–2000* (Aldershot, 2000).

Ashworth, W., *The History of the British Coal Industry: Volume 5, 1946–1982: the Nationalised Industry* (Oxford, 1986).

Benn, Tony, *Out of the Wilderness: Diaries, 1963–67* (London, 1987).

Benn, Tony, *Office Without Power: Diaries, 1968–72* (London, 1989).

Benn, Tony, *Against the Tide: Diaries, 1973–76* (London, 1989).

Benn, Tony, *Conflicts of Interest: Diaries, 1977–80* (London, 1990).

Benson, John, 'Coalowners, Coalminers and Compulsion: Pit Clubs in England, 1860–1880', *Business History*, 44 (2002), 47–60.

Beynon, Huw, *Working For Ford* (Harmondsworth, Second Edition, 1984).

Beynon, Huw (ed.), *Digging Deeper: Issues in the Miners' Strike* (London, 1985).

Bognador, Vernon, *Devolution in the United Kingdom* (Oxford, 1999).

Booth, Alan, *The British Economy in the Twentieth Century* (Basingstoke, 2001).

Booth, Alan, 'The Manufacturing Failure Hypothesis and the Performance of British Industry During the Long Boom', *Economic History Review*, 56 (2003), 1–33.

Braudel, Fernand, *The Mediterranean and the Mediterranean in the Age of Philip II* (London, 1992).

Bregman, Ahron and Jihan El-Tahri, *The Fifty Years War: Israel and the Arabs* (London, 1998).

Broadway, Frank, *Upper Clyde Shipbuilders: A Study of Government Intervention in Industry ... the Way the Money Goes* (London, 1976).

Brown, Gordon (ed.), *The Red Paper on Scotland* (Edinburgh, 1975).

Bruce-Gardyne, Jock, *Whatever Happened to the Quiet Revolution?* (London, 1974).

Bruce-Gardyne, Jock, *Scotland to 1980* (London, 1975).

Buchan, Alasdair, *The Right to Work: The Story of the Upper Clyde Confrontation* (London, 1972).

Buxton, Neil K., 'Economic Growth in Scotland between the Wars: The Role of Production Structure on Rationalization', *Economic History Review*, 33 (1980), 538–55.

Cairncross, Alec, *The British Economy since 1945* (Oxford, 1992).

Cameron, Ewen A., '"They Will Listen to no Remonstrance": Land Raids and Land Raiders in the Scottish Highlands, 1886 to 1914', *Scottish Economic and Social History*, 17 (1997), 43–64.

Campbell, Alan, *The Scottish Miners, 1874–1939: Volume One, Work, Industry and Community*; and *Volume Two, Trade Unions and Politics* (Aldershot, 2000).

Campbell, Beatrix, *Wigan Pier Revisited: Poverty and Politics in the Eighties* (London, 1984).

Campbell, John, *Edward Heath: A Biography* (London, 1993).

Campbell, John, *Margaret Thatcher: Volume One, The Grocer's Daughter* (London, 2001).

Campbell, R. H., 'The Scottish Office and the Special Areas in the 1930s', *Historical Journal*, 22 (1979), 167–83.

Campbell, R. H., *The Rise and Fall of Scottish Industry, 1707–1939* (Edinburgh, 1980).

Castle, Barbara, *The Castle Diaries, 1964–76* (London, 1990).

Castle, Barbara, *Fighting All the Way* (London, 1993).

Church, Roy and Quentin Outram, *Strikes and Solidarity: Coalfield Conflict in Britain* (Cambridge, 1998).

Claydon, Tim, 'Tales of Disorder: The Press and the Narrative Construction of Industrial Relations in the British Motor Industry, 1950–79', *Historical Studies in Industrial Relations*, 9 (2000), 1–37.

Clegg, Hugh A., *A History of British Trade Unions since 1889: Volume III, 1934–1951* (Oxford, 1994).

Coates, Ken, *Work-ins, Sit-ins and Industrial Democracy* (Nottingham, 1981).

Cole, John, *As It Seemed To Me: Political Memoirs* (London, 1995).

Coote, Sir Colin, 'Sir Walter Elliot', in E. T. Williams and Helen M. Palmer (eds), *Dictionary of National Biography, 1951–60* (Oxford, 1971).

Craigen, James, 'The Scottish TUC: Scotland's Assembly of Labour', in Ian Donnachie, Christopher Harvie and Ian S. Wood (eds), *Forward! Labour Politics in Scotland, 1888–1988* (Edinburgh, 1989).

Crossman, Richard, *The Diaries of a Cabinet Minister: Volume Two, Lord President of the Council and Leader of the House of Commons, 1966–68* (London, 1976).

Crouch, Colin, *The Politics of Industrial Relations* (Glasgow, 1979).

Devine, T. M., *The Tobacco Lords: A Study of the Tobacco Merchants of Glasgow and Their Activities* (Edinburgh, 1975).

Devine, T. M., *The Scottish Nation, 1700–2000* (London, 1999).

Doig, Jameson W., *Empire on the Hudson: Entrepreneurial Vision and Political Power at the Port of New York Authority* (New York, 2001).

Drucker, Henry and Gordon Brown, *The Politics of Nationalism and Devolution* (London, 1980).

Edgerton, David, 'The Decline of Declinism', *Business History Review*, 71 (1997), 201–7.

England, Joe, *The Wales TUC, 1974–2004: Devolution and Industrial Politics* (Cardiff, 2004).

Ewing, Winnie, *Stop the World: The Autobiography of Winnie Ewing* (Edinburgh, 2004).

Finlay, R. J., *Modern Scotland* (London, 2004).

Flanders, Allan, 'What are Trade Unions for?', in Allan Flanders (ed.), *Management and Unions: The Theory and Reform of Industrial Relations* (London, 1970), pp. 39–45.

Foot, Paul, *The Politics of Harold Wilson* (Harmondsworth, 1968).

Foster, John, 'A Proletarian Nation? Occupation and Class since 1914', in A. Dickson and J. H. Treble (eds), *People and Society in Scotland: Volume III, 1914–1990* (Edinburgh, 1994), pp. 201–240.

Foster, John, 'The Twentieth Century, 1914–1979', in R. A. Houston and W. W. J. Knox (eds), *The New Penguin History of Scotland* (London, 2001), pp. 417–93.

Foster, John and Charles Woolfson, *The Politics of the UCS Work-In: Class Alliances and the Right to Work* (London, 1986).

Foster, John and Charles Woolfson, 'How Workers on the Clyde Gained the Capacity for Class Struggle: the Upper Clyde Shipbuilders' Work-In, 1971–2', in John McIlroy, Nina Fishman and Alan Campbell (eds), *British Trade Unions and Industrial Politics: Volume Two, The High Tide of Trade Unionism, 1964–79* (Aldershot, 1999), pp. 297–325.

French, Michael and Jim Phillips, *Cheated Not Poisoned? Food Regulation in the United Kingdom, 1875–1938* (Manchester, 2000).

Gall, Gregor, 'Trade Unionism and Industrial Relations in Scotland since UCS', *Scottish Labour History*, 38 (2003), 51–74.

Gall, Gregor, *The Political Economy of Scotland. Red Scotland? Radical Scotland?* (Cardiff, 2005).

Gildart, Keith, 'Thomas Jones', in Keith Gildart, David Howell and Neville Kirk (eds), *Dictionary of Labour Biography: Volume XI* (Basingstoke, 2003), pp. 159–66.

Gilmour, Alison, 'The Trouble with Linwood: Compliance and Coercion in the Car Plant, 1963–1981', *Journal of Scottish Historical Studies*, 27 (2007), 75–93.

Gold, Michael, 'Worker Mobilization in the 1970s: Revisiting Work-ins, Co-operatives and Alternative Corporate Plans', *Historical Studies in Industrial Relations*, 18 (2004), 65–106.

Goodman, Geoffrey, *The Awkward Warrior. Frank Cousins: His Life and Times* (London, 1979).

Hall, Tony, *King Coal: Miners, Coal and Britain's Industrial Future* (Harmondsworth, 1981).

Harvie, Christopher, *No Gods and Precious Few Heroes* (Edinburgh, 1993).

Harvie, Christopher, *Scotland & Nationalism: Scottish Society and Politics, 1707–1994* (Second edition, London, 1994).

Harvie, Christopher, *Fool's Gold: The Story of North Sea Oil* (Harmondsworth, 1994).

Harvie, Christopher, *Deep Fried Hillman Imp* (Argyll, 2001).

Harvie, Christopher, 'Scotland after 1978: From Referendum to Millennium', in R. A. Houston and W. W. J. Knox (eds), *The New Penguin History of Scotland* (London, 2001), pp. 494–531.

Harvie, Christopher, *Mending Scotland: Essays in Economic Regionalism* (Argyll, 2004).

Healey, Denis, *The Time of My Life* (London, 1989).

Heath, Edward, *The Course of My Life: My Autobiography* (London, 1998).

Hechter, Michael, *Internal Colonialism: The Celtic Fringe in British National Development, 1536–1966* (London, 1975).

Hobsbawm, Eric, *Nations and Nationalism* (London, 1992).

Howell, David, *A Lost Left: Three Studies in Socialism and Nationalism* (Chicago and Manchester, 1986).

Howell, David, 'Wilson and History: "1966 And All That"', *Twentieth Century British History*, 4 (1993), 174–87.

Hurd, Douglas, *An End to Promises: Sketch of a Government, 1970–74* (London, 1979).

Hurd, Douglas and Andrew Osmond, *Scotch on the Rocks* (London, 1971).

Hutchison, Iain G. C., 'Government', in T. M. Devine and R. J. Finlay (eds), *Scotland in the 20th Century* (Edinburgh, 1996).

Hutchison, I. G. C., *Scottish Politics in the Twentieth Century* (Basingstoke, 2001).

Hutton, Guthrie, *Fife – the Mining Kingdom* (Ochiltree, Ayrshire, 1999).

Hyde, Charles K., *Riding the Roller Coaster: A History of the Chrysler Corporation* (Detroit, 2003).

Iacocca, Lee with William Novak, *Iacocca: An Autobiography* (London, 1986).

Jefferys, Kevin, *Finest and Darkest Hours: The Decisive Events in British Politics from Churchill to Blair* (London, 2002).

Jenkins, Peter, *The Battle of Downing Street* (London, 1970).

Johnman, Lewis and Hugh Murphy, *Shipbuilding in Britain since 1914: A Political Economy of Decline* (Exeter, 2002).

Johns, Stephen, *Reformism on the Clyde: The Story of the UCS* (London, 1973).

Jones, Jack, *Union Man: An Autobiography* (London, 1986).

Keegan, William, *Britain Without Oil* (Harmondsworth, 1985).

Kellas, James, *The Scottish Political System* (Cambridge, 1989).

Knox, W., 'Class, Work and Trade Unionism in Scotland', in A. Dickson and J. H. Treble (eds), *People and Society in Scotland: Volume III, 1914–1990* (Edinburgh, 1994), pp. 108–37.

Knox, W. W., *Industrial Nation: Scotland, 1800 to the Present* (Edinburgh, 1999).

Knox, W. W., and A. McKinlay, 'The Re-Making of Scottish Labour in the 1930s', *Twentieth Century British History*, 6 (1995), 174–93.

Kurlansky, Mark, *1968: The Year that Rocked the World* (London, 2004).

Lee, C. H., *Scotland and the United Kingdom: The Economy and the Union in the Twentieth Century* (Manchester, 1999).

Lee, C. H., 'Economic Progress: Wealth and Poverty', in T. M. Devine, C. H. Lee and G. C. Peden (eds), *The Transformation of Scotland: The Economy since 1700* (Edinburgh, 2005), pp. 128–56.

Lee, C. H., 'Unbalanced Growth: Prosperity and Deprivation', in T. M. Devine, C. H. Lee and G. C. Peden (eds), *The Transformation of Scotland: The Economy since 1700* (Edinburgh, 2005), pp. 208–32.

Lindblom, Charles, *Politics and Markets: The World's Political Systems* (New York, 1977).

Lindop, Fred, 'The Dockers and the 1971 Industrial Relations Act, Part 1: Shop Stewards and Containerization', *Historical Studies in Industrial Relations*, 5 (1998), 33–72, and 'Part 2: The Arrest and Release of the Pentonville Five', *Historical Studies in Industrial Relations*, 6 (1998), 65–100.

Lyddon, Dave, 'The Car Industry, 1945–79: Shop Stewards and Workplace Unionism', in Chris Wrigley (ed), *A History of British Industrial Relations, 1939–1979* (Cheltenham, 1996), pp. 186–211.

Lyddon, Dave and Ralph Hartington, *Glorious Summer: Class Struggle in Britain in 1972* (London, 2001).

Lynch, Michael (ed.), *The Oxford Companion to Scottish History* (Oxford, 2001).

McCrone, David, 'Towards a Principled Elite: Scottish Elites in the Twentieth Century', in A. Dickson and J. H. Treble (eds), *People and Society in Scotland: Volume III, 1914–1990* (Edinburgh, 1994).

McCrone, Gavin, *Scotland's Economic Progress, 1951–1960* (London, 1964).

McCrone, Gavin, and R. J. Randall, 'The Scottish Development Agency', in Richard Saville, *The Economic Development of Modern Scotland, 1950–1980* (Edinburgh, 1985), pp. 233–44.

MacDougall, Ian, *Voices from the Hunger Marches: Volume I* (Edinburgh, 1990).

MacDougall, Ian, *Voices From Work and Home* (Edinburgh, 2000).

McGill, Jack, *Crisis on the Clyde* (London, 1973).

McIlroy, John, '"Always Outnumbered, Always Outgunned": The Trotskyists and the Trade Unions', in John McIlroy, Nina Fishman and Alan Campbell (eds), *British Trade Unions and Industrial Politics: Volume Two, The High Tide of Trade Unionism, 1964–79* (Aldershot, 1999), pp. 259–96.

McIlroy, John, 'Notes on the Communist Party and Industrial Politics', in John McIlroy, Nina Fishman and Alan Campbell (eds), *British Trade Unions and Industrial Politics: Volume Two, The High Tide of Trade Unionism, 1964–79* (Aldershot, 1999), pp. 216–58.

McIlroy, John and Alan Campbell, 'The Tide of Trade Unionism: Mapping Industrial Politics, 1964–79', in John McIlroy, Nina Fishman and Alan Campbell (eds), *British Trade Unions and Industrial Politics: Volume Two, The High Tide of Trade Unionism, 1964–79* (Aldershot, 1999), pp. 93–132.

McIlroy, John and Alan Campbell, 'Beyond Betteshanger: Order 1305 in the Scottish Coalfields During the Second World War, Part 1: Politics, Prosecutions and Protest', *Historical Studies in Industrial Relations*, 15 (2003), 27–72, and 'Part 2: The Cardowan Story', *Historical Studies in Industrial Relations*, 16 (2003), 39–80.

McIvor, Arthur, 'Women and Work in Twentieth Century Scotland', in A. Dickson and J. H. Treble (eds), *People and Society in Scotland: Volume III, 1914–1990* (Edinburgh, 1994), pp. 138–73.

McKibbin, Ross, *Classes and Cultures: England 1918–1951* (Oxford, 1998).

McKinlay, Alan and Bill Knox, 'Working for the Yankee Dollar. US Inward Investment and Scottish Labour, 1945–1970', *Historical Studies in Industrial Relations*, 7 (1999), 1–26.

Macpherson, Archie, *Jock Stein: The Definitive Biography* (Newbury, 2004).

Marr, Andrew, *The Battle for Scotland* (Harmondsworth, 1992).

Marwick, Arthur, *The Sixties* (Oxford, 1998).

Maver, Irene, *Glasgow* (Edinburgh, 2000).

Miliband, Ralph, *The State in Capitalist Society* (London, 1969).

Miliband, Ralph, *Parliamentary Socialism: A Study in the Politics of Labour* (Second edition, London, 1972).

Minkin, Lewis, *The Contentious Alliance: Trade Unions and the Labour Party* (Edinburgh, 1992).

Mitchell, James, *Conservatives and the Union: A Study of Conservative Party Attitudes to the Union* (Edinburgh, 1990).

Mitchell, James, 'Scotland in the Union, 1945–95: The Changing Nature of the Union State', in T. M. Devine and R. J. Finlay, *Scotland in the Twentieth Century* (Edinburgh, 1996), pp. 85–101.

Mitchell, James, *Strategies For Self Government: The Campaigns For a Scottish Parliament* (Edinburgh, 1996).

Moran, Michael, *The Politics of Industrial Relations* (London, 1977).

Morgan, Edwin, *Selected Poems* (Manchester, 1985).

Morgan, Kenneth O., *The People's Peace: British History, 1945–1990* (Oxford, 1992).

Morgan, Kenneth O., *Callaghan: A Life* (Oxford, 1997).

Murden, Jon, 'Demands for Fair Wages and Pay Parity in the British Motor Industry in the 1960s and 1970s', *Historical Studies in Industrial Relations*, 20 (2005), 1–27.

Murray, George T., *Scotland: The New Future* (Bishopbriggs, 1973).

Newlands, David, 'The Regional Economies of Scotland', in T. M. Devine, C. H. Lee and G. C. Peden (eds), *The Transformation of Scotland: The Economy since 1700* (Edinburgh, 2005), pp. 159–83.

Nichols, Theo, *The British Worker Question: A New Look at Workers and Productivity in Manufacturing* (London, 1986).

Orwell, George, *The Road to Wigan Pier* (Harmondsworth, 1962).

Paterson, Lindsay, *The Autonomy of Scotland* (Edinburgh, 1994).

Paterson, Lindsay, *A Diverse Assembly: The Debate on a Scottish Parliament* (Edinburgh, 1998).

Paterson, Lindsay, Frank Bechhofer and David McCrone, *Living in Scotland: Social and Economic Change since 1980* (Edinburgh, 2004).

Patrizio, Andrew and Frank Little, *Canvassing the Clyde: Stanley Spencer and the Shipyards* (Glasgow, 1994).

Payne, Peter L., *Colvilles and the Scottish Steel Industry* (Oxford, 1979).

Payne, Peter L., 'The End of Steelmaking in Scotland, c. 1967–1993', *Scottish Economic and Social History*, 15 (1995), 66–84.

Peden, G. C., 'The Managed Economy: Scotland, 1919–2000', in T. M. Devine, C. H. Lee and G. C. Peden (eds), *The Transformation of Scotland: The Economy since 1700* (Edinburgh, 2005), pp. 233–65.

Phillips, Jim, 'Oceanspan: Deindustrialisation and Devolution in Scotland, c. 1960–1974', *The Scottish Historical Review*, 84 (2005), 63–84.

Phillips, Jim, 'Class and Industrial Relations in Britain: The "Long" Mid-Century and the Case of Port Transport, c. 1920–1970', *Twentieth Century British History*, 16 (2005), 52–73.

Phillips, Jim, 'The 1972 Miners' Strike: Popular Agency and Industrial Politics in Britain', *Contemporary British History*, 20 (2006), 187–207.

Pimlott, Ben, *Harold Wilson* (London, 1992).

Pitt, Malcolm, *The World on our Backs: The Kent Miners and the 1972 Miners' Strike* (London, 1979).

Priestley, J. B., *English Journey* (Harmondsworth, 1977).

Reid, Alastair J., *United We Stand: A History of Britain's Trade Unions* (Harmondsworth, 2004).

Routledge, Paul, *Scargill: The Unauthorized Biography* (London, 1993).

Saville, John, 'Arthur Horner', in Joyce Bellamy and John Saville (eds), *Dictionary of Labour Biography: Volume V* (London, 1979), pp. 112–18.

Saville, Richard, 'The Industrial Background to the Post-War Scottish Economy', in Richard Saville (ed.), *The Economic Development of Modern Scotland, 1950–1980* (Edinburgh, 1985), pp. 1–46.

Sherington, Jo, 'To Speak its Pride': The Work of the Films of Scotland Committee, 1938–1982 (Glasgow, 1996).

Slaven, Anthony, 'Sir James Lithgow', in Anthony Slaven and Sidney Checkland (eds), Dictionary of Scottish Business Biography: Volume I, The Staple Industries (Aberdeen, 1986), pp. 222–7.

Smith, David F., 'The Scientific Food Committee', in David F. Smith and Jim Phillips (eds), Food, Science, Policy and Regulation in the Twentieth Century (London, 2000).

Smith, Paul and Gary Morton, 'The Conservative Governments' Reform of Employment Law, 1979–97: "Stepping Stones" and the "New Right" Agenda', Historical Studies in Industrial Relations, 12 (2001), 131–47.

Stigler, George J., 'The Theory of Economic Regulation', in George J. Stigler (ed.), The Citizen and the State (Chicago, 1975).

Taylor, Andrew, 'The "Stepping Stones" Programme: Conservative Party Thinking on Trade Unions, 1975–9', Historical Studies in Industrial Relations, 11 (2001), 109–25.

Taylor, Andrew, The NUM and British Politics: Volume 1, 1944–1968 (Aldershot, 2003); and Volume 2, 1969–1995 (Aldershot, 2005).

Taylor, Robert, The Trade Union Question in British Politics (Cambridge, 1993).

Taylor, Robert, 'The Heath Government and Industrial Relations: Myth and Reality', in Stuart Ball and Anthony Seldon (eds), The Heath Government, 1970–1974: A Reappraisal (London, 1996), pp. 161–190.

Thatcher, Margaret, The Downing Street Years (London, 1993).

Thatcher, Margaret, The Path to Power (London, 1995).

Thompson, William, 'The New Left in Scotland', in Ian MacDougall (ed.), Essays in Scottish Labour History (Edinburgh, 1978), pp. 207–24.

Thompson, Willie, The Good Old Cause: British Communism, 1920–1991 (London, 1992).

Thompson, Willie and Finlay Hart, The UCS Work-In (London, 1972).

Thorpe, Andrew, 'The Labour Party and the Trade Unions', in John McIlroy, Nina Fishman and Alan Campbell (eds), British Trade Unions and Industrial Politics: Volume Two, The High Tide of Trade Unionism, 1964–79 (Aldershot, 1999).

Thorpe, Keir, 'The "Juggernaut Method": The 1966 State of Emergency and the Wilson Government's Response to the Seamen's Strike', Twentieth Century British History, 12 (2001), 461–85.

Tomlinson, Jim, 'Inventing "Decline": The Falling Behind of the British Economy in the Post-War Years', Economic History Review, 49 (1996), 731–57.

Tomlinson, Jim, The Politics of Decline: Understanding Post-War Britain (Harlow, 2000).

Tuckett, Angela, The Scottish Trades Union Congress: The First Eighty Years, 1897–1977 (Edinburgh, 1986).

Turner, John, Macmillan (London, 1994).

Wallington, Peter, 'The case of the Longannet miners and the criminal liability of pickets', Industrial Law Journal, 1 (1972), 219–28.

Ward, Paul, Unionism in the United Kingdom, 1918–1974 (Basingstoke, 2005).

Whitehead, Phillip, The Writing on the Wall: Britain in the Seventies (London, 1985).

Who's Who in Scotland, 1988–89 (Second edition, Ayr, 1988).

Wiener, Jon, Come Together: John Lennon in His Time (London, 1995).

Wilks, Stephen, Industrial Policy and the Motor Industry (Manchester, 1984).

Wilson, Harold, The Labour Government, 1964–1970: A Personal Record (London, 1971).

Wolfe, Billy, *Scotland Lives: The Quest For Independence* (Edinburgh, 1973).

Wood, Donna J., 'The Strategic Use of Public Policy: Business Support for the 1906 Food and Drug Act', *Business History Review*, 59 (1985), 403–32.

Worsthorne, Peregrine, 'Class and Conflict in British Foreign Policy', *Foreign Affairs*, 37 (1959), 419–31.

Worsthorne, Peregrine, *Peregrinations* (London, 1980).

Wrigley, Chris, 'The 1984–5 Miners' Strike', in Andrew Charlesworth, David Gilbert, Adrian Randall, Humphrey Southall and Chris Wrigley, *An Atlas of Industrial Unrest in Britain, 1750–1990* (London, 1996), pp. 217–25.

Wrigley, Chris, 'Strikes in the Motor Car Manufacturing Industry', in Andrew Charlesworth, David Gilbert, Adrian Randall, Humphrey Southall and Chris Wrigley, *An Atlas of Industrial Protest in Britain, 1750–1990* (London, 1996), pp. 202–9.

Young, Douglas, *Scotland* (London, 1971).

Young, Stephen and Neil Hood, *Chrysler UK: A Corporation in Transition* (New York, 1977).

Ziegler, Philip, *Wilson: The Authorised Life* (London, 1993).

Index